CURRICULUM DESIGN AND PRAXIS IN LANGUAGE TEACHING

A Globally Informed Approach

Edited by Fernanda Carra-Salsberg, Maria Figueredo, and Mihyon Jeon

Curriculum Design and Praxis in Language Teaching presents a variety of methodologies and theoretical perspectives for current and future postsecondary instructors in the areas of linguistics, second-language acquisition, and world literatures. Offering valuable insights for instructors, the materials presented in this book integrate perspectives and resources from various target languages, world regions, and cultures into areas related to teaching and learning within the field of language.

From critical assessments of the current academic curriculum to the fine-tuning of lesson planning, the essays in this collection address the innovative design and implementation of traditional, blended, and online language courses. Including inter-artistic approaches, case studies, and practical guides, this book provides theoretical and hands-on suggestions regarding how to mindfully reinforce students' socio-cultural engagement and linguistic development both inside and outside of their language-learning classrooms. The innovative ideas for language pedagogy presented in this book – including implementing technology, enhancing engaged spaces of learning, and adapting to the ever-changing field of pedagogy – represent agile ways of blending old and new approaches to carry forward into twenty-first-century postsecondary classrooms.

FERNANDA CARRA-SALSBERG is an assistant professor in the Department of Languages, Literatures and Linguistics at York University.

MARIA FIGUEREDO is an associate professor in the Department of Languages, Literatures and Linguistics at York University.

MIHYON JEON is an associate professor in the Department of Languages, Literatures and Linguistics at York University.

Curriculum Design and Praxis in Language Teaching

A Globally Informed Approach

EDITED BY FERNANDA CARRA-SALSBERG,
MARIA FIGUEREDO, AND MIHYON JEON

UNIVERSITY OF TORONTO PRESS
Toronto Buffalo London

Toronto Buffalo London
utorontopress.com

ISBN 978-1-4875-2890-4 (cloth) ISBN 978-1-4875-2893-5 (EPUB)
ISBN 978-1-4875-2891-1 (paper) ISBN 978-1-4875-2892-8 (PDF)

Library and Archives Canada Cataloguing in Publication

Title: Curriculum design and praxis in language teaching : a globally informed approach / edited by Fernanda Carra-Salsberg, Maria Figueredo and Mihyon Jeon.
Names: Carra-Salsberg, Fernanda, editor. | Figueredo, María, 1967– editor. | Jeon, Mihyon, 1971– editor.
Description: Includes bibliographical references and index.
Identifiers: Canadiana (print) 20210382376 | Canadiana (ebook) 20210382503 | ISBN 9781487528911 (paper) | ISBN 9781487528904 (cloth) | ISBN 9781487528935 (EPUB) | ISBN 9781487528928 (PDF)
Subjects: LCSH: Language and languages – Study and teaching.
Classification: LCC P51.C87 2022 | DDC 418.007–dc23

We wish to acknowledge the land on which the University of Toronto Press operates. This land is the traditional territory of the Wendat, the Anishnaabeg, the Haudenosaunee, the Métis, and the Mississaugas of the Credit First Nation.

University of Toronto Press acknowledges the financial support of the Government of Canada, the Canada Council for the Arts, and the Ontario Arts Council, an agency of the Government of Ontario, for its publishing activities.

Canada Council for the Arts Conseil des Arts du Canada

Funded by the Government of Canada Financé par le gouvernement du Canada

Canada

Contents

List of Illustrations ix

Acknowledgments xi

Introduction 3

Section I: Critical Approaches to Curriculum and Pedagogy in Language and Pre-service Teacher Education 7

1 International by Default? Global Citizenship Education in the Language Classroom 9
SHOBNA NIJHAWAN

2 Socratic Circles, Critical Literacy, and Culturally Responsive Teacher Education 21
HYUNJUNG SHIN AND GERALDINE BALZER

3 Developing Future English-Language Educators' Critical Language Awareness in Cross-College Discussions 29
ANURADHA GOPALAKRISHNAN AND LEAH SHEPARD-CAREY

Section II: Designing Classroom Resources, Activities, and Assessment Tools for Student Engagement 37

4 Teaching with Case Studies 39
LYNN BURLEY

5 Conceptualizing the Significance of Studying Translingual, Autobiographic Narratives in ESL Classrooms at the Post-Secondary Level 46
FERNANDA CARRA-SALSBERG

6 Classroom-Based Assessment Practices of College Korean-Language Teachers: A Qualitative Study 56
HYE-SOOK WANG

7 Classroom Activities for Student Engagement: "5 Minutes" and Survey Project 71
MYOUNGHEE CHO

Section III: Inter-artistic Approaches to Language Teaching 83

8 Inter-artistic Approaches to Teaching Hispanic Culture: Literature and Music 87
VICTORIA WOLFF

9 E(xpanded) Dialogues between Literature and Music: Optimizing Synaesthetic Resources for Teaching Language and Literature 97
MARIA FIGUEREDO

10 When Art and English Language Instructors Collaborate 118
TAMARA WARHOL AND KATHERINE RHODES FIELDS

Section IV: Experiential Education in Language Teaching and Learning 127

11 Communicating and Understanding the "Other" through Experiential Education: Portuguese Language and Culture in Toronto 131
MARIA JOÃO DODMAN, INÊS CARDOSO, AND VANDER TAVARES

12 Using Experiential Learning Theory as a Framework for Undergraduate Academic Communication Development 144
MARIA HERKE, SUSAN HOADLEY, AND DEANNA WONG

13 Words at Play: Language Learning at Work 158
AGUSTINA TOCALLI-BELLER

Sections V and VI: From Technology-Enhanced Teaching to Fully Online and Blended Learning Platforms 173

Section V: Technology-Enhanced Teaching 177

14 Building Capacity for Twenty-First-Century Digital Language Teaching Practices 179
GEOFF LAWRENCE

15 Digital Storytelling in the L2 Classroom: Enhanced Writing Skills 190
YUJEONG CHOI AND NA-YOUNG RYU

16 A Pedagogical Module for a Place-Based and Multiliteracies-Based Digital Storytelling Project for Language Learning 201
ANGELA LEE-SMITH

17 Using Facebook as a Resource for e-Tandem Language Learning in Higher Education 213
CHRISTINE SCHALLMOSER AND PIA RESNIK

Section VI: Online and Blended Language Learning 225

18 Students' Insights on a Fully Online Language Course 227
MIHYON JEON AND AHRONG LEE

19 Preparing Future Global Professionals: Technology-Enhanced Group PBL Pedagogy 241
MONICA BROIDO AND DANIEL PORTMAN

20 A Guide to Synchronous Online Language Teaching 250
SEUNG-EUN CHANG

Conclusion: The Future of Teaching and Learning Language in a Complex Global Setting 259

Chapter Synopses 263

List of Contributors 271

Illustrations

Figures

1.A The Hindi Nagari script 16
1.B The Urdu Nastaliq alphabet 17
12.1 Academic communication courses experiential learning spiral 151
12.2 Academic communication unit experiential learning cycle 152
13.1 Pre-test and post-test results (in percentage) for the joke 166
13.2 Pre-test and post-test results (in ST meanings) for the joke 168
15.1 Digital storytelling project: First draft 195
15.2 Digital storytelling project: Second draft 195
15.3 Effectiveness of feedback on the first draft 197
15.4 Satisfaction with revised scripts 197
16.1 The multiliteracies model 203
16.2 Project final site sample 207
18.1 First page of the course website 230
18.2 Weeks 1–3 page 231
20.1 File uploading process 252
20.2 More features on uploading files in a virtual classroom 253
20.3 Use of "note" feature 254

Tables

3.1 Google Sheet with student groups 32
6.1 Participants' demographic information 59
7.1 Two languages for a survey project 77
12.1 Course description(s) 147
12.2 Learning outcomes 149
12.3 Assessment tasks 150
13.1 VKS scoring categories: Meaning of scores 162

13.2 VKS scores for "disbarred" 165
13.3 LRE count and type for "disbarred" joke 167
14.1 A statistical impact report of student participation in an online discussion tool 185
15.1 Lesson plan for digital storytelling 194
18.1 Student survey results 232

Box

3.1 Activity sheet 33

Acknowledgments

This publication was supported by the Core University Program for Korean Studies through the Ministry of Education of the Republic of Korea and the Korean Studies Promotion Service of the Academy of Korean Studies (AKS-2018-OLU-2250001).

We would also like to thank the Faculty of Liberal Arts & Professional Studies of York University for the funding granted through the Minor Research Grant awarded in support of this publication.

CURRICULUM DESIGN AND PRAXIS IN LANGUAGE TEACHING

Introduction

As former members of the Teaching and Learning Committee at the Department of Languages, Literatures & Linguistics at York University, Canada, we have spent a significant amount of time studying our students' and colleagues' pedagogical needs. As part of our ongoing enquiry, we conducted a department-wide survey, and its results pointed to the significance of offering useful and concrete recommendations regarding successful lessons and assessments designed for in-class, blended, and online courses. Many faculty members stressed the need for creating innovative lessons that motivate students' interests, while others voiced the relevance of knowing how to incorporate technology and art into their teaching, and how to design lessons that create an active space for critical thinking and experiential learning. Our survey reinforced our understanding of the importance of sharing teaching practices, theoretical conceptualizations, and functional interpretations that pay close attention to our current realities, needs, and experiences as researchers, instructors, and learners.

Our project, which was initially guided by our intention of conducting department-wide workshops and/or webinars, grew in form and significance as we realized the complexity of the challenges that stem from teaching in an ever-changing sociocultural, political, and technological landscape. It became evident that the array and dimensions of topics we then wished to explore needed to be studied in collaboration with other pedagogues and researchers – specifically, with professionals who share our interest in addressing students' current needs and sharing practices and methodologies for contemporary language teaching. Such realizations, along with the unprecedented changes that stemmed from our most recent world health crisis, made way for the creation of this timely publication.

Curriculum Design and Praxis in Language Teaching: A Globally Informed Approach is informed by years of research and pedagogical methods. It includes twenty chapters with works from thirty contributors representing eighteen universities and research centres across the world. This includes researchers from

Canada, as well as Austria, New South Wales, Spain, the United Kingdom and the United States, covering a range of languages including – yet not limited to – English, German, Hindi-Urdu, Korean, Portuguese, and Spanish as second and heritage languages. The contributors of this volume are scholars and practitioners who are working on innovative educational pedagogy for language students and teacher candidates within the areas of language learning and teaching.

The present volume consists of a brief introduction, six main thematic sections addressing theoretical, methodological, and pedagogical issues, and a conclusion. The themes included in this volume were chosen based on the needs and interests of faculty members in our department that were identified in the aforementioned survey. Each of these sections opens with a short framing introduction, which provides the context for the ensuing individual chapters.

This volume begins with section I, "Critical Approaches to Curriculum and Pedagogy to Language and Pre-service Teacher Education." This section consists of three chapters that emphasize the significance of creating a space for the development of not only students' language skills but also critical thinking and awareness of the relation between language and power. All three chapters collectively offer theoretical and pedagogical perspectives on curricular development, focusing on the issues of dialectical interactions, language learning, and teaching.

Section II, "Designing Classroom Resources, Activities, and Assessment Tools for Student Engagement," underlines instructors' crucial role in post-secondary students' motivation and learning. The four chapters in this section combine to offer practical and theoretical guidance on how to engage students through material that is relevant to learners' interests and realities through various classroom resources, activities, and assessment tools.

Section III, "Inter-artistic Approaches to Teaching Language," consists of three chapters that demonstrate how different regions of the world can find common ground in facilitating learners' development of writing skills and cultural awareness through inter-artistic materials. Offering practical approaches, the samples drawn from courses in several universities reignite the debate about the categorization of disciplines and artistic genres. These chapters also address the way that social media has embedded contemporary conceptions of what constitutes a "text" and how this is necessarily intersected by various forms of artistic media – visual, verbal, and audio. Addressing the inter-artistic texts in language teaching examines how the flow of media and its disciplinary boundaries shift over time. In twenty-first-century pedagogy, this puts into relief the cultural approaches that define these intersections of the arts in various creative productions of the world's cultures, such as in poetry, narrative, song, and visual arts. How these are placed in relation to the acquisition of language and cultural skills is the subject of the three chapters in this third section.

The volume then moves to section IV, which focuses on experiential education in language learning and teaching. The three chapters included in this section emphasize engaging with language in cultural context. It places great emphasis on the need to foster student motivation, intercultural awareness, and sensibility, while addressing critical thinking skills. The various methods presented strive to shed light on the notion of "otherness" from within and without language.

The next two sections, V and VI, address the theme of technology and language education. Given the high level of demand and interest for the use of technology in language education, this theme is covered over the seven chapters that comprise these two sections. They provide an overview of Technology Enhanced Learning (TEL) in language classrooms and presents successful practices of TEL in the formats of digital storytelling, e-Tandem, project-based learning, and online education. All seven chapters collectively demonstrate how technology can enhance language education in general, and collaborative learning in particular. The cases of digital storytelling and e-Tandem learning and the use of Google Docs for student group projects in these sections exemplify how a specific application of technology facilitates teaching and learning experiences, while also enhancing collaboration among learners.

The volume then ends with the final conclusion, titled "The Future of Teaching and Learning Language in a Complex Global Setting." A variety of methodologies and theoretical perspectives are contained in this volume, including historical and empirical analyses; social-interactionist frameworks for language teaching; and immersionist strategies that link education technology, digital practice and new media, and affect theory and analytics. This publication is designed for current and future postsecondary instructors in the areas of linguistics and language learning. Its purpose is to offer guidance for seasoned as well as new instructors who seek fresh insights into areas related to teaching and learning within the field of language and language learning. The materials presented in this collaboration integrate perspectives and resources from various target languages, world regions, and cultures. From critical assessments of the current academic area to the fine-tuning of lesson planning, the material in this book addresses the innovative design and implementation of traditional, blended and online language courses.

Curriculum Design and Praxis in Language Teaching: A Globally Informed Approach falls outside conventional norms, while bridging practical and theoretical approaches to teaching in postsecondary courses in three areas: language, literature, and linguistics. Equally important, it provides theoretical and hands-on suggestions regarding how to mindfully reinforce students' sociocultural engagement and linguistic development both inside and outside of their language learning classrooms.

Although the contributions in this volume belong to specific places and times and we cannot claim to provide global coverage, our contributors present pedagogical practices and case studies from three continents and eight countries. While our contributions are relatively heterogeneous in terms of themes, there is a concerted effort by the contributors to provide theoretical and pedagogical approaches for facilitating students' linguistic development as well as sociocultural engagement. Despite being heterogeneous and interdisciplinary in nature, our contributions serve as a network of approaches and case studies to establish a coherent endeavour throughout the volume.

Finally, we were and continue to be inspired by the issues addressed in the array of works that became included in this volume. As language pedagogues, editors, and contributors to this publication, we are committed to making space for diverse viewpoints that have taken us from praxis to publication. Our collaboration became our means for pooling and sharing our resources and mobilizing our research. We hope our work expands into further collaborations and syntheses of approaches. We celebrate how our experiences in these teaching and learning settings have nourished current research in the fields of language, literature, and linguistics pedagogies.

SECTION I

Critical Approaches to Curriculum and Pedagogy in Language and Pre-service Teacher Education

This first section is a collaboration of pedagogical and critical methodologies centred on foreign and heritage language learning and pre-service teaching in the area of English language and literacy. Composed of three chapters, this segment pays close attention to the challenges associated with developing courses that provide a foundation for students' sense of linguistic, sociocultural, and educational preparedness inside and outside the post-secondary classroom. These chapters emphasize the significance of creating a space for the development of students' language skills, critical thinking, cultural mindfulness, and sociopolitical consciousness. This section offers practical and theoretical perspectives on the advancement of curricular knowledge within the field of dialectical interactions between host and minority language learning and teaching.

Chapter 1, "International by Default? Global Citizenship Education in the Language Classroom," examines the pedagogical implications of teaching foreign, heritage, and mixed language-learning classes at the post-secondary level. With specific attention paid to teaching introductory and intermediate Hindi-Urdu courses at York University, Shobna Nijhawan shares with her readers the pedagogical practices she developed through her years of teaching. This timely chapter blends old and new approaches. It focuses on the design and implementation of a technology-enhanced curriculum that includes components of experiential learning for blended courses. Much of chapter 1 revolves around group-oriented activities and students' active involvement in the development of course materials for the use in the classroom. While taking into account York University's international and diverse, diasporic student body, Nijhawan also examines the significance of fostering responsible global citizenship. This, she argues, is accomplished through a combination of dialogical in-class discussions and students' interviews with members of the Hindi-Urdu communities. Not limiting her pedagogical focus on language learning in its strict sense, Nijhawan highlights the benefits of implementing reflective, sociopolitical, and historical interpretations of the interconnected realities influencing the hyphened languages and cultures of instruction.

Chapter 2, "Socratic Circles, Critical Literacy, and Culturally Responsive Teacher Education," discusses the educational and interpersonal importance of developing dialectical circles in pre-service teacher education courses. As post-secondary instructors at the University of Saskatchewan's College of Education, Hyunjung Shin and Geraldine Balzer highlight the significance of incorporating Indigenous perspectives and pedagogy to the student-teacher, language and literacy curricula. These authors describe the Socratic circles as a culturally responsive, pedagogical tool through which students take ownership of their own learning. Such circles allow for future teachers to observe and share their knowledge and overall experiences as students and educators within the hegemonic field of additional language learning. Building on the diverse knowledge teacher candidates bring into the classroom, these dialogic circles are designed to challenge preconceptions and create a dynamic space for in-class discussions of decolonization and critical thinking.

In chapter 3, "Developing Future English-Language Educators' Critical Language Awareness in Cross-College Discussions," Anuradha Gopalakrishnan and Leah Shepard-Carey place great emphasis on the power of dialogue as a medium that fosters students' critical language awareness and meaning making. This chapter describes the dialogic and pedagogical relevance of cross-university and college discussions among future English-language educators. Such students are enrolled in similar teacher-education courses and reading similar texts. Gopalakrishnan and Shepard-Carey offer a clear outline of the activity. With the use of theory and a description of students' response to the cross-college activity, these authors highlight the manner in which pre-service teachers' critical learning is strengthened by their dialogic interactions and informed by their differing backgrounds, experiences, and identities.

As a whole, section I is centred on language and culture, as well as curricular and interpersonal development(s). In this way, section I is similar to the upcoming sections. It differs, nonetheless, in its approach: offering an initial overview of the curriculum-level questions and (of) the cross-collegium discussions at hand. By interweaving practical and pedagogical knowledge, its aim is to better prepare readers for the pedagogical challenges that stem from our current global, linguistic, sociocultural, economic, and political realities. Such interconnected realities are highlighted and analysed for the inevitable way in which they shape and influence individuals' experiences as learners, educators, and, ideally, agents of positive change.

1 International by Default? Global Citizenship Education in the Language Classroom

SHOBNA NIJHAWAN

Since the early twenty-first century, the Internationalizing Teaching and Learning Framework initiative (ITL) and the Cultures and Languages Across the Curriculum consortium (CLAC) have argued for responsible global citizenship education in post-secondary institutions through the teaching of language, literature, and culture.[1] This notwithstanding, "foreign" (i.e., for the Canadian context, non-English and non-French) language teaching has often been bypassed in North American universities' strategic goals and white papers laying out how the curriculum may best be internationalized at their particular institutions. A common explanation for doing so is the assumption that language courses are central to the idea of internationalization as much as to the development of Area Studies as a discipline and thus inherently international. This chapter belies such an assumption and argues for mindful global citizenship education in the post-secondary language classroom that draws from intercultural, digital, and communicative pedagogies and is institutionalized in academic and administrative internationalization policies. The following study of how language courses envision global responsibility and intercultural competency for a diverse student body is not unique to the Hindi-Urdu classroom at York University; it is part of an emerging Scholarship of Teaching and Learning (SoTL) that engages with the challenges and possibilities that foreign-language instruction faces in the age of globalization and – more recently – in a pandemic context.[2]

York University's internationalization efforts manifested among other things in the institutionalization of tenure-track positions for Less-Commonly Taught Languages (LCTL) such as Arabic, Hindi, Korean, and Persian in the early 2000s. Students from all faculties, including York University's Schulich School of Business, have since enrolled in the Department of Languages, Literatures & Linguistics' numerous course offerings and graduated with language degrees, language certificates, or used advanced knowledge of a language to fulfil the requirements of the international BA (iBA) degree. Corresponding to the principles of the CLAC that promote "transformational learning through the integration of content, language, and culture" (Soneson and Zilmer, "Developing," 2), the course offerings in the Languages, Literatures & Linguistics Department at York University are not limited to language acquisition; they include English-language courses in literatures, cultures, and linguistics.[3] Some language programs also offer study abroad initiatives to wholly integrate and embed the teaching of language, literature, and culture in international, intercultural, and global citizenship education. Such a conceptualization of language, literature, and culture courses has thrived in the department to an extent that a new degree in world languages and literatures is in development.[4] More recently, Indigenous languages have also been included in the research and teaching of the department. Faculty collaborations between the language and literature and the linguistics streams have turned internationalization and indigenization into a worthwhile and successful endeavour.

To those involved in SoTL on post-secondary language acquisition, especially the LCTL, there is no question that a trio of language, literature, and culture instruction is central to internationalization and mindful global citizenship education. Administrators, however, may think differently and refer to the latest online tools, including translation technology, as a means to bypass language instruction in a classroom capped at the relatively low number of 20–30 students.[5] Such a move isolates language from culture and puts in danger internationalization and global citizenship education at post-secondary institutions. As a caveat, it needs to be noted that a foreign language course is not by default an exercise in internationalization (Mack and Menke). In her keynote speech "The Challenge of Globalization in Foreign Language Education" (296), delivered at a conference hosted by the Centre for the Advanced Research in Language Acquisition (CARLA), Claire Kramsch calls for a "more reflective, interpretive, historically grounded, and politically engaged pedagogy" for foreign language education. She observes that despite excellent communicative pedagogy and the availability of new global technologies, there remains a gap in language taught in the classroom and language required for use in the 'real' world. Even more so, often language teaching may not be oriented towards the creation of responsible citizens, but rather towards future consumers (ibid.). In "Teaching Foreign Languages in an Era of Globalization," Kramsch argues that long-established aspects of translingual and transcultural competence need to be revisited and recontextualized in light of the demands posed by globalization and the needs towards developing global competence amongst students (304).[6] Correspondingly, this chapter explores how global citizenship education manifests in introductory and intermediate Hindi-Urdu language instruction at York University, where courses cater towards foreign-language or second-language learners as well as heritage-language learners in mixed and separate (heritage language) classrooms.[7] Special attention lies on how a responsible use of technology by instructors and students can enhance the global learning experience in virtual and face-to-face spaces alike.[8]

Responsible Use of Technology (Part I): The Cultural Importance of Script

Computer-assisted translation devices form essential tools for students, travellers, businesspeople. and inter-generational families who communicate in different languages. Arguably, the translation machine Google Translate has made it easier for students in the language classroom to work on home assignments and express themselves in group activities. Students of Hindi-Urdu are often delighted to find that Google Translate is not only capable of translating, but also transliterating from English to the Nagari script used to write Hindi. Some benefit from the option given by the site to transliterate words from the English font into the Nagari and – for Urdu – the Nastaliq or Naskh fonts or – for those unable to read these fonts – to maintain the Roman type. The knowledge of Nagari (for Hindi) and Nastaliq or Naskh (for Urdu) scripts is thus not required for navigating the site. This supposed facilitation offered by Google Translate runs contrary to language pedagogy that understands script as an essential component of language and culture and devotes several weeks of class time over a period of two years to teaching both scripts. Moreover, the transliteration on Google Translate does not follow the international phonetic alphabet (IPA) or any other standardized transliteration system but adapts a random and inconsistent phonetic notation (oo, u, uu may be used interchangeably; ū, however, is not recognized as a character). This is certainly to the advantage of the user who is not versed in the IPA but runs contrary to a holistic language pedagogy that refuses to abandon an essential component of the language and culture, that is, script.

This critique notwithstanding, the teaching of script may draw from a diversity of pedagogies and materials, including digital ones, that consider the different learning preferences of students and include in-class or virtual blackboard demonstrations by the instructor, online script tutors as those offered by the University of Oxford (UK) or the University of North Carolina (US), pencil and paper, as well as a textbook. In the process, students also explore the alphabetic conventions of three differing linguistic-cultural contexts (including the Roman alphabet). The Hindi alphabet, for example, is syllabic and arranged in phonological groups (velar, palatal, retroflex, dental, labial, sibilants, glottal sounds, etc.) while the Urdu alphabet follows its own arrangement that is based on shape similarity (see Appendices). The combination of language, script, and culture thus begins in the very first week of the academic term and continues well into the intermediate year, in which students are introduced to the art of calligraphy. As they explore the Urdu script with pen and ink, they once again develop appreciation for a writing system with its very own convention and scientific foundation. Admittedly, learning two different scripts over a period of two academic years may be cumbersome. In fact, some academic institutions bypass the teaching of script and operate with grammar and texts that use standardized transliterated Hindi or Urdu. The majority of post-secondary institutions, however, embeds the teaching of script in a global education framework that builds on communicative technology and experiential learning. At York University, students are exposed to the presence of Hindi and Urdu languages, cultures, and scripts on streets, in stores, places of worship, on the air, and at community gatherings as they explore the many neighbourhoods in Toronto and the Greater Toronto Area (GTA). They are encouraged to decipher and photograph signage, restaurant menus and advertisements in Nagari and Nastaliq/Naskh and share the images in class. Students are also introduced to the Nagari and Nastaliq/Naskh computer fonts and use these to create their personal website in Hindi, Urdu or both scripts while they are also required to submit handwritten assignments on paper.

Student Involvement in Global Citizenship Education

Hindi-Urdu at York University and many American post-secondary institutions is conceptualized as a hyphenated version of a South Asian language commonly spoken and understood in certain regions of North India, Pakistan, and – in variations – South Asian diasporas around the world (Nijhawan, "The Hindi Urdu Heritage Language Stream," 396, 404n4). The language differs from standardized, Sanskritized Hindi taught in India as much as standardized, Arabicized Urdu taught in Pakistan. Teaching Hindi-Urdu is fraught with ideologies surrounding nationalist cultures of India and Pakistan, class, caste, gender, region, and religion.[9] In the classroom, it is of importance to acknowledge the linguistic and cultural diversity of the student body and embrace students' pre-existing linguistic and cultural knowledge. That said, a common set of South Asian heritage learners may not necessarily have a connection to the Indian subcontinent as many students or their parents hail from South Asian diasporas in the Caribbean, North America, or Europe. A common point of cultural and linguistic connection remains the globally popular Bollywood movie industry. As students are encouraged to analyse the use of language and the representation of culture in movies, they develop an analytical perspective on the subject matter. Students show much interest in such activities and often even consult academic sources in English to follow up on certain class discussions concerning gender, caste, class, religion, and language. Internationalizing the curriculum thus also takes place in a language class and is not solely an activity directed at bringing languages and cultures into the traditional disciplines.

Regardless of whether the Hindi-Urdu course format is face-to-face, blended, remote, or online, it relies on a grammar book, online multimedia learning tools,[10] instructor-designed handouts, and exposure to South Asian diaspora communities in Toronto and the GTA. In addition, students become active participants in the creation of learning materials and enhancement of the learning experience. They are given the responsibility to design slideshows, in which they are encouraged to include visuals, which feed into a pool of images including people of different ages, skin shades, social status, regions, and religion that students are exposed to in class. Students also prepare drills to review and practice grammatical concepts. Hindi-Urdu songs from the Bollywood music industry are fondly used to identify a certain grammatical structure and students enjoy whenever they are streamed in the classroom or online. Occasionally they are asked to introduce a grammatical concept from the textbook to their peers. Students typically appreciate this type of interactive learning. Provided stable internet and bandwidth connections are available, classroom activities can be transferred into the remote and online context in synchronous as well as asynchronous sessions.

This glimpse into the activities taking place in the language classroom suggests that a combination of established traditional and innovative as well as integrative practices of teaching and learning contributes to mindful, responsible, and intentional global citizenship education. As I have laid out in previous publications (Nijhawan, "I got the point," "Hindi-Urdu"), the involvement of students in designing in-class activities is an essential component of Hindi-Urdu language courses at York University. Learning becomes a group-oriented activity in which students and instructor read, write, listen, and speak *with* each other.[11] While I will not explore the specific pedagogical needs of students occupying the heritage language and the mixed classroom, I quote from the course syllabus of Introductory Hindi-Urdu for Heritage Speakers to demonstrate how different types of activities cater to the diverse learning preferences of students. The syllabus acknowledges that the prototypical foreign language classroom, once integral to interdisciplinary area studies housed in the humanities and social sciences during the post-cold war era, no longer exists in the current age of globalization. All students bring different backgrounds and motivations to class:

> In language teaching, regular attendance and participation in a relaxed and non-competitive environment is most important for students' success. This course will inevitably consist of students with diverse forms of heritage knowledge, i.e., linguistic and/or cultural background on South Asia and/or the South Asian diaspora. It is the aim of this course to constructively draw from this knowledge of 'living Hindi-Urdu' and to include it in the classroom in order that students may benefit and learn from each other. Every student is expected to contribute towards the making of the course. Regardless of the "amount" of heritage knowledge, every student will be required to invest equal amount of time and effort towards this course. Homework assignments consist of drills and translation exercises, the learning of

> vocabulary and fill-in-the-blank worksheets. Small creative projects will be submitted throughout the academic year. Regular review and exercise of what was covered in class (approximately 4 hours per week outside of class) is essential throughout the academic term. Students are expected to record the time they spend with homework and review in a journal ... In the fourth week of classes, students will be grouped into moderated and supervised learning circles that meet regularly in and outside of class, at times virtually, as well as in the multimedia language centre.

Amongst the objectives laid out in the syllabus, we may identify education in the four skills of language (reading, writing, listening, and speaking) alongside experiential education and guided individual and group learning. Can it be assumed, however, that the language instructor possesses the pedagogical and technological skills for providing an education catered towards the development of global citizenship? Is it viable to hand over responsibility of developing materials for retention and introduction of language and culture to students? In giving examples of how this can be done, I argue that encouraging students' intercultural competency as it is reflected by their diverse cultural and linguistic backgrounds may serve as a viable pedagogy in language teaching.

Responsible Use of Technology (Part II): Translation Technology and Language Ideology

Long gone are the times when students of Hindi and Urdu language and literature in the foreign-language classroom had to turn the pages of dictionaries to look up the meaning of unknown vocabulary while reading through a text. In order to navigate these printed publications, language learners had to be familiar with the (Hindi) Nagari or (Urdu) Nastaliq or Naskh scripts, the latter of which run from right to left, as well as the distinct and differing alphabetical order of each script, which in no way corresponds to the Western ABC. Finding the meaning of one word in the dictionary could take minutes. Such a scenario may seem inacceptable in today's world, which is marked by high-speed data transmission and information – including knowledge – being only a "mouse click" away. I have already addressed the advantages and disadvantages of online dictionaries for Hindi-English-Hindi and Urdu-English-Urdu, which do not require the knowledge of script and pointed to multimedia and interactive materials specifically designed for the use in the language classroom.[12]

Yet, it needs to be recognized that online translation machines such as the one launched by Google have readily made their way into the post-secondary classroom. Students in fact prefer using technology that is available to them through their technical devices over purchasing printed materials. The use of Google Translate and other instant online translation services has not gone unnoticed in academia (mostly in information technology and computational linguistics) and consequently, scholars have assessed the impact and accuracy of machine-based translation sites for a number of languages.[13] While these studies acknowledge the potential and benefits of machine-based translation for learning purposes, they also point to the glitches and dangers of relying on this novel technology in academic settings, including the classroom. The challenge with translation engines for the Hindi-Urdu classroom is that Google Translate Hindi and Google Translate Urdu are two sites that promote Hindi and Urdu as official languages as they are envisioned by the respective nation states India and Pakistan. As a consequence, the Hindi word database is frequently purged of Arabic and Persian-derived linguistic variations and oftentimes also of Urdu words. Google Translate Hindi and Google Translate Urdu therefore collide with the hyphenated language taught in the classrooms of York University and other North American educational institutions.

Instead of dismissing these translation sites upfront, I suggest incorporating them in a global citizenship education framework that raises awareness not only for stylistic and linguistic detail, but also for the ideological and algorithmic decisions taken by global corporations and their cultural implications. Furthermore, Google Translate offers translations of the individual word without grammatical markers such as gender and searching for words in the plural does not yield accurate formations. How useful then is this site for the instant translation of words and phrases? After investigating the Google Translate Hindi site's usefulness in the Hindi-Urdu classroom over a number of years, I conclude that while the site may benefit heritage-language learners who wish to quickly look up the spelling of a word or find a word that they may recognize from their heritage background, it remains inadequate for sentence translation.[14] Moreover, unlike academic dictionaries, the site fails to adequately provide linguistic and cultural information on the Hindi and Urdu lexica, which has dominated Hindi-Urdu language debates since nearly two centuries.[15]

This notwithstanding, Google Translate can be included in a global citizenship education pedagogy that explores the benefits and disadvantages inherent to translation and language acquisition technology.[16] While language learners should certainly not be discouraged from using all available means that may support and enhance their speaking and writing skills, it is the responsibility of the instructor, as a global citizen, to caution, but also encourage language learners to explore technology that is not specifically designed for the classroom. Together with the instructor, students determine the etymology and connotation of words they are offered when using Google Translate. The choices offered by Google Translate Hindi for the word "teacher" (*shikschak, shikschika, adhyapak, adhyapika, ustad, ustani*), for example, require knowledge of religion, culture, gender, and the type of knowledge that is taught. Sensitizing students thereto contributes to fostering responsible global citizenship. Subsequently, students are asked to apply such knowledge in skits or in small assignments, in which the characters represent a certain language register, religious affiliation and region. One assignment that builds a word pool with awareness towards the etymology of a word may be to interview family or community members of the Hindi-Urdu speaking diaspora, with regard to the selection of words used to convey specific cultural and religious particularities. While the possibilities of creating awareness for the interconnectedness of language, literature, and culture are endless, it remains essential that instructors encourage their students to become responsible global citizens by displaying a responsible use of language.

Conclusion

This chapter explored the pedagogy and practices embedded within a global citizenship education framework for teaching Hindi-Urdu in face-to-face, online, remote, and blended courses. At York University, the language is taught as a language that emerges out of a composite culture and shared lexicon while also distinguishing itself by the use of two considerably differing scripts. Keeping in mind that Hindi-Urdu in its hyphenated version differs from the official languages as promoted by the two nation-states of India and Pakistan, the chapter described some of the pedagogical and practical decisions taken to enable responsible global citizenship education in foreign language and heritage language classrooms. Special attention was directed at the *informed* use of technology, translation technology in particular. Equally important is the acknowledgment of the linguistic and cultural diversity of the student body who brings an array of pre-existing linguistic and cultural knowledge into the classroom. Encouraging student involvement in global citizenship education from the beginning fosters global citizenship education in the classroom and beyond.

Appendix A

First five groups of consonants in the Nagari script arranged according to their position and articulation in the mouth.

Velar Consonants:	क ख ग घ ङ
Palatal Consonants:	च छ ज झ ञ
Retroflex Consonants:	ट ठ ड ढ ण
Dental Consonants:	त थ द ध न
Labial Consonants:	प फ ब भ म

Figure 1.A. The Hindi Nagari script

Appendix B

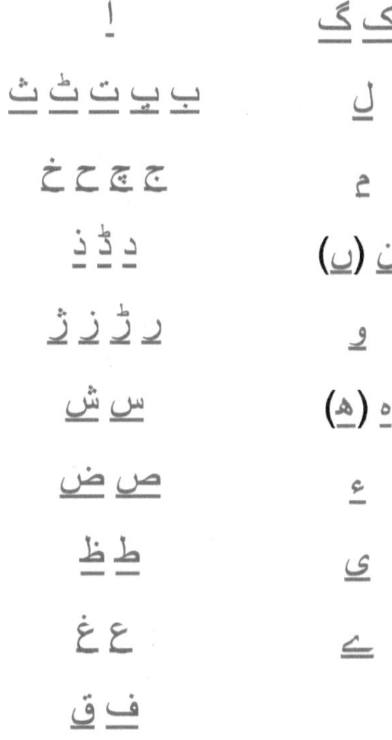

Figure 1.B. The Urdu Naskh alphabet (arranged according to shape similarity)

NOTES

1 One of many proponents of the Internationalizing Teaching and Learning framework is the University of Minnesota (Woodruff, Martin, and O'Brian, 2015) that defines internationalization as "all of the learning experiences in which students gain global and intercultural competencies." See also Clifford and the contributions in Williams and Lee. For the CLAC consortium, a non-profit, academic professional organization, see clacconsortium.org.

2 In 2012, a colloquium entitled "Foreign Languages in an Age of Globalization" addressed precisely this question. In the introduction to a collection of essays that emerged from this colloquium, Kramsch calls for foreign-language instruction to "take into account the discourse skills necessary to navigate this global world" (308). Along similar lines, but with focus on heritage language education, the Department of Languages, Literatures & Linguistics held a round table on heritage stream language education amidst innovative pedagogy and institutional challenges in February 2015.

3 See https://dlll.laps.yorku.ca.

4 The high-demand, general education course World Literatures in Perspectives is part of this planning initiative. It draws from faculty teaching in and researching on eighteen languages around the world.

5 Such as Drake University that replaced its foreign-language department with study abroad programs and individualized online instruction (Jaschik).

6 As the American Council on the Teaching of Foreign Languages (ACTL n.p.) lays out, "Global competence is the ability to: Communicate in the language of the people with whom one is interacting; Interact with awareness, sensitivity, and empathy to the perspectives of others; Withhold judgment, examining one's own perspectives as similar to or different from the perspectives of people with whom one is interacting; Be alert to cultural differences in situations outside of one's culture, including noticing cues indicating miscommunication or causing an inappropriate action or response in a situation; Act respectfully according to what is appropriate in the culture and the situation where everyone is not of the same culture or language background, including gestures, expressions, and behaviors; Increase knowledge about the products, practices, and perspectives of other cultures."

7 I use the terminology "foreign" and "second" with some unease as it doesn't accurately capture what language learning may mean to individual students and specific learner groups. For a detailed discussion of the pedagogical needs of these different learner groups, see Nijhawan, "The Hindu Urdu Heritage Language Stream," 394–5.

8 The pandemic context put new demands onto the development of a digital pedagogy for language teaching in remote and online teaching. These will form the subject of a separate article.

9 Such geo- and sociopolitically and ideologically motivated decisions are not unique to Hindi and Urdu. Zhu Hua and Li Wei address the implementation of Mandarin Chinese (rather than Cantonese taught at Confucius Institutes) as promoted by the Chinese government with its political goals concerning the nation-state.

10 Comprehensive learning sites such as A Door into Hindi (taj.oasis.unc.edu) and Darvazah – A Door into Urdu (taj.oasis.unc.edu/urdu), both developed by Afroz Taj at the University of North Carolina provide insight into everyday realities of South Asians in North India and Pakistan. New York University's Virtual Hindi (https://wp.nyu.edu/virtualhindi/) offers adapted literary readings from the *Pancatantra*, a collection of Indian fables. With the advent of fully online language courses, the language classroom has had to make adjustments to meaningfully incorporate recent developments in translation and language-acquisition technology. This is also the case for Duolingo Hindi, a free online language-acquisition course. The official launch date of Duolingo Hindi (though postponed several times over a two-year span) was set for the day that commemorated India's independence from British colonial rule. My enquiry about Duolingo's conceptualization of Hindi, that is, whether

this would be the Hindi of the Indian nation-state, a Sanskritized Hindi for the most part purged of words of Arabic, Persian and Urdu origins, or of what was conceptualized as a lingua franca of the people (the so-called Hindustani or Hin-di-Urdu), remained without response. A detailed study on Duolingo Hindi is yet to be conducted.

11 So far, Hindi-Urdu courses have not drawn from electronic chatrooms, in which students may connect with speakers from around the world.

12 See note 10.

13 For Croatian, see Brkic, Mikulic, and Matetic; for Afrikaans, see van Rensburg, Snyman, and Lotz; and for Spanish, see Jiménez-Crespo. See also Groves and Mundt and Mundt and Groves for the use of translation machines in academia.

14 Surprisingly, even simple sentences come with grammatical errors such as in the sentence "I speak Hindi": Google Translate Hindi conflates two possible pronoun options (ham or maim) and ends up with a grammatically incorrect sentence (maim hindi bolte haim) whereas Google Translate Urdu translates correctly (maim hindi bolta hum). In other cases, Google Translate Hindi and Google Translate Urdu produce the exact same sentence, such as in "This is a child" (yah ek bacca hai).

15 Over the past decades, Hindi has been infiltrated by English words, and "Hinglish" is also commonly used in the media and by students in the diaspora (Snell and Kothari).

16 Over the past decade, Google Translate Hindi and Google Translate Urdu have expanded the word choices they offer. These draw from different Hindi and Urdu language registers, but do not define their etymology. Google Translate Urdu seems to offer less word choices and often does not draw from Sanskrit-derived vocabulary while Google Translate Hindi excludes word choices from the Arabic and Persian linguistic heritage.

WORKS CITED

Brkic, Marija, Bozena Mikulic, and Maya Matetic. "Can We Beat Google Translate?" Proceedings of the ITI 2012 34th International Conference on Information Technology Interfaces, 2012, 381–6.

Clifford, Valerie. "Engaging the Disciplines in Internationalizing the Curriculum." *International Journal for Academic Development* 14, no. 2 (2009): 133–43. https://doi.org/10.1080/13601440902970122.

Groves, Michael, and Klaus Mundt. "Friend or Foe? Google Translate in Language for Academic Purposes." *English for Specific Purposes* 37 (2015): 112–21.

Jaschik, Scott. "Languages Without Language Faculty." *Inside Higher Education*, 2007. insidehighered.com.

Jiménez-Crespo, Miguel A. "The Role of Translation Technologies in Spanish Language Learning." *Journal of Spanish Language Teaching* 4, no. 2 (2017): 181–93. https://doi.org/10.1080/23247797.2017.1408949.

Kramsch, Claire. “The Challenge of Globalization in Foreign Language Education.” University of Minnesota: Centre for the Advanced Research on Language Acquisition, 2017. carla.umn.edu/presentations/OH/OH_2017.html.

– “Teaching Foreign Languages in an Era of Globalization: Introduction.” *The Modern Language Journal* 98, no. 1 (2014): 296–311. https://doi.org/10.1111/j.1540.4781.2014.12057.x.

Mack, Sara, and Mandy Menke. “International, but How? Considering Second Language Teaching and Learning from the Perspective of the Internationalizing Teaching and Learning Framework.” University of Minnesota: Centre for the Advanced Research on Language Acquisition, 2018. carla.umn.edu/presentations/recordings.html.

Mundt, Klaus, and Michael Groves. “A Double-Edged Sword: The Merits and the Policy Implications of Google Translate in Higher Education.” *European Journal of Higher Education* 6, no. 4 (2016): 387–401. https://doi.org/10.1080/21568235.2016.1172248

Nijhawan, Shobna. “The Hindi-Urdu Heritage Language Stream: Innovative Pedagogy and Institutional Challenges”. In *A Handbook on Heritage Language Education: From Innovation to Program Building*, edited by Olga Kagan, Maria Carreira, and Claire Chik, 394–406. Milton Park: Routledge, 2017.

– “‘I got the point across and that is what counts.’ Transcultural versus (?) Linguistic Competence in Language Teaching.” *Journal of the National Council of Less Commonly Taught Languages* 9, no.1 (2011): 59–81.

Snell, Rupert, and Rita Kothari, editors. *Chutneyfying English. The Phenomenon of Hinglish*. Australia: Penguin Books, 2011.

Soneson, Dan, and Caleb Zilmer, editors. *Developing Responsible Global Citizenship Through Cultures and Languages Across the Curriculum (CLAC): Selected Papers from the 2016 CLAC Conference*. University of Minnesota: Centre for the Advanced Research on Language Acquisition, 2018.

van Rensburg, Alta, Cobus Snyman, and Susan Lotz. “Applying Google Translate in a Higher Education Environment: Translation Products Assessed.” *Southern African Linguistics and Applied Language Studies* 30, no. 4 (2012): 511–24. http://hdl.handle.net/10019.1/82587.

Williams, Rhiannon, and Amy Lee, editors. *Internationalizing Higher Education. Critical Collaborations across the Curriculum*. Rotterdam: Sense Publishers, 2015.

Woodruff, Gayle, Kate Martin, and Mary Katherine B. O’Brian. “Internationalizing Teaching and Learning: Transforming teachers, Transforming Students.” In *Internationalizing Higher Education. Critical Collaborations across the Curriculum*, edited by Rhiannon Williams and Amy Lee, 47–59. Rotterdam: Sense Publishers, 2015.

2 Socratic Circles, Critical Literacy, and Culturally Responsive Teacher Education

HYUNJUNG SHIN AND GERALDINE BALZER

Introduction

This chapter explores Socratic Circles as an experiential learning activity that fosters critical literacy in pre-service teacher education. These circles are intended to better prepare teacher candidates (TCs) in their readiness to meet the needs of linguistically and culturally diverse students (LCDS). With continued increase in the number of LCDS in most schools around the globe, there is a strong need to re-orient language and literacy teacher education with the goals of better serving the diverse needs of students in today's classrooms. Yet many mainstream teacher education traditions perpetuate existing pedagogical practices and Eurocentric knowledge, as Shin and Robertson suggest, and pay insufficient attention to fostering affirming attitudes towards diversity. Curricula support for TCs that seeks the needed pedagogical assistance and resources to support LCDS is insufficient, especially outside of big cities. Existing research does not focus on how teachers respond to the increasing linguistic and cultural diversity in small suburban classrooms.

We draw from our experiences as two faculty members at a Canadian university located in a medium-sized city that has been traditionally homogeneous but is increasingly more diverse. Given its high Indigenous population and the calls to action stemming from the Truth and Reconciliation Commission of Canada, there is also an increased emphasis on incorporating Indigenous perspectives into the university curricula and pedagogies at our university. Historically, the prairie region of Canada was populated by settler farmers from the British Isles and European immigrants and refugees; diversity was evident in the many languages and cultural traditions practiced in culturally and linguistically homogenous communities. Indigenous people had been resettled on reserve lands and had minimal contact with the settler population. In the ensuing decades, communities experienced language loss and English became a hegemonizing force. Today, urbanization has led to depopulation of rural communities while recent immigration has drawn from Asia and Africa as well as Europe. Parallel to the shifting demographics caused by internationalization, the university has undertaken initiatives to Indigenize. This is, in part, a response to increased Indigenous enrolment as well as the calls to action arising from the Truth and Reconciliation Commission of Canada. Since the majority of our TCs come from Eurocentric traditions and a significant number from homogenous rural communities, engaging in literary practices that validate a diversity of backgrounds becomes increasingly important.

Our chapter begins with a brief description of Socratic Circles as a critical pedagogical tool for pre-service teacher practices. We then critically reflect on how, in pre-service teacher courses, our adoption of Socratic Circles provides students the opportunity to engage in lively, critical discussions. We look at the way in which our approach encourages students' development of critical literacies, as well as linguistically and culturally responsive pedagogies that could potentially be applied in their future classrooms. We conclude with a discussion of how Socratic Circles may serve as pedagogical tools to envision decolonizing our praxis through critical pedagogies. While it may seem counter intuitive that Socratic Circles, a method based on the pedagogical approach of a Greek philosopher, is used as a decolonizing practice, there are reasons we believe this method works in this context. Socratic Circles, as mentioned earlier, provide an opportunity to share ideas freely and engage in discussion that expands on the various ideas forwarded by students in the class. The diversity of backgrounds and experiences that TCs bring to the classroom ensure that there is a multiplicity of responses to articles they have read. The free flow of discussion encouraged by Socratic Circles allows for examination and exploration of these ideas without negative critique providing an opportunity for students to grow in their understanding of the various world views that shape the personal philosophies of their peers. Furthermore, Blaeser, Hanson, and Ong, among others, emphasize that Indigenous literacy practices often highlight oracy over literacy. We believe that the oral discussion component of Socratic Circles is a good way to familiarize students with the importance of oracy.

Socratic Circles and Critical Literacy

As faculty colleagues, we come from different backgrounds: Hyunjung is a bilingual first-generation immigrant from Korea, majoring in second language (L2) education. Geraldine is a bilingual second-generation Canadian, a descendent of Eastern European refugees. Regardless of differences, we share our belief in language and literacy education as a socially situated practice. We work towards a critical understanding of ways in which the broader sociopolitical relations among language, culture, identity, and social power play out within the classroom, as Cummins argues, in order to challenge the status quo. We also share our passion for Freire's critical pedagogy. We are drawn by the way in which his work conceives teaching as dialogues between teacher and students, highlighting the sociopolitical context of learning and teaching. Such philosophy of teaching and cultivating critical literacies has led us to adopt Socratic Circles in our pre-service teacher education courses.

Socratic Circles provide opportunity for students to raise difficult questions and discuss complex issues in a judgment-free, non-conflictual environment. Unlike debates, Socratic Circles are not concerned with proving points but with broadening the discussion by bringing forward as many ideas as possible. Copeland notes that "modern education appears obsessed with answers – both correct and incorrect. It is questions, however, that drive the human mind in critical thought" (7). Our pre-service teacher education classrooms are filled with students eager to become the best teachers possible and who continually look for the right answer or right method to adopt in their classrooms. While they recognize the goal of educating critical and creative thinkers, or as described by bell hooks, "enlightened witnesses … those who are critically vigilant both about what is being told to us and how we respond to what is being told" (8), they are caught in an education system that rewards correct answers and discourages challenging questions. Copeland draws on the tradition of Socratic questioning as "a systematic process for examining the ideas, questions, and answers that form the basis of human belief … recognizing that all new understanding is linked to prior understanding, that thought itself is a continuous thread woven through our lives rather than isolated sets of questions and answers" (7–8). Copeland stresses that "all thinking is flawed and incomplete, that all ideas can be further developed and better explained" (8). With this philosophy as a base, we use Socratic Circles to expose the flawed nature of our preconceived understandings, and to challenge and build on the knowledge that students bring with them to the classroom. Socratic Circles encourage the increase of in-class student participation. These enable critical discussions that provide opportunities for students to construct their own knowledge and consider how they might, in turn, provide these opportunities to their future students. While TCs are more concerned with the practical than the theoretical aspects of teaching, the practice of Socratic Circles inserts theory into practice. The questions that are raised through these circles become a form of problem-posing, a method advocated by Freire and designed to raise critical consciousness.

Socratic Circles and Linguistically and Culturally Responsive Teaching

In classrooms, Socratic Circles provide a learning opportunity where students, not teachers, take ownership. In the quest for democratic, student-centred education, Socratic Circles create a space for participants to express their conceptualizations, build on the ideas of each other, question those ideas, and develop new ways of seeing the world. Copeland's Socratic Circle model is a method we have used in our teaching. It follows a discussion-feedback-reversal format, as detailed below. Implementation of the Socratic Circle begins with a reading that is common to an entire class. We prefer to choose an article that challenges the pre-service teachers' understanding of a commonly held perspective. TCs are asked to read the article and formulate several questions based on their reading and their understanding of the article. This initiates the discussion stage of the circle. The class is then divided in two, with half forming an inner circle and the remainder forming the outer circle. The role of the inner circle is to begin the discussion: one participant poses a question and the remainder of the participants in the inner circle respond to that question. When dialogue wanes, another question is posed.

During this time, the outer circle observes the flow of dialogue, considering what contributes to or detracts from the dialogue, while preparing for the feedback stage. Students are often reminded that the exercise is a discussion, not a debate – there are no winners or losers, and all ideas are valid and worthy of exploration. After a specific time period, the inner circle ceases their discussion, and the outer circle provides feedback. As instructed, the feedback focuses on the dialogue itself: turn taking, the flow of ideas, and member participation, not on the ideas and questions raised. The reversal stage occurs when the two groups exchange places, and the process repeats itself.

Initially, students are challenged by the free-flowing nature of the conversation. Students who are used to expressing themselves are often critiqued for not allowing quieter students an opportunity to speak. Since the smallness of the inner circle makes their silence obvious, quieter students are challenged to speak. Through their observations, the outer circle gains a better understanding of effective discussion and are able to comment on behaviours that advance or silence ideas. This feedback process enables students to improve their own contributions to the discussion. An important role of the outer circle is to comment on these processes. The role of the teacher is limited to ensuring that dialogue and not debate occurs, and to add additional questions should the conversation fail. Following the Socratic Circles, a full class discussion can ensue where the teacher expands and adds to the ideas generated by the group.

Socratic Circles in Practice

Hyunjung successfully introduced Socratic Circles into her Secondary Literacy course. The topic of this course was planning for diversity and the development of positive attitudes towards linguistic and cultural diversity among TCs. For this session, TCs were asked to explore how they may incorporate Indigenous literacy and perspectives into their own diverse classrooms. Before class, students were assigned four short readings related to the topic. In class, students were informally grouped into topics based on the articles they had read. An adapted jigsaw discussion ensued to prepare students for upcoming discussions in Socratic Circles. Once the students familiarized themselves with all four readings, Hyunjung presented the framework of a Socratic Circle for a connected discussion opportunity. She also facilitated the shift in students' energies into a situation where they formed two Socratic Circles. For their Socratic Circle discussion, both groups chose the article entitled "Whose English counts? Indigenous English in Saskatchewan schools," by Sterzuk. During the discussion, many TCs mentioned that they had not realized Indigenous *Englishes* are legitimate forms of English, instead of dialects. Since this was the first-time students were introduced to this technique, after the completion of the demonstration - including the feedback and the reversal stage, Hyunjung debriefed this practice with the entire class. The discussion included ideas about scaffolding group participation through both the opportunity to speak, and the chance to observe. This was followed by discussions of how TCs might adopt this technique in their own classrooms. A final focus on classroom discussions was presented to remind TCs of some overarching ideas related to creating ideal environments for this type of discussion: encouraging listening, establishing goals for discussion, focusing discussion, and avoiding squelching discussion.

At the time, Hyunjung had a colleague visit her class for a peer teaching observation. This colleague reported in her feedback letter that during the break, she heard many students talking very animatedly about the Socratic Circle discussion technique. She also highlighted how students appreciated the Indigenous content that was being discussed including language-based inequalities whereby speakers of certain languages or certain varieties of languages are differently positioned in the social hierarchy. She commented that through this activity, Hyunjung was able to "guide students' responses into quite difficult territory, navigating a number of highly sensitive topics including white privilege and racism," while being "respectful to students in their developing views," "nudged the students into examples of critical literacy outcomes that they would wish to replicate in their own classroom learning environments," and "presenting deeper information in regards to subjects such as power and relationships." She also noted how much she herself enjoyed learning this new framework and stated, "I am now planning to give it a try in my own courses." In group presentation assignments later in the term, many TCs chose to implement Socratic Circles in their teaching demonstration to see possibilities for their own classrooms and generated meaningful discussions in fun and engaging ways. Students' comments included "[Socratic Circle] offers active learning opportunities," "gives everyone a chance to listen, reflect, and express their own ideas," is "a valuable tool both for myself and for my future students to make better, more engaging lessons," and "a great way to have group discussions and for planning projects."

Geraldine also uses Socratic Circles for another section of the same course, Literacy Across the Secondary Curriculum. This course is required for secondary TCs in all subject areas. TCs majoring in math or the sciences struggle to see the relevance of literacy to their disciplines. By choosing a diversity of articles to initiate the discussion, the links to cross disciplinary literacies can be made. For example, in Mason's paper entitled "A Kinder Mathematics for Nunavut," TCs consider ways of seeing mathematics from a non-traditional perspective. Mason references ethnomathematics, which "suggests that the mathematics of different people are different not just in form or the context in which it is enacted, but in its nature" (136). Pre-service TCs had difficulty imaging mathematics that did not stem from a Eurocentric perspective and struggled to consider what ethnomathematics might look like. Students generated this question to begin their Socratic circle dialogue: Seeing as how mathematics is the basis behind a large portion of top paying jobs in North America, would it be okay to sacrifice the enjoyment and success of math for some in order to give a bigger opportunity for success in the working world for others? The Socratic Circle format enabled students to explore a diversity of ideas without arriving at a fixed conclusion. While Mason's article focused on the complexities of math education, it also provided a springboard into a discussion of literacies and how they are impacted by context and place. TCs struggled with ideas. Through their dialogue, however, they furthered their understanding of multiple literacies and developed their language skills. Mason challenged them to consider that "curriculum not be based on universal truths, but on the local and specific realities of particular communities and cultures" (139). Socratic Circles provided a methodology that facilitated open dialogue and enabled students to ponder difficult questions to which there was no right answer. TCs described their experiences with Socratic Circles as "thought provoking discussions," and an "opportunity to learn within the community of the class." For TCs, the Socratic Circles provide an opportunity for them to construct their own knowledge through problem-posing and dialogue. Ultimately, through the realization that there may be a multiplicity of answers and methods, students are more likely to be the "enlightened witnesses" by encouraging each other and their future students to be critical and creative thinkers.

Conclusion: Decolonizing Language and Literacy Teacher Education

We have examined Socratic Circles as an experiential learning activity to build critical awareness towards linguistic and cultural diversity. We argued how this is a quality essential for linguistically and culturally responsive teaching amongst our TCs who grew up in relatively homogeneous contexts. Language learning almost always involves learning about the social context within which the language is used. In Canada, the social context within which the teaching and learning of official languages and other minority, heritage, or Indigenous languages occur cannot be separated from settler colonialism and the unequal settler-Indigenous relationship. Thus, language learning and teaching is embedded in sociopolitical and economic relations of power, and hence plays a key role in the construction as well as the transformation of inequality between the privileged and the underprivileged. Fung suggests that "[the] Canadian experience cannot be removed from the Canadian imaginary, which, as a by-product of culture being produced in this country, continues to serve and protect a white masculine settler-colonial hegemony" (18), further marginalizing immigrant and racialized Canadians. Academics such as Loomba and Smith claim that colonial systems continue to elevate settler populations and subjugate Indigenous populations in today's world, and Donald notes that Canadian teachers who remain largely white, female, and middle-class act as gatekeepers by controlling ideas, knowledges, and texts. Battiste reiterates these conclusions: "Education is a process by which a culture expresses its reality and values, processes its culture, and transmits it to each generation" and identifies "the need for a serious and far-reaching examination of the assumptions inherent in Eurocentric curricula" (104). Similarly, we argue that the colonial discourses and ideologies around the representation of Indigenous peoples and their languages and culture must be a clear focus for the study of language learning and teaching. Through the use of Socratic Circles, we are able to introduce articles that challenge the status quo and thereby challenge our TCs to rethink their understandings of knowledge and the curriculum that shaped their thinking. We hope our discussion presents one possible pedagogical intervention to engage with the problems generated through colonial histories and by perpetuating colonial discourses around Indigenous languages and knowledges in order to decolonize language and literacy teacher education.

WORKS CITED

Battiste, Marie. *Decolonizing Education: Nourishing the Learning Spirit*. Saskatoon, SK: Purich, 2012.

Blaeser, Kimberly. *Writing Voices Speaking: Native Authors and an Oral Aesthetic. Talking on the Page: Editing Aboriginal Oral Texts*. Toronto: University of Toronto Press, 1999.

Copeland, Matt. *Socratic Circles: Fostering Critical and Creative Thinking in Middle and High School*. Stenhouse, 2005.

Cummins, Jim. *Language, Power and Pedagogy: Bilingual Children in the Crossfire*. Bristol: Multilingual Matters, 2000.

Donald, David. "Forts, Curriculum, and Ethical Relationality." In *Reconsidering Canadian Curriculum Studies: Provoking Historical, Present, and Future Perspectives*, edited by Nicholas Ng-A-Fook and Jennifer Rottman, 39–46. London: Palgrave, 2012.

Freire, Paulo. *Pedagogy of the Oppressed*. London: Continuum, 2000.

Fung, Amy. *Before I Was a Critic I Was a Human Being*. Hong Kong: Book*Hug Press, 2019.

Hanson, Aubrey. "Relational Encounters with Indigenous Literatures." *McGill Journal of Education* 53, no. 2 (2018): 312–30.

hooks, bell. *Cultural Criticism and Transformation*. 1997. www.mediaed.org/transcripts/Bell-HooksTranscript.pdf.

Loomba, Ania. *Colonialism/Postcolonialism*. Milton Park: Routledge, 1998.

Mason, Ralph. T. "A Kinder Mathematics for Nunavut." In *Curriculum as Cultural Practice: Post-colonial Imaginations*, edited by Yatta Kanu, 131–49. Toronto: University of Toronto Press, 2006.

Ong, Walter. *Orality and Literacy*. New York: Routledge, 2021.

Shin, Hyunjug, and Kaitlyn Robertson. "Immigrant and Minority Parent Engagement: A Participatory Approach in Pre-service Teacher Education Program." In *Home-School Relations: International Perspectives*, edited by Yan Guo, 267–84. Singapore: Springer Nature Singapore Pvt Ltd., 2018.

Smith, Linda Tuhiwai. *Decolonizing Methodologies: Research and Indigenous Peoples*. London: Zed, 1999.

Sterzuk, Andrea. "Whose English Counts? Indigenous English in Saskatchewan Schools." *McGill Journal of Education* 43, no. 1 (2008): 9–19. https://doi.org/10.7202/019570ar.

3 Developing Future English-Language Educators' Critical Language Awareness in Cross-College Discussions

ANURADHA GOPALAKRISHNAN AND LEAH SHEPARD-CAREY

Introduction

This chapter describes an inter-college discussion activity that aims at fostering critical language awareness (CLA) in future English-language educators. Implemented in two teacher education programs, this activity created discursive spaces for participants to reflect on how they can act as "moral agents of change" (Kubanyiova and Crookes, 119) in their future teaching contexts. Critical language awareness is defined as the knowledge of linguistic practices in the world with acknowledgment of how "these practices are shaped by, and shape, social relationships of power" (Clark et al., 249). In a multilingual society, raising future educators' CLA before they enter the profession is imperative. Teachers must critically examine and engage with the tensions surrounding the globalization of English, present-day colonialism, and standardized notions of language, such as "native speaker" proficiency (Canagarajah, 3; Motha, 45).

Critical language awareness pedagogies do not derive from a prescribed list of methods; rather, teachers can draw on several frameworks that support the critical examination of language and power. For the activity in this chapter, we drew upon two theoretical framings to help us plan and implement our activity: Kumaravadivelu's conceptualization of postmethod in language teaching and the notion of dialogue (Bakhtin, 291; Freire, 17). Kumaravadivelu's framework emphasizes the situated nature of teaching ("Towards a Postmethod Pedagogy," 538). It moves away from a singular method of teaching languages and further conceptualizes L2 teaching and learning as opportunities to explore sociopolitical consciousness, identity, and possibilities for societal transformation ("Language Teacher Education," 10). One characteristic of postmethod pedagogy and other critical pedagogies is the notion of dialogue (Bakhtin, 291; Freire, 17). Dialogue is recognized as an ongoing process of meaning making, informed by experiences and identity. Future teachers are constantly in dialogue with their experiences and ideologies as they make sense of the world around them and as they conceptualize their future teaching practice. We position actual dialogue, or interaction, as integral for gaining critical awareness, acknowledging Kumaravadivelu's assertion of providing ongoing, dialogic opportunities for future educators to reflect upon their identities and future practice ("Toward a Postmethod Pedagogy," 552).

Drawing upon our theoretical frameworks, we sought to raise students' CLA, both in and across our respective teacher education contexts. At the time, we each taught courses with similar texts and goals, yet at separate institutions: in the Midwest at a small undergraduate liberal arts institution, and at a large metropolitan university. One of the texts used included *Motha's Race, Empire and English Language Teaching: Creating Responsible and Anti-Racist Practice.* This text became central to students' learning in each course. Cognizant of the many differences in student backgrounds and the teacher education contexts themselves, we wondered how each class of students would engage differently with the text and related course topics, and how they might learn from each other. As such, we created a cross-institution discussion opportunity related to the Motha text in order to facilitate CLA amongst our students. The following sections describe the context and activity in detail and provide implications for implementing this type of activity in language teacher education programs.

Context

In this chapter, we employ the term "future English-language educators" broadly, as we are cognizant of the varied educational contexts in which English-language instruction occurs. In our teacher education programs, our students were preparing to teach the English language in a number of settings in the United States and abroad. These included elementary school classrooms, secondary school classrooms – inclusive of various content areas – English as an additional language in public schools, and English as a foreign language abroad. In addition, some future teachers wished to be involved in the same contexts in other ways: some showed interest in being social workers at international schools, speech pathologists, aides working with immigrants and refugees, and others in developing teaching materials. Thus, the term "future English-language educators" refers to any student in our programs preparing to teach students of the English language or involved in working with English-language learners in any capacity.

Saint Teresa College

Saint Teresa College – a pseudonym – is a private, religiously affiliated liberal arts institution with approximately 3,400 undergraduate students, with most being from the Midwest United States. The teacher education program offers a minor in teaching English as a Second Language (TESL). This program supports K-12 licensure for work in state schools. Students may opt to concentrate their coursework in TESL without licensure. This usually attracts students who want to teach English abroad or learn more about teaching English learners in K-12 schools. The class in which this activity was situated broadly focused on theories of language acquisition and cultural considerations for teaching English learners. There were five female students, four of whom were from the surrounding area, and one from another state. All students were preparing, in some form, for state teaching licensure. Four of the students were obtaining their TESL K-12 licence in addition to another licensure area. One of the students was preparing to be an elementary teacher, yet took several classes from the TESL minor program. Although Saint Teresa College is relatively homogeneous in student race and cultural backgrounds, Leah's class did not reflect the majority. There were three students of colour in the class, two students were second-generation immigrants, and one student identified as a first-generation refugee. The remaining two students identified as being of white European descent. In this class, many of the students were introduced to critical pedagogies and CLA topics for the first time, which seemingly culminated in much growth in CLA over the course of the semester.

Midwestern University

Midwestern University – also a pseudonym – is a large university in the United States that welcomes international students to its many undergraduate and graduate programs. The number of undergraduate students currently exceeds 30,000. This university promotes liberal values and claims no religious affiliation.

The TESL minor program offers courses in preparing students to teach English, both within the United States and abroad. This program offers a certificate in teaching English and therefore attracts both degree and non-degree students. The class in which the activity was implemented included twenty students, with sixteen female and four male students. The focus of this course is developing students' intercultural awareness as they enter new cultures and countries to teach English. Some of the topics discussed included language socialization, identity formation in language learners, racio-linguistics, context-specific teaching, and culturally sensitive language materials. There were three international students, and amongst the other students many had travelled abroad to study or to teach English. Students came from both rural and urban backgrounds and had diverse schooling experiences. Most of the students expressed an interest in becoming English-language teachers. Some wished to become social workers who might still need to interact with and possibly teach refugees and immigrants with limited to no English knowledge.

Table 3.1. Google Sheet with student groups

1	Group	Name	Class/section/ college/university	Email address	Group meeting time (11/26–12/2)
2	1	Student 1	Institution 1		
3		Student 2	Institution 2		
4		Student 3	Institution 2		
5					
6	2	Student 1	Institution 1		
7		Student 2	Institution 2		
8					
9	3	Student 1	Institution 1		
10		Student 2	Institution 2		
11					
12	4	Student 1	Institution 1		
13		Student 2	Institution 2		

Activity

The activity began with assigned weekly readings on the topics of race, language, and identity in English-language teaching. Most readings were chosen to match well with the contexts in which students planned to work in the future. An assigned, common reading for both groups was *Race, Empire, and English Language Teaching: Creating Responsible and Ethical Anti-racist Practice* by Suhanthie Motha. The reading was spread over several weeks with intermittent in-class discussions about central issues that were prevalent in the chapters. Once both groups had completed reading the book, the discussion activity was introduced to them.

Set-Up Phase

Towards the middle of the semester, students were introduced to the activity. Students were provided detailed explanations of what the activity entailed, the rationale behind it, and the timeline for its completion. In preparing for the activity, students were divided into pairs or triads. As instructors, we were familiar with the backgrounds of our students, which included an awareness of their strengths and vast experiences. We intentionally grouped them in a manner so that every pair or triad possessed ample variety in terms of personality, country of origin, future goals, languages known, immigrant background, and teaching experience. These student groups were entered into a Google Sheet (table 3.1) and shared with both sets of students. Students were required to add their email address to the Google Sheet so that their partners could contact them. Students were instructed to reach out to their partner(s) and agree on a convenient time for them to meet to discuss the book, as well as to decide whether they would meet online or in-person. If they were meeting online, the online platform they planned to use had to be mentioned in the Google Sheet.

Discussion

Once all the information about the meeting had been entered, we explained the details of the activity. An activity sheet (see box 3.1) with guiding discussion questions was given to all students. We suggested that they should begin the discussion with a self-introduction and some icebreaker questions (introduction questions in the activity sheet).

BOX 3.1. ACTIVITY SHEET

Discussion

Meet your group member(s) at the designated time to discuss the Motha book. Given below are some questions that can guide your discussion. These questions are meant to act as prompts, but feel free to follow the flow of your discussion or to focus on one question deeply. You are expected to discuss the book for a minimum of 45 minutes. Ensure that everybody in the group is offered sufficient opportunities to express their thoughts. We encourage you to take notes on interesting points, thoughts, questions, etc. even as you are engaged in discussion or right after the discussion ends. This will help you with the post discussion task.

Introduction Questions (first 10 min)

- Name, major/minor, future plans for teaching or being involved in education
- Talk about your college, what it's like
- Anything else you'd like to share

Book Discussion

- Motha argues that the English language has a contested past. What was so contested about how English was used or taught in the past?
- Motha points out that we continue to see remnants of the colonial past in the learning and teaching of the English language in our schools, in educational policies, and in our society at large. What are some ways in which we see these remnants?
- Do you see any of these in your immediate contexts and/ or your personal experiences (e.g., study abroad, teaching, service learning, volunteering, your own language learning experiences, etc.)?
- The teachers in the book had varying experiences, identities, and ideologies that changed as they became teachers. How do you think your language ideologies and cultural background will impact your teaching practices?

- If you have an idea of your specific future context, do you predict ideological clashes between yourself and your teaching context? Do you have strategies and ideas for working in culturally and linguistically diverse settings?
- Do you see yourself applying some of Motha's suggestions for pedagogy (Ch. 6)? How so? What do anti-racist pedagogies look like in your future context?

Once the students were ready to begin the discussion, they had the option of using (or not) the questions provided under "Book Discussion" to guide their conversation. These questions were framed in such a way as to elicit key points contained in individual chapters, as well as the overall arguments of the author. Students were told that, while these questions could help guide their discussion, they were free to follow the flow of their conversation. Alternatively, students were also allowed to produce questions and highlight points of interest from the book that were not included on the activity sheet. We recommended that the students take notes, either independently or together, in a common document as they engaged in discussion. Any important points or questions that were brought up during the discussion could be recorded, and possibly used to aid in their post-discussion reflection.

Post-Discussion Reflection

In order to allow for some introspection, students were asked to write a one-page individual reflection on the activity following the book discussion. We emphasized that this reflection did not necessarily have to be about the book itself, as they had discussed it in class and with peers from the other institution. Instead, this reflection was based on the activity itself. Students were instructed to reflect on two different aspects: how the activity improved their understanding of the book and what they thought of the activity. To aid their writing, they were given the following prompts:

1. How did this conversation enhance your understanding of:
   - racialized practices in English language teaching?
   - implementing anti-racist pedagogies?
   - the impact of your identity on teaching?
   - any other insights and questions that came up during your conversation?
2. Tell us your thoughts about engaging in a conversation with students from a different institution.

Students' Reactions

The post-discussion reflections included a final section where students were asked to share their thoughts on the activity. All students reacted positively, with reasons ranging from it was fun to gaining a deeper understanding of the topics. Many pointed out that interacting with students that they did not know was surprisingly beneficial. First, students expressed that initially they had been sceptical about conversing with someone they did not know. Yet the unfamiliarity with the partner and their fresh perspectives made the conversation interesting. Second, despite the diversity in the students' backgrounds, classes, and education, there was one underlying similarity in all student groups: their professional goal to work with students learning English. This common goal and interest fostered engaged and active participation among the students.

Third, students in both institutions aimed to work in different contexts, including: English as a second language, English as a foreign language, content-based English classes, and adult basic education. In their reflections, many students indicated that the diverse teaching contexts in which they and their partners intended to work brought out meaningful interpretations of the book. Students' contrasting arguments stemmed from the relevance of the reading and significance to each of these contexts, thereby enriching the conversation. In their reflections, students also claimed that other differences, such as whether or not they were native speakers of English, international or local students, and the state where they were raised, contributed to the diverse perspectives in their conversations.

The most significant comment came from a few students who mentioned that their conversations improved their awareness of their biases towards the topics of discussion. The interactions on the book and related topics brought to light how their social, cultural, and educational upbringing had shaped their thought processes. The conversation made explicit their individual biases and triggered the students to think about why they harboured such biases.

Implications and Conclusion

As we prepare future language educators to teach in a multilingual society, we agree with Kubanyiova and Crookes in their call to develop language teachers as moral agents. More specifically, teachers must be able to examine critically the relationships between language, power, and race, as well as problematize the practices that result from specific ideologies of language teaching. We contend that raising students' CLA through a variety of intentional ongoing, dialogic opportunities will help them acknowledge their role as a "moral agent" (Kubanyiova and Crookes, 119) capable of transformative practice in their own classrooms. The activity presented in this chapter is just one of many that may facilitate CLA. We hold that opportunities to engage in critical conversations must be consistent throughout a teacher education program. Additionally, without opportunities to build community and recognize the discomfort of engaging in CLA work in our separate contexts, this activity would cease to be meaningful for students. However, there are implications of engaging in cross-institutional activities for future English-language educators, as there seems to be an untapped potential in collaborating with other teacher education programs. Broadly, the distinctions between the teacher education programs enriched the students' discussions in various ways, as students had different experiences and content in their programs.

The variety of students' future teaching contexts, which also connected to the distinctions in program context, provided opportunities for students to reflect collectively on how issues of race and language may impact their teaching in different ways. Specifically, some students had different and extended experience with critical frameworks, and thus, conversations amongst students with differing experiences provide new perspectives and points for further thinking. As we move forward, we suggest that all teacher education programs should explicitly address issues of language, race, and power via intentional CLA pedagogies. We also assert that future teachers need multiple opportunities and outlets to problematize such topics. With the significant number of culturally and linguistically diverse students in public schools today, as well as in primary and secondary licensure programs, planning for conversations and experiences surrounding CLA throughout the teacher education program is particularly important. We further recommend that establishing cross-institutional relationships and activities are potentially effective ways to do so, paying careful attention to the students, the platform, and the organization of the activity. While attending to the impacts of power, globalization, and contact of languages and language varieties in our classes, we must recognize the potential of contact across teacher education programs and how these cross-institutional opportunities can facilitate critical language awareness for all students and teachers.

WORKS CITED

Bakhtin, Mikhail M. *The Dialogic Imagination*. Austin, TX: University of Texas Press, 1981.

Canagarajah, Suresh A. *Resisting Linguistic Imperialism in English Teaching*. Oxford: Oxford UP, 1999.

Clark, Romy, et al. "Critical Language Awareness Part I: A Critical Review of Three Current Approaches to Language Awareness." *Language and Education* 4, no. 4 (1990): 249–60. https://doi.org/10.1080/09500789009541291.

Freire, Paulo. *Pedagogy of the Oppressed*. London: Continuum, 1970.

Kumaravadivelu, B. *Language Teacher Education for a Global Society: A Modular Model for Knowing, Analyzing, Recognizing, Doing, and Seeing*. Milton Park: Routledge, 2012.

– "Toward a Postmethod Pedagogy." *TESOL Quarterly* 35, no. 4 (2001): 537–60. https://doi.org/10.2307/3588427.

Motha, Suhanthie. *Race, Empire, and English Language Teaching*. New York: Teachers College Press, 2014.

SECTION II

Designing Classroom Resources, Activities, and Assessment Tools for Student Engagement

From host and foreign language learning to teaching applied linguistics, this section recognizes pedagogues' pivotal role in students' learning processes. It pays close attention to the significance of creating well-informed assessments and engaging learners with critical material that is of interest and relevance to their own realities and interests. With a focus on differing qualitative aspects of language learning at the postsecondary level, this segment is comprised of the following four chapters.

Chapter 4, "Teaching with Case Studies," illustrates the significance of student engagement. Lynn Burley highlights the benefits of using real-life situations as a pedagogical tool for undergraduate students in the field of linguistics. This pedagogue offers a description of activities involving case studies and supports how such use increases students' interest, in-class participation, and involvement. She stresses the way in which an enquiry-based method of teaching enhances students' scientific literacy as well as their critical thinking, interpersonal, collaborative, and ethical decision-making skills.

Chapter 5, "Conceptualizing the Significance of Studying Translingual, Autobiographic Narratives in ESL Classrooms at the Post-Secondary Level," considers the importance of reinforcing students' reading and writing skills through the introduction and discussion of translingual auto-narratives. With a focus on teaching English as a second language at the postsecondary level, Carra-Salsberg underlines the didactive meaning of studying published, host-language learning reflections in the form of essays and poems, and contextualized sections of migrant memoirs. The author looks at the subjective significance of creating a space to engage students in critical discussions that relate to identity formations and transformations within the problem of language, socio-geographic relocations, and host-language learning. Carra-Salsberg argues that, through such relevant material, learners become intrinsically and socially motivated to work individually and collaboratively through exercises that have the layered purpose of improving their host-language skills, while aiding in students' understandings of their own linguistic relocation(s).

In chapter 6, "Classroom-Based Assessment Practices of College Korean-Language Teachers: A Qualitative Study," Hye-Sook Wang centres her discussion on literacy assessments and literacy practices in foreign language teaching. As a Korean-language instructor at Brown University, Wang looks at the importance of conceptualizing the educational value of assessing students' learning effectiveness and progress. She studies the need to understand instructors' general perceptions regarding evaluations, for pre-service and service instructors' assessment training, for knowledge distribution of current postsecondary evaluation practices, and for further pedagogical studies that are crucial for language learning. Wang's discussion centres on the realm of Korean foreign and heritage-language learning. Needless to say, her chapter is of much relevance to postsecondary instructors of all languages and levels of instruction.

Chapter 7, "Classroom Activities for Student Engagement: '5 Minutes' and Survey Project" by Myounghee Cho, presents the importance and logistics of pre-class engagement activities. In her chapter, Cho argues that providing learners with informal, pre-class, additional exposure to the target language and culture in the form of videos and post-video discussions results in a productive rapport between students and the instructor. Such informal exposure establishes a relaxed, low-stress, yet productive learning environment that increases students' motivation. It also establishes a positive teacher-student rapport and enhances students' proficiency in interpersonal, interpretative, and presentational modes of communication. Grounded in her own experiences as a postsecondary instructor of Korean at the elementary and intermediate levels, Cho explores the manner in which students' learning potential is increased when they are not fully cognizant of the targeted learning task to which they are exposed.

As described above, this section pays close attention to post-secondary instructors' crucial role in students' motivation, agency, and learning. Its topics range from a qualitative study that points to the utmost significance of instructors' assessment literacy to theoretical and practical guidance on teaching within the fields of language socialization and host and foreign language acquisition. Activities presented in this section engage students prior to and following the commencement of scheduled lessons. Aside from highlighting the significance of formal and informal teaching, this section stresses the value of working with timely material that is relevant to students' overall interests. Together, chapters 4, 5, 6, and 7 point to the pedagogical implications of developing circumspect assessments and lessons that inform, while reflecting, learners' acquisition of language(s) or language-related subject(s).

4 Teaching with Case Studies

LYNN BURLEY

Introduction

Case studies have long been a teaching tool in business, law, the sciences, and the social sciences, but they are largely absent in teaching linguistics. Perhaps this is because many courses in an undergraduate linguistics program focus on learning phonetics, phonology, morphology, syntax, and semantics – that is, areas that do not lend themselves very well to a case study approach. However, much of the applied linguistics in an undergraduate curriculum is perfect for the case study method since we find inherent in it the elements that make for a good case study: a problem or question set in a real-world situation that can be approached using analytical tools and ethical decision-making skills. In courses where language and culture, language policy and management, language and education, language documentation, and language and social issues are examined, teaching with a case study offers a systematic method that is highly engaging for students, while also teaching scientific literacy and critical thinking skills. Using case studies, an enquiry-based method of teaching, has been shown to increase students' critical thinking skills over more traditional teaching methods, and is an excellent way to enhance student learning of linguistics (Thaiposria and Wannapiroon, 2138).

What Is a Case Study?

A case study can take several different forms, but the kind that teaches scientific literacy, ethical decision making, and uses analytical tools is ideally suited to teaching linguistics. Language is fundamental to an individual's or a group's identity, and, as such, making decisions involving language use, rights, policy, or management always has an ethical dimension that must be considered. The case study presents a question or poses a problem for students to investigate, and does so in an engaging way, preferably through stories of real people and actual situations. It provides, moreover, a guide of reading materials, activities, and assessments to be followed over a course of time, from two weeks to an entire semester, although four to six weeks is a good target for undergraduate linguistics courses as such a length of time allows for in-depth analysis and reflection yet does not turn the course into a seminar, if that is not what the course is intended to be.

A case study is the collection of materials and a guide to engaging with those materials. The question or problem begins the case study, followed by the student learning outcomes (SLOs) (see below), so that students know what they are expected to do. The instructor writes a section introducing the issue, including any background information the student needs to put the issue in context. This can best be done by providing narratives of a person or group who has encountered this conflict or faced this question. At the heart of the matter should be an ethical conflict where values, rights, or beliefs are called into question. As Kenneth Winston of the Kennedy School of Government at Harvard University states:

> only the detail of a real case situates ethical conflict in such a way as to encourage the exercise of moral imagination in the search for innovative solutions. Without knowledge of the constraints and opportunities present in the environment, reasoning is either sterile (having no real application) or artificial (producing solutions all too easily). (3)

This is part of utilizing high-impact practices, where students feel they have a stake in the outcome and an ethical dilemma encourages a high level of engagement in discussion and collaborative activities. The case proceeds by asking questions that challenge students to reflect, to analyse, to question their own assumptions, and to share their answers in discussions. The case materials that the instructor has chosen will need to be organized so that students move through the complexities one point at a time, finally concluding with students being able to formulate an argument and provide evidence for their conclusions, usually in an essay or a formal presentation.

Why Use a Case Study?

The case study is well-suited to courses that are part of the high-impact strategies that many universities are embracing (see, for example, Kuh[1] or Fink[2]). One high-impact strategy is the first-year seminar: courses taken by first semester students where instructor to student ratio is low (15–25 students), and where the focus is on critical enquiry and collaborative learning using writing intensive assignments in any subject area. With the lower number of students, instructors can more easily monitor several small-group discussions taking place at once or have whole-class discussions. Also, with fewer students, the instructor can require more written work where students respond to prompts in one- to two-page assignments.

Another common high-impact strategy is the learning community, where students are grouped together by majors, living space such as a residence hall, or a common attribute such as first-generation students or transfer students. These communities of students take two or more courses together, often centred on a theme or "big question" that is cross-disciplinary in nature. The case study in linguistics is ideal because it begins with a language question (first discipline), then asks students to work with data and evidence requiring scientific analysis (second discipline), and poses an ethical dilemma (third discipline). Linguistics courses are easy to pair with many other disciplines – psychology, English, composition, culture, education, sociology, anthropology, philosophy – and the case study can be designed to combine those two course disciplines in the learning community.

High-impact strategies also include writing-intensive courses and collaborative assignments in areas that focus on diversity or global issues, and the case study is a great tool to incorporate these into assignments and forms of assessments. Writing assignments can vary in length and in type and be done by individual students or in groups. Most important, simply having students write more is not enough. Anderson and others found that three features of writing tasks increase student learning (3). One feature is to ensure that students interact with at least one other student – either orally or in writing – before writing a final draft. Students working in small groups can collaborate through discussion on elements of the case study and present their findings to the class or in writing to the instructor. A second feature is that the writing task has to engage the students in integrative, critical, or original thinking, which is the primary purpose of the case study. Third, the instructor must ensure that students clearly understand what they are being asked to do in an assignment, as well as how they will be evaluated for each writing assignment. The structure of the case study with explicitly stated student learning outcomes enables the instructor to make sure that every assignment is tied to the SLOs and that rubrics can be made for each one.

Writing and Using a Case Study

Unlike disciplines that have long been using case studies, linguistics does not have a repository of published and accessible case studies, so for now we must write our own. The only one I am aware of is my own, "Should English Be the Official Language of the United States?," which was written through the Association of American Colleges & Universities' Scientific Thinking and Integrative Reasoning Skills (AAC&U's STIRS) Scholar Program in 2015 and can be found on their website[3]. This case study was designed for a first-year general education course – Linguistics, Culture, and Society – sometimes taught as a first-year seminar and sometimes as part of our residential college program, a first-year learning community. I teach it over six weeks in a class that meets three times a week. Some of the links in this version are broken, and because case studies are meant to be timely and deal with real situations, there are newer materials that would be better starting points to engage students in this issue. Nevertheless, the goals, questions, and data are all still relevant and useful. I will discuss the process I utilized as a guide to writing a case study.

The first step is to pose a question or present a problem that is a current issue concerning any area of language: language policy, education, ethics, rights, etc. This issue should be controversial, informed by course content, and must require the use of evidence to help come to any conclusions, ideally including scientific evidence that students can either collect themselves, or that can be provided. One of the main goals of using a case study is to require students to evaluate evidence – its sources and how they can be used. One must also consider the students' level, meeting the course objectives, and, in order to prompt a high level of engagement, the issue should be interesting to students. The more relevant the issue is to their lives, the more likely they will be able to understand the multiple perspectives they will encounter.

The second step is to determine what students should learn and then write that out in the form of student learning objectives. This will guide the instructor in organizing the case study and focusing on what kinds of assessments will be best to use. SLOs are observable and measurable outcomes of what students will be able to do as they complete the case study, ranging from lower-level skills to higher levels. In a case study designed for longer periods of time, the instructor can include SLOs about content as well as using data and evidence ranging from the lower-end skills (defining concepts, explaining issues, summarizing, articulating relationships) to the higher end (interpreting data, developing hypotheses, evaluating policies, and formulating arguments).

The next step is to compile the case by finding materials for students such as readings, videos, documents, podcasts, websites, and whatever else will aid them in understanding and problematizing the issue. The materials are then organized in such a way as to guide the students through a logical way of thinking about the question or problem. The level of complication of the question or problem, as well as how many SLOs there are, will dictate how much class time to devote to the case study. Ideally, two weeks would be the minimum so that students have time to work together and reflect upon, present on, or write on the questions the case study proposes. A case study could last an entire semester, if it is comprehensive enough for the subject of the class and the final product merits that time, such as a formal presentation or a research paper. In any case, four to six weeks seems to work well in keeping students engaged and in varying the kinds of tasks they are asked to perform.

The last step is to write the guide. The question or problem itself and your own expertise in teaching will help you determine which materials and information your students need at various points and what activities work best to engage your students. In my case study, the title was the following question: Should English be the official language of the United States? After listing the seven SLOs, in which I made sure to choose both lower and higher-level skills (define, articulate, explain, develop, evaluate, interpret, and formulate), I had the students read several short articles and web pages: two advocating for English as an official language, two against, and the Linguistic Society of America's statement on language rights. I also wrote an introduction with some background on what an official language was and presented a lecture in the opening class period on national languages throughout the world.

There were three main sections that seemed a natural way to structure the case study and lead students to come to their own conclusions. The first was an examination surrounding the issue of speaking English in the United States – national identity, unity and disunity, and bilingualism. Each time I have taught this case study, I have had students whose first language is not English or who had at least one parent or grandparent whose first language was not English, and most had friends or schoolmates who learned English as a second language. Sharing their stories allowed everyone in the class to have a personal connection and hear firsthand about some of the problems real people encountered who do not speak English, in addition to hearing about the attitudes they faced from others and developed themselves. This section typically takes two weeks, where students have four more readings and four more questions to answer in varied ways: either in small-group discussions, presenting answers to the large group informally, or as written homework. Class time was spent mostly on discussion with some PowerPoint lectures on the issues.

The second section introduces students to real data from the US Census Bureau's American Community Surveys detailing languages spoken in the home and how well they are spoken, broken down by demographic factors. Then we look at the same data over a span of forty years. These two weeks are spent on scientific enquiry and critical thinking to interpret the data, so we discuss how data is collected and how reliable we can expect that data to be. We crunch the numbers together as a whole class because, generally speaking, first-year students have not yet been exposed to the sort of math needed for this step. In trying to figure out how serious the problem of not being able to speak English is, we also must discuss age as a factor in learning a language, our school system, and what this means in the labour market. The final section for the next two weeks has additional readings and data on the costs involved to individuals, to schools, to government, and to society as a whole, balanced by examining the rights US citizens have as defined in the Constitution and US laws, and as human rights. Students grapple with ethical questions that are always part of the problem when looking at how best to spend tax dollars. The final assessment is an essay in which students answer the question about whether English should be the official language of the United States and use evidence to support their answer.

One consideration of great importance in teaching the case study is to be prepared to guide students through issues of human rights and social justice. Most of us are not prepared to teach ethics, but the case study requires an ethical dimension; it is probably the key component that engages the student. Ladke and Houck, in writing on teaching ethics in business management, state that the focus in teaching cases and ethics should be to help students understand their own attitudes and beliefs and to share these with others in order to gain a better understanding of their own values (157). The classroom should be a safe place where students can voice their ideas, discuss them with their peers, and offer an opportunity to reflect upon ethical decision making. At the very least, students can be made aware of the values practiced in the field and why those values matter to linguists. In my case study, students begin by reading the Linguistic Society of America's statement on language rights, which does not explicitly mention English as an official language. Students can begin to discuss and reflect upon what linguists value and why and apply that as they consider their values.

Conclusion

Teaching linguistics using case studies provides many benefits to student learning. Students practice problem-solving skills and critical-thinking skills through discussion and writing, working with data, and learning to evaluate and interpret it, all while being challenged by ethical dilemmas. The case-study method allows instructors to guide students through complex issues, making sure to cover multiple perspectives and help students learn to make decisions. There is a considerable time investment in writing a case study and in devoting weeks of class time to teaching it, but a good case study is worth that to meet the goals of student learning.

NOTES

1 www.aacu.org/leap/hips
2 files.eric.ed.gov/fulltext/EJ1104478.pdf
3 See www.aacu.org/stirs for more information.

WORKS CITED

Anderson, Paul, et al. "How to Create High-Impact Writing Assignments that Enhance Learning and Development and Reinvigorate WAC/WID Programs: What Almost 72,000 Undergraduates Taught Us." *Across the Disciplines* 13, no. 4 (2016). wac .colostate.edu/docs/atd/hip/andersonetal2016.pdf.

Burley, Lynn. "Should English Be the Official Language of the United States?" *Association of American Colleges & Universities*. 2015. www.aacu.org/stirs/casestudies/burley.

Fink, L. Dee. "Five High-Impact Teaching Practices." *Collected Essays on Learning and Teaching* 9 (2016): 3–18. https://doi.org/10.22329/celt.v9i0.4428.

Kuh, George D. "Excerpt from High-impact Educational Practices: What They Are, Who has Access to Them, and Why They Matter." *Association of American Colleges and Universities*. 2008. www.aacu.org/leap/hips.

Laditka, Sarah B., and Margaret M. Houck. "Student-Developed Case Studies: An Experiential Approach for Teaching Ethics in Management." *Journal of Business Ethics* 64, no. 2 (2006): 157–67. doi: 10.1007/s10551-005-0276-3.

Language Rights. Linguistic Society of America. 1996. www.linguisticsociety.org/files/lsa-stmt- language-rights.pdf.

Scientific Thinking and Integrative Reasoning Skills (STIRS). Association of American Colleges & Universities. 2013. www.aacu.org/stirs.

Thaiposri, Patamaporn, and Panita Wannapiroon. "Enhancing Students' Critical Thinking Skills Through Teaching and Learning by Inquiry-based Learning Activities Using Social Network and Cloud Computing." *Procedia: Social and Behavioral Sciences* 174 (2015): 2137–44. doi: 10.1016/j.sbspro.2015.02.013.

Winston, Kenneth. "Teaching Ethics by the Case Method." Case Program, Harvard Kennedy School. 1995. https://case.hks.harvard.edu/content/Teaching%20Ethics%20by%20the%20Case%20Method.pdf.

5 Conceptualizing the Significance of Studying Translingual, Autobiographic Narratives in ESL Classrooms at the Post-Secondary Level

FERNANDA CARRA-SALSBERG

Learning a new language is more than just an acquisition of a new linguistic system. It is an experience interlinked with questions of culture, involving the transformation of the way of thinking, feeling and acting.

– David Block, *Second Language Identities*, p. 58

Introduction

At the post-secondary level, English as a second language (ESL) curricula may incorporate readings that expose students to sociocultural, economic, historical, and political matters affecting host countries. With such material, students are guided in active reading, critical thinking, formal and informal discussions, and academic writing. The objective is for language students to acquire and eventually transfer skills that promote and support their success within and outside our post-secondary classrooms. Centred on such pedagogical outcome, and while accounting for "the intimate connection between education and literature" (Kellner and Share, 369), this chapter offers an alternative to student engagement: it focuses on the didactic significance of tapping into the emotionality of students' collective and individualized language learning experiences through the study of translingual auto-narratives.[1]

This work is centred on the importance of creating a space for students to conceptualize published descriptions of host-cultural immersions and host-language learning experiences. While highlighting the pedagogical, social, and intrinsic significance of reflexive, oral, and written expressions, this chapter offers curricular suggestions that actively engage post-secondary students and foster their language skills. It draws attention to the developmental and pedagogical significance of working with publications that may relate to students' own experiences within languages and cultures.[2] It also highlights the value of furthering research in the area of reflexive cross-cultural discourse as a pedagogical tool in the area of host-language acquisition.

A Close Look into the Significance of Language and the Socio-emotional Effects of Host Immersions and Language Learning

An internalized language is integral to our learning and self-other relations. It is central to our social organizations (Pavlenko, "In the World of the Tradition," 319), and key to the construction, deconstruction, and reconstruction of our identities (Block, 47). In agreement with Kramsch, language constitutes the very core of the self (4). It is a medium through which speakers perceive themselves and are perceived by others within specific communities of practice and figured worlds. This connection between language and identity is significant for our understanding of the socio-subjective transformations undergone by individuals immersed within a host foreign language and culture. By taking a post-structural approach to the study of identity formations, we conceptualize identities as fluid, multiple, constantly moving, changing, and often conflicting. Identity constructions, deconstructions, and reconstructions evolve naturally throughout our lives. Often, life changes are not sudden, anxiety-evoking experiences. Yet, with host-foreign immersions, the suddenness and degree of change in individuals' environments, self-other relations, and subject positions creates a rupture in individuals' sense of temporal continuity (Akhtar, "Strange Lands," n.p.). This explains why, after geographic, socio-cultural, and linguistic relocations and following the initial period of elation (Brown cited by Block, 60)[3], individuals may describe feeling disoriented, and/or existing within a never-ending haze (Carra-Salsberg, "A Psychoanalytic Look," 30). In time, as individuals adjust to their newly imposed reality, this inner and social crisis is brought into relief following the process of synthesis and adjustment to their new reality (30).

Newcomers' sensed unease is not only born from the tensions that arise from the sudden changes in their socio-cultural and linguistic environments. It does not solely stem from individuals' exposure to new belief systems, behaviours, and ways of life, either. Their crisis is also rooted in significant language learning, specifically in learners' inability to make relations and secure meaning (Carra-Salsberg, "Aggression," 37). Though differing in source, the emotionality of language learning is also addressed by Karpinski. In *Borrowed Tongues*, Karpinski argues that becoming proficient in a host language and giving up of one's language's instrumental function involves becoming transformed or remade within the flow of the foreign other (1–2). This loss, she suggests, concerns linguistic displacements that relate to individuals' dislocation within language and within the self. Karpinski points to the challenges learners encounter when translating or attempting to translate themselves within a host language (3). The feelings uprooted from language learning could be understood from a psychoanalytic lens: since our mother tongue is linked to our maternal imago (Akhtar, "A Third Individuation," 1069), a host language learner's crisis may also be linked to unconscious guilt: to the feelings that rise from needing to replace or socially demote the language that is interwoven with their remembered and seemingly forgotten history of affect (Carra-Salsberg, "A Psychoanalytic Look," 14).

By turning our attention to language socialization theory, we may note that the emotionality of host immersions, second language learning, and identity shifts are also tied to an alteration in language learners' group membership. Lambert argues that "the more proficient a person becomes in a second language, the more [she] may find that [her] place in [her] original membership group is modified." Lambert also suggests that at the intermediate and advanced levels of language acquisition, a speaker "experiences feelings of chagrin or regret as [she] loses ties with [her original] group" (cited by Block, 48). Block expands Lambert's argument by addressing the concept of anomie. This feeling, according to Block, is defined by experiences of internal conflicts and feelings of "moral chaos" (48–50). Such conflicts are born from the link between language and affect. They are also associated with speakers' identity shifts and self-other relations.

Karpinski, Lambert, and Block are among the many academics who examine the feelings of guilt and confusion that stem from developing new socio-emotional attachments, switching languages, and attempting to interact in a tongue that is yet to offer its speaker a sense of comfort in displacement. The socio-affective aspects of host-foreign immersions and language acquisition are central to ESL students' experiences. Hence, reading, discussing, and sharing published descriptions and theories that may be of relevance to students' own lives may increase students' inclination to learn, reflect, engage in research, write, and participate in formal and informal classroom discussions.

Working with Translingual Auto-narratives in the ESL Classroom

Translingual or cross-cultural auto-narratives in the form of essays, sections of book-length memoirs, or poems are self-representations of transformative experiences within the area of second-language learning. Through such publications, second-language speakers are encouraged to define an alternative space between incommensurable languages and cultures (Kramsch, 93). These resources of data collection[4] bring into conversation the dynamic plasticity of identity constructions and the affective nature of linguistic disruptions. Such self-reflections describe writers' attempts at understanding and organizing dislocated occurrences within languages (da Conceição Passeggi,, 293). Equally important, these published auto-narratives are spaces of reinvention, ownership, and legitimization of experiences. They are spaces in which linguistic markers such as accents become erased (Pavlenko, "In the World of the Tradition," 320), where the many voices are offered a stage to share their experiences within the complexity of second-language learning. Through the analysis of these narratives, readers reflect on their lives. By doing so, students may embrace or reject publications' claimed experiences within languages.

Working with auto-narratives in the ESL classroom allows instructors to focus on the intellectual, social, and creative aspects of active reading, critical thinking, research, and writing. This genre enables the private and public expression of students' perceived realities. It becomes a medium for students to understand, embrace or reject, interpret, and claim their own stories. Instructors may choose to work with the many topics that are brought to light through published descriptions. Through the understanding and discussion of auto-narratives, students may be guided to conduct their own research in areas within – or beyond – the themes of socio-geographic moves, culture, education, gender, and identity. Auto-narratives may also create a space for the discussion and research of the short- and long-term private and social effects of cultural pluralism and the manner in which newcomers' attempts at integration and/or acceptance are either embraced or rejected by a host country.

Examples of In-Class Exercises

There are many activities that may be linked to the introduction and ongoing discussion of translingual literature. Many may become scaffolding exercises that eventually lead to a summative assessment in the form of a midterm or final essay. Written below are two brief examples of such formative, in-class exercises.

Exercise 1:

This proposed exercise is best suited for groups of two to three students. That being said, prior to dividing the class into small groups and introducing translingual literature, students should be asked to research key theoretical concepts that relate to translingualism. Examples include:

- the subjective meaning of language
- identity and foreign linguistic immersions

- culture and culture shock
- inter-subjectivity

After introducing a chosen reading, the class should be divided into small groups and asked to answer questions that build on concepts that are directly linked to the presented literature. By taking Gustavo Pérez Firmat's "Dedication" as an example, students may be asked to briefly research this writer's life and answer the following open questions:

- Why do translingual writers place emphasis on their experiences within languages?
- What does language represent for an individual and its community of speakers?
- What does the author mean when he states: "the fact that I am writing to you in English, already falsifies what I wanted to tell you"?
- What exactly is he trying to tell his readers?
- How may the writer's identity be defined through his language(s)?
- How may we explain the writer's need to share and publish his reality between languages?
- How do the writer's descriptions of his experiences within language relate or not relate to your own? Please explain.

Ideally, questions should be uploaded on a shared online platform such as Google Docs for students to write their individual responses through a common drive, before sharing their findings with the class.

Exercise 2:

For this second exercise, students are introduced to a new cross-cultural auto-narrative. An example of such could be "The Condition of Exile: An address" by Joseph Brodsky. Before coming to class, students are asked to:

- read the discursive resource chosen by the instructor
- take careful annotations when reading[5]
- come prepared with questions and record the reading's most prominent themes (with page numbers)
- research, describe, and contextualize each recorded theme

In class, students' (home)work is to be shared with members of their groups, uploaded onto a shared online platform, and later discussed as a class.

(Individual) Assessment Component for Exercises 1 and 2:

Following the completion of the aforementioned in-class exercises, students are asked to complete a two-paragraph summary and response piece at the end of each aforementioned exercise. The first paragraph is informative – that is, a summary of the reading. In this paragraph students are asked to also contextualize, highlight, and describe the main themes presented in the reading and discussed in class. The second paragraph is a reflection.

The following are brief instructions for students. Ideally, this should be part of an individual online assignment.

Paragraph 1: Informative Paragraph

- Introduce the main idea found in the reading, provide the title of the reading and the author's name
- Summarize the main themes discussed in the reading. These should include examples and a supporting discussion
- Ensure that all sentences flow well together and discuss the same main topic
- Provide a clear reflection thesis

Paragraph 2: Reflection Paragraph

- Students may be asked to consider at least one of the following group of questions

First Group of Questions

- Does the article challenge you socially, culturally, emotionally, or theologically?
- If so, how?
- Why does it bother you, impress you, or catch your attention?

Second Group of Questions

- Has the article changed your way of thinking?
- Did it conflict with beliefs you had before?
- What evidence did it provide for you to change your opinion on the topic?

Important Note: The Reflection Paragraph should include a concluding sentence in which each student states how s/he feels about the main topic and themes discussed. This concluding sentence should support the thesis or main idea provided in the introduction paragraph.

Each writing piece (one per reading) should be explained in class and presented with a rubric that includes a brief description of the expectations and grading breakdown. An example of such a rubric is presented below:

Student Name:

Grade: /22

Reflection Assignment

Evaluation

INTRODUCTION (1 paragraph)	
Does this paragraph offer a topic sentence?	/1
Does the student give information about the author and the essay/literature from which the new information/idea is taken?	/1
Is the topic or idea (chosen from the article) clearly stated at the beginning of the reflection?	/2
Does the student summarize the main idea in 2–5 sentences (still as part of the introduction paragraph)?	/3
Does the student make a connection between the chosen idea and his/her response to it (thesis)?	/2
REFLECTION (1 paragraph)	/3
Does the student express his/her opinion/reflection on the above stated summary in a cohesive, well-organized (ensuing) paragraph?	
Does this paragraph also offer a topic sentence?	/1
After describing his/her personal and subjective response, does the student give a brief synthesis	
stating his/her conclusion?	/2
Is the thesis re-stated and supported with a concluding sentence?	/2
Does the concluding sentence flow well with the entire piece (both paragraphs)?	/1
MECHANICS AND LANGUAGE (for the entire reflection piece)	
Did the student maintain an appropriate academic tone?	/1
Did the student ensure that the reflection has correct grammar and spelling?	/2
Was the article with which the student worked cited using APA style?	/1

Final/Summative Exercise

After repeating exercises 1 and 2 with three to four more translingual autonarratives, students are to be guided on writing a reflexive essay or an expository essay that focuses on themes related to in-class discussions and their own research. A reflection essay and its accompanying rubric could be a modified, extended version of the shorter assessments explained above.[6]

As described thus far, working through topics of relevance to students' own experiences and interests may become part of a motivational force for research and dialogic expressions. Hence, in classrooms, following the reading and discussion of the themes accessed through specific self-narratives, instructors may guide students to produce their own writing. This could be achieved through structured summaries, collaborative or individual research, and reading responses that incorporate students' own language socialization experiences in the forms of reflection or exploratory essays.

Conclusion

There are pedagogical benefits to incorporating translingual auto-narratives to the ESL curricula. This focus on language and the way it forms and informs our amplified biography provides a glimpse of host-language learners' experiences. With an emphasis on the intersection of literature and education, this chapter has drawn attention to the affective, epistemological, and pedagogical significance of creating spaces for students to engage with concerns that relate to their inner and social realities as host-language learners.

Our goal as ESL post-secondary instructors is to advance students' active reading, critical thinking, oral expression, and academic writing. It is to create lessons and assessments that reinforce their oral and written skills, in hopes these become transferred to other courses within academia. Understanding auto-narratives' pedagogical potential supports the need for further research on the benefits of teaching with translingual narratives.

NOTES

1 When referring to auto-narratives, this chapter uses the terms translingual and cross-cultural interchangeably.

2 In *Switching Languages*, Steven Kellman defines a translingual writer as someone who writes in a language that is not his or her primary tongue (xviii). Paola Bohorquez defines translingualism as a psycho-emotional and linguistic condition of living in transition between two or more symbolic codes. A translingual subject is an individual who experiences an imbalance between languages (2). For this chapter, translingual literature refers to narratives written by first, 1.5, and second-generation migrants who live or have lived through the abovementioned state of transition.

3 Brown describes three stages of language acquisition: the period of excitement and euphoria over the newness of the surroundings; the "culture shock" that emerges as the individual feels the intrusion of cultural differences into the image of self and security; and acceptance, in which the speaker begins to accept the differences

in thinking and feeling that surround them. In this stage the individual slowly begins to feel empathetic towards the other culture: "near or full recovery," which is the stage of assimilation or adaption (cited by Block, 60).

4 In her article "Autobiographic Narratives as Data in Applied Linguistics," Pavlenko delineates the three interconnected types of information that may be gathered from auto-narratives: subject reality, life reality, and text reality. Subject reality is a look into how events were understood by the narrator, life reality is a study of how things are or were, at the factors that influenced and may continue to influence writers' ideologies and perception of events, and text reality is an examination of how occurrences are narrated by writers (165).

5 A seminar and sample assignment on active and critical reading and note taking should precede this lesson and related exercise. As a suggested source for such a seminar, readers may refer to Steve Marshall's *Academic Writing: Making the Transition* (2011).

6 Preparing ESL students by providing a seminar (or separate seminars) on paragraph writing, writing and supporting a statement, writing an introduction and a conclusion, in-text citations (APA, MLA, or Chicago Style), and writing a reference section are necessary preliminary steps for all in-class writing assessments.

WORKS CITED

Akhtar, Salman. "A Third Individuation: Immigration, Identity, and the Psychoanalytic Process." *Journal of American Psychoanalytic Association* 43 (1995): 1051–84. https://doi.org/10.1177/000306519504300406

– (2012, September). Strange Lands: Location and Dislocation: The Immigrant Experience. 18th Annual Day in Applied Psychoanalysis, Toronto, Ontario.

Arendt, Hannah. *Between Past and Future*. Australia: Penguin, 2006.

Block, David. *Second Language Identities*. London: Continuum, 2007.

Bohorquez-Arcila, Paola. *Living Between Languages: Linguistic Exile and Self-Translation*. PhD. diss. York University, 2008.

Britzman, Deborah. "A Note on Identification with the Aggressor." In *Novel Education: Psychoanalytic Studies of Learning and Not Learning*. New York: Peter Lang, 2006.

Britzman, Deborah, and Pitt, Alice. "Pedagogy and Clinical Knowledge: Some Psychoanalytic Observations on Losing and Refinding Significance." *JAC Online* 24 (2004), 353–74. http://www.jaconlinejournal.com/archives/vol24.2.html

Brodsky, Joseph. "The Condition We Call Exile: An Address." In *Altogether Elsewhere: Writers on Exile*, edited by Marc Robinson. San Diego: Harcourt Brace, 1994.

Carra-Salsberg, Fernanda. "Aggression and the Telos of Learning: A Psychoanalytic Study of Significant Language Learning." *Journal of Language and Psychoanalysis* 4, no. 2 (2015): 34–49. doi: http://dx.doi.org/10.7565/landp.2015v2

– "A Psychoanalytic Look into the Effects of Childhood and Adolescent Migration in Eva Hoffman's *Lost in Translation*." *Journal of Language and Psychoanalysis* 6, no. 1

(2017): 10–32. doi: http://www.language-and-psychoanalysis.com/article/view/1837/pdf_31

da Conceição-Passeggi, Maria. “Reframing Discourses: Autobiographical Narratives in Education.” *Auto/Biography Studies* 32, no. 2 (2017): 293–5.

Derrida, Jacques. *Monolingualism of the Other and the Prosthesis of Origin*. Translated by Patrick Mensah. Palo Alto: Stanford UP, 1996.

Karpinski, Eva. *Borrowed Tongues: Life Writing, Migration and Translation*. Waterloo, Canada: Wilfrid Laurier University Press, 2012.

Kellman, Steven. *Switching Languages: Translingual Writers Reflect on Their Craft*. Lincoln: University of Nebraska Press, 2003.

Kellner, Douglas, and Jeff Share. “Toward a Critical Media Literacy: Core Concepts, Debates, Organizations, and Policy.” *Discourse: Studies in the Cultural Politics of Education* 26, no. 3 (2005): 369–86. https://doi.org/10.1080/01596300500200169

Kramsch, Claire. *The Multilingual Subject: What Foreign Language Learners Say about Their Experience and Why It Matters*. Oxford: Oxford University Press, 2009.

Marshall, Steve. *Academic Writing: Making the Transition*. Toronto, Canada: Pearson, 2011.

Pavlenko, Aneta. “Autobiographic Narratives as Data in Applied Linguistics.” *Applied Linguistics* 28, no. 2 (2007): 163–88. doi: 10.1093/APPLIN/AMM008

– “In the World of the Tradition, I Was Unimagined: Negotiations of Identities in Cross-Cultural Autobiographies.” *The International Journal of Bilingualism* 5, no. 3 (2001): 317–44. https://doi.org/10.1177%2F13670069010050030401

Perez-Firmat, Gustavo. “Dedication.” In *Switching Languages: Translingual Writers Reflect on Their Craft*, edited by Stephen G. Kellman, 295–8. Lincoln: University of Nebraska Press, 2003.

6 Classroom-Based Assessment Practices of College Korean-Language Teachers: A Qualitative Study

HYE-SOOK WANG

Introduction

It is a truism that teachers play a pivotal role in students' general learning process, but their role becomes especially critical in assessment. This is not only because teachers' "meaningful" assessment feedback is believed to enhance their learning but also because teachers fulfil their responsibility as graders. While making overall assessments is one major task that all teachers are engaged in, grading is something that they do almost on a daily basis.

There are sound reasons, then, why teachers' practices need to be examined, given the place that assessment holds. Rea-Dickins underscores the "teacher agency in assessment," as she states:

> [T]he teacher as assessor both engages with and creates discourses of assessment at different levels: the individual teacher(s), the cultural context of the classroom, at professional and institutional levels, all of which – in turn – reflect the different political as well as social contexts in which the teachers work. (255)

Teachers' assessment practices are not only affected by classroom and institutional context but also deeply influenced by the teachers' beliefs, philosophy, views, attitudes, and preferences regarding assessment. Therefore, it is natural that much attention has been paid in recent years to the importance of "assessment literacy" as one of the crucial qualities required of any teacher as an agent of assessment. It is a common understanding and expectation that foreign-language teachers are generally well trained in assessment because most graduate programs offer course(s) on language assessment, although the breadth and depth of the coverage may vary from school to school and program to program. However, studies (e.g., Malone; Montee et al.) report that this might not be the case, especially for so-called less-commonly-taught languages, of which Korean is one, and suggest the need for training in assessment for in-service teachers.

Each institution or professional organization offers in-house professional development workshops for in-service teachers, but such training opportunities often are limited or perceived to be insufficient by the teachers. They are even more limited for Korean-language teachers.

In Korean-language education in US higher-education context, it appears that very little is known as to how teachers perform this important task of assessment in their respective classrooms. The American Association of Teachers of Korean made assessment one of the conference themes in 2017 and 2018,[1] but teachers' assessment practices did not receive much attention in general. In fact, most previous discourse and discussion on assessment has been predominantly focused on assessing specific skills (e.g., writing). Furthermore, qualitative studies on teachers' assessment practices in a Korean as a foreign language (KFL hereafter) setting are virtually non-existent.

The main goal of this study is to increase our understanding regarding assessment in the current practices of KFL teachers in US colleges and universities, which will be undertaken through a set of three research questions. First, what are college Korean-language teachers' general perceptions and beliefs regarding assessment? That is, what are their perceptions of their preparedness for this task – including self-assessment of their assessment literacy, how important do they view assessment in the entire teaching context, and what do they perceive as the challenges and best practices regarding this issue? Second, what do teachers consider to be a fair or sound assessment method (i.e., their definition of it), as well as the purposes of assessment? Third, what are their views of the relationship between assessment in general and grading in particular? That is, how do teachers see grading in the general context of assessment? In an institutional context and classroom setting, grading is a necessary component of the assessment, unlike in a non-institutional setting. What types of assessment tools do they use in their classes in determining grades, and how do they differ from teacher to teacher?

Literature Review

The majority of the assessment literature focuses on ESL/EFL, although there are some studies done on other foreign languages. In fact, many studies have examined teachers' assessment practices on different subjects (i.e., language vs. non-language) at different school levels (i.e., secondary schools vs. higher education) in different countries (i.e., China, Hong Kong, Australia, and Malaysia).

Assessment practices, however, appear to be relatively "underexplored" or "under-researched" topics in a KFL context. The lack of research may be due to a common perception or belief that teachers are all proficient assessors of students' learning, who possess not only sufficient knowledge of what assessment is about but also are equipped with necessary skills and tools to perform the required assessment. There is also a "taboo mentality" that suggests that what takes place in one's classroom should be left to the teacher and therefore should not be meddled with.

As far as assessment is concerned, the vast majority of studies in KFL focus on a specific type of test (e.g., a placement test or proficiency test). This is probably because these tests are in higher demand. Proficiency tests are far more popular, and a well-established system exists especially for assessing oral skills (i.e., ACTFL's Oral Proficiency Interview). Placement tests serve school-specific needs for school-specific audiences, and thus are not universal. Institutions with high enrolment in Korean programs (e.g., University of Hawaii, University of California at Berkeley, University of California at Los Angeles, Columbia University, etc.) use their own placement tests, while smaller programs use other means (e.g., personal interviews) in lieu of such formal tests. Unlike these two test types, however, achievement tests have received relatively less attention and consequently the research volume is also notably scarce.

Chang's review is especially useful since it offers a holistic view of research trends on Korean-language assessment from 1981 through 2011. This study reviewed 146 works published in Korea over the past three decades, including degree theses (MA and PhD), journal articles, books, and special project reports on this topic. The review shows that research on Korean language assessment is largely categorized into studies on 1) assessment in general, 2) proficiency tests, 3) TOPIK (Test of Proficiency in Korean, which is a standardized test that measures one's general Korean proficiency), 4) achievement tests, and 5) other assessment methods (e.g., assessment of Korean for Academic Purposes, web-based assessment, performance assessment, etc.). Among these, according to Chang, studies on proficiency tests far outnumber other types of tests. Studies on achievement tests, as Chang's review also reveals, are relatively few, focusing mostly on the effectiveness of a specific institution's assessment tools, analysis of current practices of various institutions, or ways to assess a specific language modality such as writing. There does not appear to be a similar study that reviews the research trend of assessment in Korean-language education in the United States, reflecting low scholarly attention on assessment in general as well as assessment practices in particular.

The Study

Data Collection and Procedures

The main data set used in this study is comprised of interviews with seven teachers, who are all full-time regular faculty currently employed at US

Table 6.1. Participants' demographic information

	Gender	Age	Teaching experience	Terminal academic degree held	Status/ position title	Type of schools employed
Participant #1	M	50s	20+ yrs	PhD	Sr. Lecturer	State
Participant #2	F	30s	11–15 yrs	PhD	Lecturer	State
Participant #3	F	40s	11–15 yrs	PhD	Lecturer	State
Participant #4	F	40s	16–20 yrs	PhD	Asst. Prof.	State
Participant #5	F	40s	16–20 yrs	PhD	Assoc. Prof.	State
Participant #6	M	40s	16–20 yrs	PhD	Lecturer	State
Participant #7	F	50s	16–20 yrs	MA	Lecturer	Private

higher-education institutions. The above table displays the participants' demographic backgrounds.

To summarize, while their status varies from lecturer to associate professor, all the participants have more than ten years of experience in Korean language teaching in US post-secondary institutions, and many have more than sixteen years of experience. They all have PhDs, except for one participant who has two master's degrees. All except for one participant are running the Korean-language program as the program head in their respective institutions, either as a multi-staff program or single-handedly running the program. Based on the demographic information presented above, it would be reasonable to state that all participants are seasoned teachers who have garnered much experience over the course of their long careers.

The researcher contacted each individual teacher via email to invite them to participate. The invitees were provided with an explanation of the main purpose of the study, as well as what was expected of them. If they accepted the invitation, the follow-up interview was scheduled. All the interviews took place between 17 December 2018, and 10 January 2019, and they were conducted in Korean via phone. Each interview lasted between sixty and ninety minutes. Before the interview, the participants had to return the signed consent form and survey questionnaire.

One of the most common assessment tools that has been widely used in studies investigating teachers' assessment practices in the literature is the Assessment Practices Inventory (known as API). API is a survey questionnaire that consists of seventy items encompassing all aspects of assessment in three main sections: practices related to assessing literacy standards, beliefs about assessment principles, and frequency of carrying out the above items. This measurement tool is most useful for collecting a large amount of data for the purpose of capturing a general tendency in teachers' assessment practices across the board.

Even though many studies, especially ESL/EFL ones, adopted API as their data collection method, this study elected not to because it was deemed not to serve the objective of this study appropriately. Instead, the researcher devised her own questionnaire based on several forms used in other studies (Montee et al.; Shohamy et al.), with some modification to fit the purpose of this study. This questionnaire was used as a template for the personal interviews.

Findings and Discussion

The first research question has to do with Korean-language teachers' general perceptions and beliefs regarding assessment. To answer this question, the interviewees were first asked to self-evaluate their assessment literacy and preparedness for this task. Except for one participant who answered he/she is "completely confident," as well as another participant who answered "somewhat unconfident," the majority responded that they feel "somewhat confident" in their assessment in general. The one who reported to be "completely confident" had indeed plenty of experience in terms of attending workshops, which might account for her high level of confidence. All the participants have attended some assessment-focused or assessment-related workshops during their time as a Korean-language teacher in their current institution or in their professional organization(s) with which they are affiliated.

In the absence of universally accepted and officially recognized forms of credentials related to assessment, it is difficult to evaluate teachers' overall confidence. For this reason, the OPI certificate was considered one objective criterion that can gauge one's qualification, thus the question was asked. As for OPI training, three of the seven participants have attended both an OPI workshop and have a certificate, while two of them have attended an OPI workshop but do not have a certificate. Two of them have neither attended an OPI workshop nor have a certificate. Obtaining a certificate requires a series of ensuing steps from the attendees, and those who did not obtain it cited time constraints as the main reason why they failed to complete the process. Given the long history and "added premium" associated with OPI in the foreign-language teaching field, OPI training seems to have been an essential credential for Korean-language teachers as well. Institutional support, including financial support and strong encouragement, was cited as necessary because the participants who have a certificate mentioned that they were motivated by the expectation (and perhaps implicit pressure) of their department or program to be certified. The department culture also plays a role in which Korean teachers are to be well aligned with Chinese and Japanese teachers. Irrespective of the reasons why Korean teachers obtained their OPI certificate, it became apparent during the interviews that those with the certificate were evidently more confident than those without it.

One of the most fundamental aspects of assessment is learning about teachers' views on "fair and sound" assessment, since this will most likely influence their overall assessment practices (assuming that they all strive to conduct fair and sound assessment). One may come up with "textbook" classical answers (e.g., valid, reliable, authentic) but the researcher was interested in the participants' responses to this question. Their definitions include:

- an objective, procedurally fair assessment corresponding to initial statements about assessment components and procedures
- an assessment that shows students' usual ability, an assessment that does not make students feel like they are being assessed but one that makes them feel like they are part of the learning process
- assessment that is comprehensive rather than specific to a certain area
- fair and sound assessment should not be equivalent to grading
- an assessment that provides teachers and students with what students learned and how much they achieved
- fair and sound assessment measures what is supposed to be measured (i.e., students should be aware of how their performance will be assessed)
- fair and sound assessment should be aligned with the lesson objectives and course goals, measuring students' progress and efforts throughout the given time period

While described in different ways, these answers touch upon a few major aspects of assessment. That is, the participants consider procedural fairness as a precondition for sound assessment. It is also interesting that the relationship between grading and assessment is addressed as a response to fair and sound assessment. Participants seem to be highly concerned about the role and purpose of assessment regarding learning goals and learning outcomes when defining fair and sound assessment, indicating their understanding of assessment as an ongoing process.

Teachers' perceptions of the relationship between assessment and grading are indeed one of the questions this study aims to explore. The place and importance of grading in assessment in an institutional setting – in a classroom setting in particular – pre-suppose unavoidable strains in teachers' assessment practices, as discussed in several studies. For example, McMillan and Nash examined how elementary and high school teachers made decisions on assessment and grading (i.e., the nature of their decisions, influencing factors on such decisions, and justification of such decisions) in classrooms.

Their study reports that there was a tension between internal factors (e.g., their philosophy, beliefs, and values) and external factors (e.g., state mandates, district grading policies, parents) and that the teachers attempt to strike a balance between those factors. Similarly, Cheng and Sun examined teachers' decision making on grading in Chinese schools, which raised questions as to whether classroom assessment and grading should be based exclusively on learners' achievement or whether other non-achievement factors such as study habits or attitudes should also be considered. They found a significant relationship between the factors that teachers considered and the types of assessment they used for grading. Oscarson and Apelgren reported similar results that non-language factors carried considerable weight in teachers' grading. While these studies were done in a secondary-school context, participants in this study expressed the challenges they faced in assessment practices, with assigning grades being a major one.

Teachers assign scores or grades for each requirement of the course, be it lesson tests, vocabulary quizzes, skit presentations, written essays, and so on. Each of these is graded based on an assessment scale, normally in the form of a rubric. A rubric is a standard assessment tool commonly used by teachers today. Although the majority of the participants said that they use a rubric, this is not to suggest that they had full confidence in them. They were not certain that using a rubric would ensure the objectivity of the assessment, as one can still be subjective in choosing a score column. The language used in rubrics is often seen as too abstract, or not concrete enough. Moreover, given that one interviewee "confessed" that his program did have rubrics in place, but that they were not for actual use but rather for the program review, supports the idea of doubting the effectiveness of rubrics.

Teachers' concerns over grading are reflected in their responses to the purposes of assessment. The overwhelming majority (six out of seven) chose students' learning as the most important purpose. And when asked to rank these purposes in comparison to each other, four out of those six marked grading as the second most important purpose. Grading was ranked higher than teachers' planning of the course or curriculum adjustment.

The course requirements, which are the basis for assigning grades and for assessing the entire course, do not vary much regardless of the level each participant most frequently teaches on a regular basis. Role play is only used in the lower levels, for understandable reasons, while portfolio was not used by most participants. The weight assigned to each assessment criterion does not vary much either other than regular written tests (e.g., lesson tests, midterm exam, and final exam), for which they range between 20 and 45 per cent. Some teachers rely more on conventional paper-and-pencil tests than others. Other assessment criteria look similar: homework ranges between 15 and 20 per cent, projects range between 10 and 20 per cent, quizzes range between 10 and 20 per cent, essays range between 8 and 10 per cent, and presentations range between 5 and 10 per cent. These outlooks suggest that teachers use a variety of assessment tools, between five and eight criteria depending on the level they teach. However, it was also revealed that only three participants use either peer assessment or self-assessment, implying that assessment is heavily teacher dependent. Similar results were reported in Seden and Svaricek about EFL teachers in Czech schools that, "although the majority of the teachers used a wide range of sources to construct their subjective theories of assessment, most of their assessment practices are still based on old-fashioned routines" and that "grading, testing, questioning, and verbal feedback were used often, while self-, peer, written, and portfolio assessments were the least exercised options" (119).

All of the participants, except for one, are the head of their respective Korean-language programs. Some have three to four colleagues, while others have one to two colleagues in their program. Unless they co-teach a course as the lead instructor, they do not get involved in their colleagues' assessment, granting complete authority to the course instructor. The interviews revealed that it was common practice that teachers are very much on their own when it comes to assessment and they rarely collaborate or communicate with each other for feedback, advice, or even discussion. A number of reasons for that can be speculated upon, but one major one appears to be workload (i.e., busy schedule) and time constraints. It is not that they were not interested in sharing their thoughts and practices; rather, it is more because they simply could not find the time and room to do so. Some participants indeed expressed their wish to engage in such practices.

Even though the program heads consider assessment to be one of the most important and yet challenging tasks, they tend not to "meddle" with their colleagues on the team. One interviewee, the eldest among the group, stated that, "as the head of the program, it is important to respect my colleagues' independence and individuality" and that "as I am old, my interference might make them feel uncomfortable," suggesting that he tries to maintain a certain degree of distance from his colleagues. Although for different reasons, other program heads seemed to take a similar stance when it comes to the degree to which they get involved in the assessment process.

However, supervising and collaborating need to be distinguished. The fact that every teacher is completely independent in their assessment practices raises a reasonable degree of concern. Rea-Dickins, when reviewing Davison's research on teacher assessment practices in Hong Kong and Australia, echoes Davison and emphasizes "the importance of creating opportunities for teacher interaction about assessment issues" (253). A dialogue between or amongst teachers in the same program will not only be beneficial for a better understanding of assessment framework and criteria to be used for specific assessment areas but also further explore any doubts and questions that they might have about interpreting learners' performance. The conclusion of Zhang and Burry-Stock's widely cited study also supports the need for increased communication among the program members, as they found that "teachers with measurement training report a higher level of self-perceived assessment skills" in all aspects they tested including "using performance measures, standardized testing, test revision, instructional improvement, and communicating assessment results than those without measurement training" (323). Teaching experience is an important asset in instruction, but it might not necessarily make one proficient with respect to assessment. One way to implement this practice is to regularize a discussion session as part of monthly program meetings.

Assessment is viewed as challenging by teachers, even those very skilled ones, since it encompasses broad dimensions. The reality is that teachers should be experts (or possess a reasonable amount of expertise) in all assessment criteria that they exercise for any given course. Data collected in the pre-interview survey show that the number of requirements for a course ranges between five and eight for both beginner levels and intermediate levels. Among the seven interviewees, five regularly teach lower-level courses (i.e., first year and second year). The assessment tools they use that are described as course requirements do not differ much. Regular paper-and-pencil tests, quizzes, essays, portfolios, projects, homework, and presentations are common components of these courses, although the weight of each requirement varies.

The challenges cited by the participants include: 1) the burden of grading and ensuring the objectivity of the assessment, 2) mismatch or gap between students' daily performance and assessment (i.e., tests) and how to deal with it, 3) assessment of intercultural competence and the difficulty of assessing against course goals (in a large state university where the enrolment is high in each class), 4) assessing pragmatic competence (e.g., use of honorifics and intercultural competence), and 5) gaps between the learning goals set at the beginning of the semester and learning outcomes (e.g., actual performance) at the end of the course (they differ by semester).

Two teachers specifically mentioned the difficulty of assessing intercultural or pragmatic competence. This is a valid concern given the rapidly changing teaching and learning environment in an increasingly globalized world. As pointed out in Scarino, intercultural orientation in language learning has gained more ground, which necessitates "a reconceptualization of the constructs and alter the very nature of assessment" (18) that may well apply to KFL. It would be unfortunate if this essential aspect of assessment was pushed to the side, especially for a language like Korean for English-speaking learners given the linguistic and cultural distance between the two. Although there does not seem to be a readily usable system of assessing intercultural competence in a classroom setting, the Intercultural Development Inventory (IDI)[2] can be explored. It is one of the most widely used assessment tools currently available for intercultural competence assessment but has not received due attention in KFL, especially in North America (59–61).

Another challenge shared by the participants is a perceived gap between learning goals and learning outcomes. This was viewed as more of an issue for teachers working at state universities, which happened to be the majority in this interviewee pool, than the participant teaching at private universities. It is generally the case that the range of students' performance is wider at state universities than it is at private universities. Teachers set the learning goals for the course at the beginning of the year based on the level they teach – typically using the OPI scale as an exit goal – and yet they see students who do not achieve expected learning outcomes at the end of the year. This is not only an individual learner issue but also a program issue that concerns the course instructor.

When asked about their perceived best practices in assessment that was open in nature, the majority of the participants displayed immediate hesitance, a reflection of Korean culture that promotes the virtue of humility. This question might have surprised them, unless the teachers had been reflecting upon their practices on a regular basis as to what they are doing right as well as what they need to do to improve on in their practices. They were reluctant to call what they think they were doing right, or to state with confidence that theirs represented best practices. Two aspects emerged from their answers. One is that they make special efforts to provide as much detailed feedback as they can, especially on students' writing. Apparently, teachers who teach at a private university, where an enrolment cap for each class is relatively low, are in a much better position than those who teach at a large state university. They explicitly mentioned the need and value of teachers' feedback on learners' sustainable improvement in writing while also acknowledging the enormous time commitment this requires on their part. In fact, it is interesting to note that providing detailed feedback on writing is viewed as a best practice for teachers at a private school, while the inability to do so against their desire is cited as a challenge for those who teach at public schools. This suggests that the instructional environment affects teachers' perceptions to a certain degree.

The significance of writing among four skill modalities increases as learners advance to higher levels where writing proficiency is emphasized, especially for Korean for academic purposes. Writing requires more guided training and organic feedback than other skills, not only for improving learners' linguistic proficiency (i.e., knowledge and usage of grammar and vocabulary) but also for genre knowledge, content organization, and writing conventions. Perhaps due to this multi-dimensional nature, as well as the assessor's high degree of subjectivity, writing is perceived to be most challenging to assess. Providing detailed feedback is challenging because of the time commitment involved, but the participants seemed to believe strongly that their detailed feedback would enhance learners' writing proficiency as long as they were able to provide it. They also seem to believe that there is a strong connection between their feedback and their assessment.

While detailed feedback might be beneficial to learners, written feedback can be useful and meaningful when it is selective, specific, and focused on materials previously taught and studied, like Cumming suggests. Contrary to what teachers believe, excessive feedback (e.g., editing every error) can actually overwhelm learners and thus may be more deleterious than advantageous for the learner. Targeting only "treatable" aspects selectively and purposefully is what has been suggested in previous studies. Such a strategy would likely lessen teachers' burden of correcting "everything," while at the same time help teachers focus on what really needs to be assessed.

The other aspect that the interviewees cited as their best practices is their efforts of implementing an integrative assessment by taking all aspects of learners' performance into account, rather than relying on a certain assessment tool (e.g., tests). In fact, several teachers knew about Integrated Performance Assessment (IPA), had training in, or were using the IPA approach to a varying extent in their practices. Similar to the way in which performance-based learning has been valued for its strong implications for real-life situations in recent years, IPA also has been advocated by researchers and adopted by conscientious teachers.

Limitations and Implications

Assessment is a complex topic that encompasses various sub-topics in a variety of educational settings. This study is limited to a KFL context in a college classroom setting. The study also chose to deploy a qualitative approach as the research methodology over a quantitative one for the sake of gaining deeper insights into actual practices beyond what surveys can reveal. While the results of the interviews with the seven teachers will not be representative of the entire group, it is nonetheless hoped that they will offer some perspectives into what teachers do and how they feel about assessment. Since the study is intended to be qualitative, the questions are broader and more inclusive than specific and focused. Also, the study is intended to be practice-oriented rather than theory-oriented, as well as descriptive rather than analytical. While assessment should take place throughout the entire learning process, the one that takes place at the end of the semester carries a special weight because of its culminating nature.

Some researchers stress the importance of continuous and ongoing assessment by differentiating "assessment *for* learning" (usually equated with "formative assessment") from "assessment *of* learning" (usually equated with "summative assessment"). That is, assessment should focus more on the learning process than on learning outcomes. This has been debated amongst scholars in regard to what should be considered in assessment. Some scholars (e.g., Guskey and Bailey, cited in Brown) advocate that the combination of the three components of *process* (work habits, study skills, etc.), *product* (achievement, performance, academic products), and *progress* (amount of learning) is desirable. Although the study does not clearly show that this is what most teachers are doing, they are indeed taking all of these aspects into consideration when they undertake assessments of their learners. The question should be more about how they perform these assessments than whether they do them or not.

A few participants communicated with the researcher after the interview, while others stated during the interview that it was an invaluable opportunity for them to seriously reflect on and reengage themselves in the topic of assessment. One participant mentioned that she put far more thought than usual into the writing of a course syllabus that started shortly after the interview. Another participant stated that she was very strongly motivated and determined to be more proactive in attending workshops and other similar training opportunities in the future. This discussion is worthwhile in that it has provided an opportunity for teachers to be more reflective and vigilant about their current practices. As discussed earlier, an important implication borne out of this study is that there is an urgent need for greater dialogue amongst the teachers themselves within programs. The culture of the teaching environment needs to change from closed practices to more open ones.

In addition to the new realization of an individual teacher at the personal and institutional level, the role of professional organizations (i.e., the American Association of Teachers of Korean in Korean-language education in America) in training and empowering in-service teachers cannot be emphasized enough. AATK, as the sole organization exclusively focused on issues related to Korean-language education in North America, is best positioned to carry out this task, given almost all of the teachers teaching in colleges and universities in America and Canada are members of AATK.

On average, approximately 150 members attend the annual meeting in any given year, and this is undoubtedly the best outlet for teachers to discuss and learn from each other on a particular agenda-like assessment. There are many competing demands for the organization, but assessment is one area that will truly benefit its members. In fact, the participants' suggestions on topics that they would like to see covered if such workshops were offered through AATK were diverse. They include the following: IPA training using specific examples, actual assessment forms and tools that other teachers use, and a standardized assessment manual; research involving FL assessment; assessment of writing skills (making rubrics, giving meaningful feedback, diagnosis of improvement); and test development (achievement tests as well as a standardized placement test).

It has become clear through the interviews that teachers employed at schools that have a well-established coordination system are in a much better situation than those who do not. It was also clear that those participants were carrying a heavy burden without substantial guidance or support from their respective units. This is where an organization like AATK can step in and play a facilitative role.

Conclusion

This study explores various aspects related to the assessment practices of Korean-language teachers in colleges and universities through in-depth interviews with teachers in an attempt to ascertain their views of assessment and classroom practices. In using a qualitative research methodology, it was hoped to reveal what the teachers' daily assessment practices were like, what their views and concerns were, and what their perceived needs were. Similar challenges were mentioned, while others were more individual and school or program specific. Despite teachers' efforts to assess their students' learning effectiveness and progress as objectively as possible, many issues in assessment remain unanswered. Different social and institutional contexts undoubtedly affect and define teachers' practices to a great extent. Ultimately, it is the responsibility of each classroom instructor to assess these factors and to engage in the best practices that they can. It is important for the teachers to seriously reflect and critically assess their practices, as well as make any necessary adjustments to help yield the best possible results.

Assessment is more than giving scores and assigning grades. As agents in the assessment process, teachers should realize the gravity and multifaceted nature of this responsibility and welcome any opportunities to update their knowledge and make their practices more informed. Like many other aspects of teaching, there is a gap between what teachers know as an assessor and their day-to-day actual assessment practices. There seems to be a gap between how they feel about assessment and what they actually do. Thus, it is also important for the researchers to look into what Looney and others called "teacher assessment identity." This "encompasses not only a range of assessment strategies and skills, and even confidence and self-efficacy in undertaking assessment, but also the beliefs and feelings about assessment that will inform how teachers engage in assessment work with students. This focuses not simply on what teachers do, but on who they are" (Looney, 15).

NOTES

1 The 2017 conference theme at University of Southern California was "Promoting Global Competence for Diverse Learners in the 21st Century: Implementing World-readiness Standards in Language Curriculum, Instruction and *Assessment*." The 2018 conference theme at University of Toronto was "Innovation and Accountability in Korean Language Assessment and Program Evaluation."

2 The IDI consists of fifty statements (agree or disagree on 5-point Likert scales) that measure "culture-general" intercultural competence of learners.

WORKS CITED

Brown, Alan. "Understanding the Relationship between Language Performance and Course Grades." *Foreign Language Annals* 46, no. 1 (2013): 80–7. https://doi.org/10.1111/flan.12014.

Chang, Euna. "Korean Education Assessment Studies." *Bilingual Research* 47 (2011): 351–82.

Cheng, Liying and Youyi Sun. "Teachers' Grading Decision Making: Multiple Influencing Factors and Methods." *Language Assessment Quarterly* 12 (2015): 213–33.

Cumming, Alister. "Connecting Writing Assessments to Teaching and Learning: Distinguishing Alternative Purposes." Plenary talk delivered at the American Association of Teachers of Korean annual conference. University of Toronto, June 2018.

Hamp-Lyons, Liz. "The Impact of Testing Practices on Teaching: Ideologies and Alternatives." 2006. www.researchgate.net/publication/242022707.

Hill, Kathryn. "Understanding Classroom-Based Assessment Practices: A Precondition of Teacher Assessment Literacy." *Papers in Language Testing and Assessment* 6, no. 1 (2017): 1–17.

Jang, Hyejin. "Exploring the Development of Intercultural Competence of Korean Language Learners at University Level." *International Journal of Korean Language Education* 4, no. 2 (2018): 49–80. https://doi.org/10.1177/1028315315596580.

Kang, Sahie. "Linking Assessment and Learning via Performance and Proficiency Assessment." *International Journal of Korean Language Education* 2, no. 2 (2016): 97–123.

Lee, Icy. "Research into Practice: Written Corrective Feedback." *Language Teaching* 46, no. 1 (2013): 108–19. https://doi.org/10.1017/S0261444812000390.

Looney, Ann, et al. "Reconceptualizing the Role of Teachers as Assessors: Teacher Assessment Identity." *Assessment in Education: Principles, Policy & Practice* (2017): 1–27. https://doi.org/10.1080/0969594X.2016.1268090.

Malone, Meg. "Training in Language Assessment." In *Encyclopedia of Language and Education*, edited by Nancy Hornberger, 429–62. New York: Springer, 2008 .

Montee, Megan, et al. "LCTL Teachers' Assessment Knowledge and Practices: An Exploratory Study." *LCTL Journal* 13 (2013): 1–31.

Oscarson, Mats, and Britt Marie Apelgren. "Mapping Language Teachers' Conceptions of Student Assessment Procedures in Relation to Grading: A Two-Stage Empirical Inquiry." *System* 39 (2010): 2–16. https://doi.org/10.1016/j.system.2011.01.014.

Rea-Dickins, Pauline. "Understanding Teachers as Agents of Assessment." *Language Testing* 21, no. 3 (2004): 249–58. https://doi.org/10.1191/0265532204lt283ed.

Scarino, Angela. "Developing Assessment Literacy of Teachers of Languages: A Conceptual and Interpretive Challenge." *Papers in Language Testing and Assessment* 6, no. 1 (2017): 18–40.

Seden, Kinley, and Roman Svaricek. "Teacher Subjectivity Regarding Assessment: Exploring English as a Foreign Language Teachers' Conceptions of Assessment Theories that Influence Student Learning." *CEPS Journal* 8, no. 3 (2018): 119–39. https://doi.org/10.26529/cepsj.500.

Shohamy, Elana, et al. "Investigating Assessment Perceptions and Practices in the Advanced Foreign Language Classroom." Center for Advanced Language Proficiency Education and Research, Penn State University, Report No. 1108. 2008.

Zhang, Zhicheng, and Judith A. Burry-Stock. "Classroom Assessment Practices and Teachers' Self-Perceived Assessment Skills." *Applied Measurement in Education* 16, no. 4 (2003): 323–42. https://doi.org/10.1207/S15324818AME1604_4.

7 Classroom Activities for Student Engagement: "5 Minutes" and Survey Project

MYOUNGHEE CHO

Introduction

This chapter introduces two classroom activities that were conducted in Korean as a foreign language classes in a US college: 1) a practice of showing a video for five minutes before class that was effective in creating an engaging classroom environment, and 2) a survey project that worked well to implement national standards that govern communicative and functional forms of language learning. The practice of using five minutes before class was designed to provide students with additional exposure to the target language and culture. This established a productive rapport between the teacher and students that facilitated learner motivation and created an engaging learning and teaching environment. A survey project was designed with the purpose of familiarizing students with indirect speech. By identifying the language components that students needed in the project (designing a survey form and conducting group discussions) and for the project (giving a presentation and reporting the results of the survey), students enhanced their proficiency in interpersonal, interpretive, and presentational modes of communication. This chapter discusses the logistics and significance of these activities.

Activity #1: Creating an Engaging Language Learning and Teaching Environment during the "Five Minutes before Class"

The design of the practice of "using five minutes before class" originated in a Japanese-language class that I had observed where the instructor played a video before class. Watching the video appeared to relax the students, leading them to talk about the video with their classmates before class. Many studies suggested that playing a video in a classroom can provide an environment in which students can be exposed to visual and aural information regarding the target language and culture present in the video (Flowerdew and Miller, 175;

Ishihara and Chi, 31). When the video materials are either fun or engage the interests of the students, the practice can set a relaxed mood before class. When the video contains class materials, moreover, playing a video before class adds to the activities of reinforcing the class materials and acquainting the students with the target language and cultural aspects (Negishi, 1). In conducting the practice I noticed additional benefits to those presented in other studies. The practice built up a productive rapport between a teacher and students that led to a more engaging classroom environment.

Logistics

Class. The practice was conducted in introductory and intermediate Korean classes in a US college. The classrooms at the college were equipped with a projector or large TV monitor that teachers could use to display video materials. I went to the classroom approximately five minutes before class, played a video, and left it playing while I was greeting students and returning their homework as they entered the classroom. I stopped the video when it was time for the class to begin.

Video Materials. A wide range of video materials related to Korean language and culture were easily found on YouTube. The materials that were used for practicing are categorized as follows:

- Popular culture (e.g., music, films, dramas, and entertainment shows)
- TV commercials, news
- Advertisements to celebrate or promote cultural events (e.g., Korean Alphabet Day, Korean Thanksgiving Day, etc.)
- Interviews with Korean celebrities and foreign celebrities visiting Korea
- Entertaining videos (e.g., ones created by foreigners that highlight the differences between Korean culture and their own)

The choice of video materials was strategic, with the purposes being to set a positive mood for class, reinforce the class materials, and discuss ongoing issues related to Korea.

Uses of Video Materials. Video materials that included the target learning material (e.g., words, expressions, grammar structures, and cultural aspects) were played in line with the progress of the class. For example, in showing a college promotion video, words related to college and campus life were used that the students were learning at that time. In another instance, a video of a Korean idol group called BTS, which was popular among the students, was shown to celebrate their performance at the 2018 American Music Awards. Videos that celebrate things such as Korean Alphabet Day and Korean Thanksgiving Day were also played before each class.

Some videos that were played before class were used again in class for a focused instruction. For example, a video in which a Korean male celebrity sang a happy birthday song was used in class again on a student's birthday, and the whole class practiced and sang the song together. This provided repeated exposure to the target language and culture, in addition to adding fun to the class and getting students more engaged in class.

Findings: Unexpected Benefits of This Practice

This section focuses on the unexpected benefits that this practice brought to the class throughout the semester.

Development of Rapport. One day a student sent me an email with the title "Request," asking me to play a song that he liked during the five minutes before class. This led to more students requesting specific video materials be played before class. Many of the students wanted to share video materials that they found, because the videos were either fun or included the words and structures that they were learning in class. Some students wanted to share video or audio that they had personally made. This practice provided an opportunity for students to share their interests with the rest of the class, as well as the teacher (me).

Engaging Class Environment. Building a rapport between the teacher and the rest of the class made the students feel comfortable interacting with the teacher and their classmates. Students actively cooperated with each other while doing class work and enjoyed a very relaxed environment during the semester. Students did not appear to be embarrassed by any mistakes they made. On the contrary, mistakes or errors often served as a "joke-jerker," rather than a tear-jerker. Students appeared to incorporate the sort of free interactions that they had outside of class into class time, all while using and practicing Korean. This environment led to active learning and enriched the class activities that are outlined below.

Active Learning. A particular student wanted to share an image that she made using a meme generator– that is, an online image maker that allows people to add custom text to images. The student included a Korean sentence (that means "<I> studied a difficult grammar structure and…") that she produced with a grammar structure she learned in class. Many students requested that I play Korean popular songs that they liked, because the lyrics repeatedly included grammar structures and words that they learned in class. I played the songs together with the lyrics on a PowerPoint slide. The practice became a multi-functional medium through which students could share their interests, actively notice what they learned in class in real life, and facilitate their learning.

Enriched Teaching. Students' active engagement in this practice also provided additional resources for the teacher to use for in-class instruction. A student wished to share a fun video that displayed naughty, yet adorable panda bears in a zoo. The video was used to encourage the students to respond in Korea to the question, "What are the panda bears in the video doing?" using a progressive form that they were learning at that time. The student's contribution allowed the whole class to enjoy a fun video, practice a target grammar structure, and expand their vocabulary to the words relating to the panda bears' behaviours in the video.

Students' Responses. The students' reactions to this form of practice ranged from complete indifference (e.g., not paying that much attention to the video while being into their own personal work) to active engagement (e.g., being very attentive to the video, talking with other students about the video, and swaying or grooving to the music). At the end-of-semester discussion regarding the pros and cons of this practice, all forty-one students of both the introductory and intermediate level classes responded that I should continue this practice, since it made them feel good. They felt relaxed before class, especially when the video was entertaining. With regard to their study of Korean, thirty (out of forty-one) students said that the practice was useful because it allowed them to listen to the Korean language and watch Korean culture. Thirteen students expressed that the practice helped them learn Korean better, while also motivating them to continue learning Korean.

Discussion

Significance of the Practice. The benefits of this exercise are supported by many works in the extant literature. Lightbown and Spada (41) claimed that language learners need multiple forms of exposure to a language in order to solidify their learning. Among the "ten commandments" that Dörnyei and Csizér (215) suggested to motivate language learners, this practice met at least three of them in that it created a relaxed atmosphere in the classroom, helped to develop a good relationship between the teacher and the students, and provided an opportunity for students to familiarize themselves with the target language and culture. Many studies suggested that student anxiety has a negative effect on their level of achievement (Hortwitz, 115; Young, 426). Young (432) suggested that teachers' friendly interactions with students can help to reduce anxiety, as opposed to when they stick to a typical role to direct students to perform. Horwitz also claimed that the teacher support that students perceive is related to the level of students' feeling of anxiety, so "sometimes the classroom atmosphere, rather than specific in-class instructional activities, can reduce students' anxiety level" (119). Specifically, on having practices before class, Lang ("Five minutes") and Volk ("Minutes before class") claimed that having warm-up minutes or being active before class provided rich opportunities to provoke more participation during the class.

Suggestions. This practice is not, however, one size fits all. Using the five minutes before class can be done in many different ways, according to teachers' purposes, classroom environments, and students' proficiency levels. For example, any of the following would be appropriate: teachers can simply play music on a music player or a cell phone; display pictures, images, or posters from magazines with quotations (Negishi, 6); or allow time for free conversation for advanced-level language learners, as suggested by an Arabic language teacher that I met at a conference. More suggestions for the practice are provided in Lang ("Five minutes") and Volk ("Minutes before class").

Activity #2: Standards-Based Project for Enhancing Language Learning: A Survey

Stoller has suggested that project work is a "natural extended form of content-based instruction (CBI) and is an approach to develop fully integrated and content learning beyond CBI" ("Project work"). Project work involves more than one lesson for a longer period of time than task-based instruction (TBI) (Bilsborough, "TBL and PBL"). Therefore, it is also regarded as a learner-centred and action-based teaching approach that combines content and tasks to accomplish a visible goal (Lier, 48). Miller claims that project-based instruction (PBI) is an approach to meet national standards, especially facilitating communication and the functionality of language (cited by Mikulec and Miller, 81). The survey project was initially created to help to familiarize students with indirect speech (e.g., quotation). A survey project requires students to create a survey instrument and then collect, analyse, and present data gained from informants. Therefore, the project involves all language skills. In this particular project, students need to use indirect speech in reporting survey results and their reflections on the results.

Logistics

Class. The survey project was assigned to students in the first semester of an intermediate-level Korean class in the same US college as the practice of "five minutes before class" was conducted. The class included fifteen students, which were divided into five groups of three students. The teacher assigned a survey project with an umbrella question, "What is Korea in the University of (the name of the school)?" The project aimed to investigate the standing of Korean culture within the school. The students were required to examine the perceptions that non-Korean students at the school had about Korean culture, such as whether they had encountered Korean culture and, if so, what they thought of it. Students chose one cultural aspect of Korea, conducted a survey on non-Korean students at the college, and gave a presentation in class.

Purpose of a Survey Project (in the Target KFL Class). One key purpose of the survey project was to familiarize students at an intermediate level of proficiency with the concept of indirect quotation, which is frequently used in our daily communications to report one's own ideas or information gained from other sources. Korean has different speech levels, ranging from an intimate speech style that Koreans use with their friends or others close to them to a deferential speech style that they use to address seniors in a very formal context. Plain speech style, the base of (direct and) indirect quotation, is usually introduced to an intermediate Korean class, and introduction to various uses of indirect quotation follows in the same or next level class. Students who have an intermediate level proficiency in Korean, therefore, do not show the equivalent proficiency in their use of indirect quotation. Kim (208) suggested that even Korean-language learners with an advanced-level proficiency seldom incorporate indirect quotation in their speech and writing in comparison to native Korean college students.

Key Elements in Designing a Survey Project. There are several factors that need to be considered when designing a project assignment beneficial to students' learning.

Grouping: Students can choose their own group members or teachers can use Super Teacher Tools, an online grouping tool. If necessary, teachers can try the tool before class until they find an ideal grouping result based on the learning dynamics of a group once individual group members' proficiency levels and relation to other members is taken into consideration.

Two languages for a survey project: Folse claimed that teachers should set guidelines for two types of language use when they give students a task – "language in the task" and "language for the task" (23) – and provided an example of each (25). Teachers are generally good at providing language that students need in the task (language in the task), but often miss providing language that students need for speaking activities (language for the task). Therefore, students tend to revert back to their native language to perform the task (25). In the same vein, a survey project needs language in the task to prepare for a survey form and a presentation, while language for the task is used to accomplish their speaking activities for group discussions and giving a presentation. Both languages include the use of indirect quotation (see table 7.1).

Guidelines for the project: Students received a set of guidelines regarding what they should do to carry out the project. These included the items below:

- What to do for the project (e.g., choose a topic, make at least five survey questions, conduct the survey on at least twenty non-Korean students, use both Korean and English for survey questions, use Korean for group discussions, etc.)
- What to include into their presentation (e.g., why the group chose the topic; when, where and how many times the group members met for the project; the results of the survey, if necessary, with charts or other visual aids; and their reflections on the results)

Table 7.1. Two languages for a survey project

Language in the task	Language for the task
(For survey forms) * words for survey forms * Likert Scale	(For group discussions) What topic do you want to choose? What about ________? How shall we conduct the survey? Who will make the survey form? When and where shall we meet? (etc.)
(For a presentation script) * plain speech style * indirect quotation * words, phrases, expressions for presentation	(For giving a presentation) Hello, everyone! Our group researched what students at our college think about _______. ________will introduce the next section. ______ students out of _______ students responded that ____________. Do you have any questions? Thank you for listening. (etc.)

- Two languages (e.g., required expressions that students should use and useful expressions that they might want to use when they give a presentation)
- Timeline (e.g., dates to submit a survey form and presentation script for the teacher's feedback, to complete the survey, to submit final materials for an in-class presentation, and to give a presentation)
- Rubric: There are a lot of online rubric tools that teachers can use, such as RubiStar. One key item that can motivate students while doing the project work is to include extra points for whether or how often presenters initiate an interaction with the "audience" (i.e., other students), and whether or how often the audience asks the presenters questions.
- Survey form example: With a survey form example, students can be guided on the basic structures of a survey form and other requirements (e.g., indicating and assuring informants that the survey would be used only for a classroom presentation and that informants' personal information would not be retained or used in any other way, the inclusion of a thank-you note, etc.)

Repeated practice of two languages: Language learners need multiple exposures to secure their learning (Lightbown and Spada, 175). According to the timeline that the teacher provided, the survey project was a seemingly one-month long project, from the teacher's announcement of the project to students' presentation in class at the end of the semester. Students, however, practiced indirect quotation in many different ways throughout the semester.

Before the survey project was announced:

- Introduction to the plain speech level and indirect quotation was given at the beginning of the semester, regardless of where it appeared in the textbook.
- For two months, students engaged in a short conversation activity in pairs – "What did you do last weekend?" – at the beginning of every Monday class, and one student reported what his/her partner said to the whole class using indirect quotation. Students used an informal polite ending form (-어/아요'), which was the primary speech level that was used in the elementary and intermediate level classes.

After the survey project was announced:

- Students used, during the short Monday conversation activity, a deferential speech style ending form (-ㅂ/습니다) that is used in formal settings (e.g., giving a presentation).
- Students were guided in their use of the two languages (and other required and useful expressions) for the survey project and practiced them in class.
- Students also practiced the two languages (and other expressions) individually outside the classroom on the class's Quizlet site where those languages and expressions were uploaded.
- Every week until they gave a presentation, students practiced key sentence structures that would be useful for their presentation.

Discussion

Significance of a Survey Project. Mikulec and Miller suggested that language learning occurs best when all four language skills are developed interdependently and "when learners use the language in meaningful tasks and use the language for real-life purposes" (82). The survey project required planning, collaboration, and delivery. Students worked in meaningful tasks to answer the umbrella question of the project. Students used all language skills – reading, writing, speaking, and listening – while they organized their project work through group discussions, produced their materials, organized their presentation materials, and gave the presentation. Students also used multi-disciplinary skills that they brought from other subjects and their creative and critical thinking when they designed and conducted their survey, analysed their data, presented the results, and gave their reflections on the results. The survey project helped students to enhance their Korean proficiency in interpersonal, interactive, and presentational mode of communication.

Students' Work. Students' efforts in organizing their data, designing their PowerPoint slides, and delivering the results and their reflections on the results all showed a great deal of thought and effort. For the survey project, students also brought diverse skills and abilities beyond their abilities in Korean. Students chose diverse topics related to Korean culture (e.g., food, clothing, TV programs, etc.). Some groups used an online survey form and distributed it by email to non-Korean students that they knew. Some groups used paper survey forms and distributed them to non-Korean students in the library or at their dorms. Students arranged the required contents that the guideline instructed in their presentation slides in a well-organized manner. All groups included charts or tables of their own design.

Students' Perceptions of the Survey Project. At the end-of-semester discussion about the survey project, students said that the project helped them practice Korean and improve their Korean proficiency, in particular with regard to giving their reflections on the results and delivering others' ideas. The project made them use their knowledge and skills to design a survey and to organize and interpret data. Many students liked the project. The project required them to use more complex structures and be more involved in teamwork. It also required that students use a more open-ended content and structure, and it helped to improve their other abilities, in addition to learning Korean. A couple of students liked the project, especially because they had the new experience of presenting and delivering results in Korean. In terms of difficulty, most of the students initially felt the project would be challenging but considered it as manageable after they completed it. Students claimed that the guidelines and repeated practice in class helped the most to prepare them for the project.

Conclusion

This chapter shared two useful and practical classroom activities for language teachers to use with their students: 1) strategically using the five minutes before class begins, and 2) a survey project. Creating an environment in which students come to class prepared to learn and engage with a teacher and the instructional materials is often critical for success in a class session but creating this environment can often be difficult. The practice of playing a video for "five minutes before class" is not an official in-class activity, but it helped to lower students' anxiety, set a positive mood for class, and built up a productive rapport between the students and the teacher that created an engaging learning and teaching class environment. The practice can be easily adopted in other foreign-language classrooms through simple modifications, if necessary. Although the practice requires an additional commitment on the part of the teacher, it is worthy of a trial for teachers who are seeking new ways to motivate their students to be more engaged in class.

The 2017 National Standards in Foreign Language Education stated that "effective curriculum design supporting learners involves meaningful learning experiences that incorporate communication, cultures, connections, comparisons, and communities (5Cs)" (ACTFL). The survey project is compatible with many aspects of the national standards. Students engaged in real-life tasks and used the target language to answer the umbrella question that the project proposed. The project involved group discussions, designing a survey form, and giving a presentation in class, which encouraged students to use all kinds of language skills. Students carried out the survey project as a community of Korean-language learners within the school. They used and demonstrated their knowledge of Korean culture and used their knowledge in other areas and critical thinking in analysing the data, preparing the presentation, and giving their reflections on the survey results. The survey project helped students enhance their proficiency in interpersonal, interpretive, and presentational modes of communication.

ACKNOWLEDGMENT

Special thanks to Professor Makoto Negishi at Northern Arizona University for allowing me to observe his Japanese language class in 2014.

WORKS CITED

American Council on the Teaching of Foreign Languages (ACTFL). "ACTFL 2017 Call for Proposals: Submission Guidelines." *2017 Annual Convention and World Languages Expo*. www5.aievolution.com /tfl1701/files /content /docs/ ACTFL_Submission_Guidelines.pdf.

Bilsborough, Katherine. "TBL and PBL: Two Learner-Centered Approaches." *BBC: Teaching English*. July 2013. www.teachingenglish.org.uk/article /tbl-pbl-two-learner-centred-approaches.

Dörnyei, Zoltan, and Kaya Csizér. "Ten Commandments for Motivating Language Learners: Results of an Empirical Study." *Language Teaching Research* 2, no. 3 (1998): 203–29. https://doi.org/10.1191 /136216898668159830

Flowerdew, John, and Lindsay Miller. *Second Language Listening: Theory and Practice*. Cambridge: Cambridge UP, 2005.

Folse, Keith. S. *The Art of Teaching Speaking: Research and Pedagogy for the ESL/EFL Classroom*. Peninsula: University Press of Michigan, 2006.

Horwitz, Elaine K. "Language Anxiety and Achievement." *Annual Review of Applied Linguistics* 21 (2001): 112–26. https://doi.org/10.1017 /S0267190501000071.

Ishihara, Noriko, and Julie C. Chi. "Authentic Video in the Beginning ESOL Classroom: Using a Full-Length Feature Film for Listening and Speaking Strategy Practice." *English Teaching Forum* 42, no. 1 (2004): 30–5.

Kim, Hyunah. "Syntactic Complexity in the Writing of Korean Heritage Learners in the United States." *Korean Language in America* 21, no. 2 (2017): 186–217. https://doi.org/10.4324/9780429244384.

Lang, James M. "Small Changes in Teaching: The Minutes Before Class." *The Chronicle of Higher Education*. 15 Nov. 2015, www.chronicle.com/article/Small-Changes-in-Teaching-The/234178.

Lier, Leo Van. "Action-Based Teaching, Autonomy and Identity." *Innovation in Language Learning and Teaching* 1, no. 1 (2007): 46–65. https://doi.org/10.2167/illt42.0.

Lightbown, Patsy M., and Nina Spada. *How Languages Are Learned*, 3rd ed. Oxford: Oxford University Press, 2006.

Mikulec, Erin, and Paul Chamness Miller. "Using Project-Based Instruction to Meet Foreign Language Standards." *The Clearing House: A Journal of Educational Strategies, Issues and Ideas* 84, no. 3 (2011): 81–6. https://doi.org/10.1080/00098655.2010.516779.

Negishi, Makoto. "Making Productive Use of the Five Minutes Before Class Begins." *AZ-TESOL News* 3, no. 5 (2013): 15–16.

Stoller, Fredricka L. "Project Work: A Means to Promote Language Content." *English Teaching Forum Online* 35, no. 4 (1997). dosfan.lib.uic.edu/usia/E-USIA/forum/vols/vol35/no4/p2.htm.

Volk, Steve. "The Five Minutes Before Class Begins." *Center for Teaching Innovation and Excellence at Oberlin College*. 1 Feb. 2016. languages.oberlin.edu/blogs/ctie/2016/01/31/the-five-minutes-before-class-begins.

Young, Dolly Jesuita. "Creating a Low-Anxiety Classroom Environment: What Does Language Anxiety Research Suggest?" *The Modern Language Journal* 75, no. 4 (1991): 426–39.

SECTION III

Inter-artistic Approaches to Language Teaching

This section addresses inter-artistic approaches to learning and teaching languages and literature, bridging various cultural milieus and curricular formats. The trio of chapters offers concrete ways to promote language acquisition; develop writing acumen for creative, academic, and professional fields; and build confidence and abilities in oral communication skills. They also reveal time-tested ways to enhance the research capacity and (inter-)cultural awareness in learners through the analysis of inter-artistic materials. Offering practical approaches, the samples drawn from courses in several universities reignite the debate about the categorization of disciplines and artistic genres. Music, visual arts, digital media, and aesthetics are presented here alongside and in counterpoint to literature, language, and culture as vital components of import to current pedagogical concerns. They explain the processes of transculturation in concert with an examination of various pedagogical objectives, mediated in the ways inter-artistic approaches are proposed so that students can more fully understand the complexities and richness of multilingual identities and the socio-cultural connections of self to the world. The chapters show how to engage students in higher orders of critical thinking by utilizing various multisensory approaches to language and literary studies. This brings together aurality, orality, and new forms of reading to envision more clearly how local and global imaginaries unfold in relation to each other. These inter-artistic pedagogical paradigms inspire and engage by identifying how these innovations media across time relate to what matters to twenty-first-century learners and their ways of being in the world.

While other pedagogical treatises on teaching language and culture address these aspects from one language area or from a global approach to theory or curriculum issues, this section examines how geographically dispersed regions of the world can find methodological ground in common to achieve sustained pedagogical objectives. The Modern Language Association (MLA) series in teaching has offered in the past a series called Approaches to Teaching World

Literature. These include suggested teaching strategies for such canonical literary texts as *Approaches to Teaching Gabriel García Márquez's One Hundred Years of Solitude* (1990) or *Approaches to Teaching Don Quixote* (2015). These very fine texts nevertheless do not to address specific inter-artistic approaches, as we do in our volume. Although the MLA has published works such as *Teaching Literature and the Other Arts* and *Teaching the Oral Traditions*, these relate mainly to English language texts and traditions (American and the United Kingdom) or European ones, with greater emphasis placed in these editions on providing overviews of syllabi, rather than specific strategies for teaching and learning language skills through the texts in question.

Prior research in the inter-artistic areas applied to pedagogy has tended to provide more examples from survey courses in undergraduate level curricula, rather than on upper-level undergraduate courses taught in the specific interactions of text, music, and other arts, within a cultural context that is Latin America, South American, the Caribbean, and areas less represented in the current pedagogical literature in these interstices. Other existing publications, such as *Global Issues in the Teaching of Language, Literature and Linguistics* (Díaz Pérez, Peter Lang), address some of the "globalized" issues, but also to so predominantly for teaching ESL or from an English-language perspective only. In this section, we move further into the findings of studies in other less-represented languages, whose data are rich with information that cross language divides and cultural regions.

In chapter 8, "Inter-artistic Approaches to Teaching Hispanic Culture: Literature and Music," Victoria Wolff focuses on methodologies and successful practices for teaching the intersection of literature and music to better understand Hispanic culture. This contribution offers practical advice and suggestions for both undergraduate and graduate classrooms. Furthermore, its applications are intended for teaching Hispanic culture in the target language (Spanish), or for more general use (in English). Wolff begins by considering the established practices of connecting literature and music, as well as newer approaches that consider popular music and the relationship of music and society through experiential and community-engaged learning. Another important frame of reference is transatlantic studies, which seeks to uncover cultural linkages between Spain and Spanish America. Examples come from diverse countries of the Hispanic world. Finally, Wolff's discussion is informed by theoretical perspectives from the sociology of music. The principal idea of this academic subfield is that musical art is the result of collaborative social and artistic interactions. As applied to the classroom environment, activities and outcomes are also defined by collaborative and artistic actions. Media, such as recordings and film, are included as additional resources that help bring new dimensions to the material.

Chapter 9, "E(xpanded) Dialogues between Literature and Music: Optimizing Synaesthetic Resources for Teaching Language and Literature" by Maria

Figueredo, approaches the teaching of advanced literature and language through connections to sound, music, and cultural expression. As part of a Spanish program, the sample course studies significant movements and interactions of literature and music as authentic expressions of cultural identity in Hispano America and the Caribbean by examining the textual and performative contexts in which musical forms are adopted in literature and literature is set to music. In a similar way to chapter 4, here Figueredo draws examples drawn from course activities, assignments, and group work. These reflect key questions that arise from course syllabus construction over decades (since 2005), student feedback, and test scripts that provide empirical data from which to examine "best practices" for engaging with cross-disciplinary materials. This course does so in a cross-regional and trans-historical framework as it involves all Hispanic countries in Latin America, but also examines the roots of musical subgenera from Europe and Africa that inform the precolonial roots of those linguistic, verbal, and rhythmic forms. The structural element in language appropriation, regional cultural expressions, and inherent patterns of speech appear in scaffolded assignments that bridge macro- and micro-contextual frameworks. The students' personal engagement with the musical elements also forms part of the creative aspects and reflective analysis of the examined literary (in print, song, hypertext, and video). Although geared mainly towards upper-level undergraduate students, Hispanic studies and literature courses, the approach is also transferable to graduate studies in literary analysis, critical and postcolonial cultural studies, and language in cultural context. As it pertains to language studies, the dialogue between literature and music in today's internet-imbued world expands the ways that students can interact with a medium that is familiar to them (that of popular and other music), and by offering this motivation, also develop skills to address local and global concerns via community-engaged activities and events related to their course work.

The final chapter in this section moves from music into visual arts. In "When Art and English Language Instructors Collaborate," Tamara Warhol and Katherine Rhodes Fields discuss a case study that arose from the collaboration between an art and English-language instructor in an Intensive English Program (IEP) at a public university in the southeastern United States. The instructors constructed and implemented a curriculum that required students to create fine-art projects and write a blog about the cultural differences amongst students. As the course was based in an IEP, the English-language instructor was not teaching language to help students successfully participate in a university art course. Instead, the art instructor taught visual arts techniques to support English-language learning. Although not without its challenges, the curriculum and the collaborative pedagogy provided students with creative tools that have the potential to help them improve their multimodal English skills. This case illustrates how collaboration between English-language and disciplinary specialists need not only be designed to support content learning through additive language instruction but may also be designed to enhance English-language learning by teaching disciplinary skills.

The three chapters in this section reveal cutting-edge research that takes multi-artistic approaches to update them in current technology-driven contexts. There are few, if any, pedagogical volumes that address the integration of using sound and music, songs and other such texts, in approaching curriculum design and teaching language and literature in conjunction. This approach views the inclusion of songs or other musical elements into the classroom not as unique materials to use intermittently, but to inform an overall approach that involves activating higher orders of learning, such as those espoused in Bloom's taxonomy. The current gaps in research on the pedagogical efficacy of incorporating movements of musical connections to literary developments or of artistic theory to the teaching of language offer here some insights into deepening our engagement with these artistic resources in new ways. Even if some of the origins of the links of these arts are seen as traditionally rooted, the ways that the internet has reinvigorated their application since the 1980s bears discussion here, as does the review of teaching methods to employ digital and sound resources, connected with the synthesis of the intersection of the senses in their application with the widespread engagement of our students with technology, music, and social media.

8 Inter-artistic Approaches to Teaching Hispanic Culture: Literature and Music

VICTORIA WOLFF

Literature and music combine to add a much needed depth to human comprehension; separately and together, they have the intrinsic power to reach beyond the surface of history and individual consciousness into the wellspring of the human mind. In doing so, they help us probe the human condition.

– Robert Spaethling, "Literature and Music," p. 59

Introduction

German professor Robert Spaethling, in his chapter for the volume *Teaching Literature and the Other Arts*, argues for using literature and music together in the university classroom to engage students and increase their understanding of the arts, both separately and together (59). This essay will focus on methodologies and successful practices for teaching the intersection of literature and music to better understand Hispanic culture. My contribution will be developed so that it offers background and suggestions for both undergraduate and graduate classrooms. The applications are for teaching Hispanic culture in the target language (Spanish) or for more general use (in English).

I begin with the established practices of connecting literature and music, as well as newer approaches that consider popular music and the relationship of music and society through experiential and community-engaged learning. One important theoretical frame of reference is transatlantic studies, which seeks to uncover cultural linkages. As English professors Susan Manning and Andrew Taylor explain: "Complex interchanges between the Americas, Europe and Africa, with all the forces of 'global' markets and movements of people, are a fundamental feature of modern life, one that makes clear the futility of continuing with nation-based studies developed in a world whose parameters looked very different" (3). Examples, therefore, will be drawn from diverse countries of the Hispanic world with connections beyond national borders. Finally, my commentary is informed by the theoretical perspectives of sociology of music. The principal idea of this academic subfield is that musical art is the result of collaborative social and artistic interactions. Musicologist Ivo Supičić explains that "music is regarded above all as a participant in social life … musical art appears as an integral part of collective experiences" (60). As applied to the classroom environment, activities and outcomes are also defined by collaborative and artistic actions. Media, such as recordings and film, will be included as additional resources that help bring new dimensions to the material.

Conceptualizing Music and Literature

While a course on literature and music is an enriching area of study, its discussion must nevertheless be anchored in solid methods. Critical distinctions set forth by German and comparative literature scholar Steven Paul Scher in his essay "Literature and Music" allow us better to understand the complexity of this particular inter-arts relationship.

Scher divides musico-literary phenomena into three categories: music in literature (the "musicalization" of literature), literature and music ("literary text and musical composition are inextricably bound"), and literature in music (the "literarization" of music) (173–201).[1] These categories can serve as useful ways to organize a course on literature and music that moves away from traditional course designs that are based on historical and chronological, genre, or national tradition foci.

Music in Literature (Short Stories and Novels in Peru)

Beginning with music in literature is ideal for arts and humanities students. Scher explains that music in literature "is the only one of the three areas of interrelation that encompasses exclusively literary works of art" (179–80). More specifically, Scher defines "verbal music" as "any literary presentation (whether in poetry or prose) of existing or fictitious musical compositions… such poems or passages often suggest characterization of a musical performance or of subjective response to music" (188). One of the best examples I can think of to illustrate verbal music to students is through the short stories and novels of Peruvian writer José María Arguedas (1911–1969). As an ethnographer, Arguedas focused on music as an important cultural expression linked to nature, cultural resistance, as well as to an enduring source of Indigenous and mestizo identities. The music in his short stories and novels comes from Arguedas's personal and professional knowledge of Andean musical practices. His use of verbal music not only documents songs, but also recreates the effects of their performance for readers.

For undergraduate students, I suggest Arguedas's short story collection *Agua* (1935). Although all three stories in the collection are precursors to Arguedas's most famous novel, *Los ríos profundos* (1958), my first choice for undergraduate students would be "Warma Kuyay" (*amor de niño*), and my second choice would be "Agua." The protagonist of both of these two stories is named Ernesto. This narrator and alter-ego for the author persists in *Los ríos profundos*. In both stories, students observe that Arguedas transcribes within the narrative the words of songs in Spanish.

"Warma Kuyay" is constructed as a remembrance. Ernesto narrates his boyhood search for his own cultural and personal space, and the music reflects the emotions of the characters in the story. In "Agua," Arguedas highlights a specific genre of music called a huayno. Huaynos are the most popular and far-reaching musical genre in the Andean world. This type of music is characterized by improvisation, and its performance, through both song and dance, can take place at any time and within a variety of contexts (Romero Cevallos, 363). Huayno songs, transcribed within the story, prove significant as they represent the important process of mestizaje or cultural mixing through which Arguedas seeks to express modern Peruvian identity and culture. With origins in the post-contact period, huaynos are considered a cultural phenomenon that brings together tradition and innovation, the individual and collective experience, as well as Peru's past and present. Huaynos will be a defining example of music in Arguedas's later novels. For graduate students, after reading the stories of Agua, I recommend the novel *Los ríos profundos*. In addition to a seminar on music in literature in the writing of Arguedas, this novel could also be included in courses connecting his work to indigenismo or the Latin America novel in general.[2] *Los ríos profundos* can also be found in English translation for a cross-listed graduate seminar. There are extensive secondary sources on Arguedas to develop a graduate-level course and to enhance an instructor's understanding for teaching undergraduates. For the undergraduate student seeking to read the stories of *Agua* in English, there is, unfortunately, no published translation of the collection. However, there are translations of "Warma Kuyay" and "Agua" in journals, on the web, and in theses.

In terms of activities, for undergraduates, I suggest a compare and contrast exercise of the songs in the stories from *Agua* with songs documented in *Canto Kechwa* (1938) – Arguedas's published collection from the same period. The songs in *Canto Kechwa* are in Quechua and in Spanish translation; students could seek out songs in the collection that are similar to or relate to the songs from the stories. Additionally, Arguedas's use of music in literature could be compared to the short stories of Argentine writer Julio Cortázar (for example, "Las ménades" or "El perseguidor"). For graduate students, this could lead to a discussion of the controversy and public debate (1967–9) between Arguedas and Cortázar about the nature of Latin American literature. Another exercise useful to graduate students would be to seek out information related to Arguedas from a music perspective. In the past, my students have had orientation sessions to the music library on campus, thereby becoming familiar with the general and specific resources that can better help them understand the music in the literature of Arguedas. These resources include recordings. There are beautiful recordings of Arguedas singing and reading. I recommend *Arguedas: Canta y Habla* (vols. I and II) from the *Escuela Nacional Superior de Folklore José María Arguedas* (Lima, Peru). Finally, an exceptional vision of the musical worlds of Peru and the impact of José María Arguedas can be found in the documentary *Sigo Siendo, Kachkaniraqmi* (2013) by Javier Corcuera.

Literature and Music (Musical Theatre in Spain)

According to Scher, the area of interrelation between the arts that embraces perspectives from both literary studies and music is "literature and music." Literature and music, taken together, is particularly known as "vocal music," where text and music are combined in single works, such as opera, zarzuela, art songs, and a myriad of other forms through different time periods and traditions (175). How literature and music interact in vocal music is best exemplified, I think, in the Spanish language classroom through the study of *Adiós a la bohemia*, a short, one-act opera.

Our classroom's understanding of this work begins with literature. Spanish writer Pío Baroja (1872–1956) first composed a short story in 1899 (published in 1900) called "Caídos." In terms of context, students will need to understand that this story, written in dialogue form, was created during an intense period of capitalist modernization in Spain. It is one of many artistic and cultural depictions of the counterculture of bohemianism that arose in reaction to the new values of fast-changing, modern societies. Specifically, it represents the final meeting of two "fallen" bohemians, Ramón and Trini, who once shared an artistic, non-conventional life together.

Baroja later revisited and rewrote the story, this time as a play entitled *Adiós a la bohemia*. Published (1911) before it was first performed (1923), the dramatic work called for two musician characters to play music in the background of the café where Ramón and Trini have their last encounter. In 1926, Baroja's play made its way to San Sebastián, where the young musician Pablo Sorozábal (1897–1988) participated in the performance as the violinist. The significance of this second step in the development of Baroja's work should be made explicit to students. First, literary creation is frequently a process of re-creation. In contrast to viewing texts as "closed," reconsiderations and rewritings of a literary work in different moments and for different motivations should be underscored. Second, the story's transition into a play creates both fictional and real spaces in which literature and music can intersect. The violinist is both a character in the play and a real-life musician performing melodies for the audience. Sorozábal, trained in both Spain and in Germany, was not only a musician; he was also a burgeoning composer in the world of Spanish musical theatre.

For students, the discussion of the writer and his literature now naturally unfolds into a discussion of the social status of the professional musician. Also, an account and brief history of the most common examples of musical theatre in Spain and in Spanish America – opera and zarzuela – is valuable to students. In the 1930s, Sorozábal was an established composer who longed to move away from what he believed to be the simplistic storylines and frivolous characters of Spanish lyric theatre. He was convinced that the modernization of musico-dramatic works could be done through music based on libretti that moved away from certain set formulas. Furthermore, Sorozábal was interested in creating works with more emotion tied to the realities of modern life. As such, he began to seek out new literary foundations for his musical compositions. It was during this time that he recalled Baroja's play *Adiós a la bohemia.* For a deeper understanding of the life and work of Pablo Sorozábal, I recommend selections from his memoir *Mi vida y mi obra* (1986).

Baroja served as librettist and Sorozábal served as composer. The ópera chica *Adiós a la bohemia* premiered in Madrid at the Teatro Calderón in 1933. Baroja and Sorozábal planned future collaborations but were separated by the Spanish Civil War and its aftermath. Writer and composer eventually reunited in 1944 to collaborate on a second revised version of *Adiós a la bohemia.* This second version premiered at the Teatro Apolo in Barcelona in 1945. That same year, Sorozábal was hired to take a company of Spanish musicians and performers to South America (1946–7). *Adiós a la bohemia* was performed in Buenos Aires, Argentina, and in Montevideo, Uruguay.

A unique activity that generates for students an understanding of the relationship between literature and music is called "Creating the Libretto: A Group Adaptation Project," available online from the Utah Festival (Opera and Musical Theater). Students could follow the suggested process by taking a Spanish story and rewriting it as a libretto based on developing the characters through NEWUB (needs, emotions, wants, and underlying beliefs). If the Spanish language-literature class has the opportunity to collaborate with students from the Faculty of Music, the libretto could even be put to music. Music students could assist literature students in understanding the core concepts of recitative, scene, action, aria, duet, trio, quartet, and chorus in relation to the writing of the libretto.

For the comparative literature and culture classroom, Baroja and Sorozábal's visions of Spanish bohemianism could be read alongside other European interpretations, such as Henri Murger's collection of short stories *Scènes de la Vie de Bohème* (1848) and the opera *La bohème* (1896) by Giocomo Puccini (librettists Luigi Illica and Giuseppe Giacosa). A city-based course could compare and contrast Madrid and Paris. For a Spanish graduate seminar, the discussion of Baroja's story, play, and short opera could be read alongside Theodor Adorno's essays on music (for example, "Music in the Background" c. 1934).

Alternatively, graduate students of Spanish could read Baroja's depiction of Spanish bohemianism alongside his other works (for example, the novel *Aventuras, inventos y mixtificaciones de Silvestre Paradox*, the poem "Espectros de bohemios," or the essay "Bohemia o seudobohemia"). Baroja's interpretations could also be studied alongside those of Ramón del Valle Inclán (*Luces de bohemia*), Rafael Cansino Assens (*La novela de un literato*), or the poetry of Manuel Machado and Rubén Darío (a transatlantic Hispanic connection).

Popular Music (Chavela Vargas: Costa Rica, Mexico, Spain)

Comparative literature scholar Ulrich Weisstein notes: "Chances are that the student of the libretto as literature will get a fair return for his [her] investment in time and effort" (21). But what about popular song lyrics? Spanish professor Elizabeth Gackstetter Nichols and English colleague Timothy Robbins state that "[p]opular culture, simply put, is the culture of everyday life" (xiii). Out of all the popular culture forms for study, I have observed that popular music has the most everyday impact on the lives of students. Furthermore, Latin American popular music in particular has become an important part of the lived experience of undergraduate and graduate students alike. However, as noted by philologist J. Rubén Valdés Miyares, beyond popular music studies, cultural studies, and musicology, "popular song lyrics are seldom considered an object for literary study" (162). This is unfortunate, since not undertaking the study of popular music lyrics in Spanish is a lost opportunity for learning the language, as well as important aspects of Hispanic literature and culture.

One way in which I teach the connections between popular song lyrics, music, and biography is through Mexican mariachi, ranchera, and the career of Isabel Vargas Lizano, better known as Chavela Vargas (1919–2012). After gaining background in the popular music genre, students work directly with a variety of song lyrics to compile a list of principal themes of the genre (love, honour, pride, patriotism, landscape etc.) across artists. For example, *The Mexico Reader* (2003) includes lyrics from José Alfredo Jiménez and Cuco Sánchez. José Alfredo Jiménez was a major influence on the career of Chavela Vargas. The documentary *Chavela* (2017) is an intriguing way in which to engage students with the life and work of a female singer of Mexican rancheras. Song lyrics, for example those of Vargas's most famous songs ("La Llorona," "Marcorina," and "Que te vaya bonito") can be related to the biographical story related through the documentary, what Valdés Miyares calls the "star text" (161). Through the documentary, we see Chavela Vargas's strong ties with Spain and there are direct connections with the poetry of Federico García Lorca and the films of Pedro Almodóvar. The popular music of Chavela Vargas intersects with issues of gender and sexual identity; nationalism and cultural imperialism; the globalization of culture and regional identities; economics; and social class.

The discussion of lyrics as literature can be connected to music and poetry. The fact that Bob Dylan won the Nobel Prize for Literature in 2016 could generate debate on how songs relate to poetry. Likewise, students could serve as imaginary committee members who select which artists could be recognized "for having created new poetic expressions within the great [Latin] American song tradition."[3]

Music and Society (El Sistema: From Venezuela to the World)

Community engagement is a form of service teaching and learning that builds bridges to the organizations and people beyond the walls of the university. As English professors Laurie Grobman and Roberta Rosenberg note, "service-learning helps students see themselves as part of a collective whole and value both their own well-being and that of others" (15). Language and literary studies can be greatly enhanced through community partnerships. According to Fulbright Specialist scholar Aileen Hale, "a community can provide a powerful setting for genuine communicative practice and skill-building" (17). Professor of music Patrick Jones highlights music's "inherently social nature" and argues "that globalization has made the development of skills and dispositions for civic engagement and intercultural understanding some of the most crucial things that people must develop for our era and for the foreseeable future" (131). The benefits and possibilities for community engaged learning for literature and music are clear; but how could all three intersect for the Hispanic studies classroom? I suggest community-engaged partnerships with local El Sistema music education programs.

El Sistema is the Venezuelan youth orchestra program founded in 1975 by politician, economist, and conductor José Antonio Abreu (1939–2018). Through the promise of using music in the service of society, El Sistema has garnered political and economic support to expand across Venezuela through the establishment of music education centres called núcleos. As of 2013, there were twenty-two El Sistema–inspired music education programs in Canada; the majority are in Ontario, but they can also be found in the provinces of Alberta, British Columbia, Manitoba, New Brunswick, Quebec, Saskatchewan, and in the territory of Nunavut (Petri, 9). As might be expected, the number of El Sistema–inspired music education programs in the United States is even greater. Both my undergraduate and graduate Hispanic studies students have studied the El Sistema music education phenomenon and completed community-engaged projects with our local El Sistema Aeolian program in London, Ontario, Canada.

To connect community and music to literature, I have my students read and deconstruct narratives written about El Sistema in Venezuela and beyond. News media reports, documentaries, books, and a long list of international awards with available speeches are some examples of what has been written and archived in relation to this musical movement. For example, I begin with an overview of the foundational narrative of El Sistema in Venezuela as documented in the speeches of José Antonio Abreu and the published chronicle *Changing Lives: Gustavo Dudamel, El Sistema, and the Transformative Power of Music* by Tricia Tunstall. The concept of "foundational fictions" as studied by Doris Sommer in *Foundational Fictions: The National Romances of Latin America* is applicable. I aim to show students that culture in the service of nation building continues to be an important trend in the twentieth and twenty-first centuries in Latin America (and beyond). However, the dominant narrative surrounding El Sistema promotes music, not literature, as a means through which development may occur. Literature was once a way to inspire reflection; music, through El Sistema, has been constructed as the way in which to catalyze action. Graduate students, in particular, benefit from also reading Geoffrey Baker's *El Sistema: Orchestrating Venezuela's Youth*. Baker shows that, in Baroque fashion, the spectacle of El Sistema has won over the hearts of global audiences while, at the same time, suppressing critical thinking about the project (254). His study points out that the dominant narrative on El Sistema is largely constructed, promoted, and perpetuated by the program itself, when in fact there are multiple narratives that must also be considered (17). Baker's book seeks to go beyond the official account of the program to consider the perceptions and experiences of participants in the program (19).

Through community engaged learning projects, students at all levels have the opportunity to compare and contrast official and unofficial narratives in relation to the program. They take on the role of observer-participant – assessing the programs, its organizers, educators, volunteers, and students – while also reflecting upon their own role as they take part in the placement. As indicated by Grobman and Rosenberg, knowledge and knowledge-sharing ("mutual learning") happens through classroom-community projects that may include grant writing assistance, bibliographies, interviews, facilitating discussion groups, generating publicity, mapping, policy research, recording oral histories, and surveys, among other activities, as dictated by the community organization based on their needs (5).

Summary

The examples provided here seek to provide instructors with useful ideas and inspiration to acquaint students of different levels and backgrounds to a range of recognized and more recent approaches of connecting literature and music. Extensions can be made, moreover, to teaching literature and the other arts. Interdisciplinary teaching is one important way through which interrelations – connections between instructors, students, and community – can be developed and enhanced.

NOTES

1 Scher's systematic typology of the basic relationships of literature and music explains that the last category of "literature in music" designates works of a primarily musical genre (program music) and clearly falls in the realm of musicology. However, he also states: "Though … a primarily musical genre, program music invites the scrutiny of the literary scholar insomuch as it often exhibits an impact of literature on music" (177). As a primarily musical genre, teaching literature in music will not be developed as a separate section in the body of this essay. However, as instructors, we can reflect on the possibilities of including a discussion of literature in music in relation to the Hispanic world. What Hispanic works of literature have influenced music? How does the composer seek to evoke the images, succession of events, or the story through sound? As suggested by Spaethling, this section of the course encourages the participation of a colleague from the Faculty of Music in the form of team-teaching or as an invited guest lecturer: "A collaboration of this sort would enhance the pedagogical aspects of the course and help provide a sound professional footing" (59).

2 I recommend Garth William's contribution "Teaching Arguedas" in *Teaching the Latin American Boom* (Modern Language Association).

3 Quote adapted from the Nobel Prize Committee's motivation for honouring Dylan "for having created new poetic expressions within the great American song tradition" (www.nobelprize.org/prizes/literature/2016/dylan/diploma).

WORKS CITED

Gackstetter Nichols, Elizabeth, and Timothy R. Robbins. *Pop Culture in Latin America and the Caribbean*. Santa Barbara, California: ABC-CLIO, 2015.

Grobman, Laurie, and Roberta Rosenberg. "Introduction: Literary Studies, Service Learning, and the Public Humanities." In *Service Learning and Literary Studies in English*, edited by Laurie Grobman and Roberta Rosenberg, 1–39. New York: The Modern Language Association of America, 2015.

Hale, Aileen. "Service-Learning and Spanish: A Missing Link." In *Construyendo Puentes (Building Bridges): Concepts and Models for Service-Learning in Spanish*, edited by Josef Hellebrant and Lucía T. Varona, 9–31. New York: American Association for Higher Education, 1999.

Jones, Patrick M. "Developing Social Capital: A Role for Music Education and Community Music in Fostering Civic Engagement and Intercultural Understanding." Proceedings from the International Society for Music Education (ISME) 2008 Seminar, edited by Don. D. Coffman, 130–44. ISME Commission for Community Music Activity.

Joseph, Gilbert M., and Timothy J. Henderson. *The Mexico Reader: History, Culture, Politics*. Durham, North Carolina: Duke University Press, 2003.

Manning, Susan, and Andrew Taylor. "Introduction: What Is Transatlantic Literary Studies?" In *Transatlantic Literary Studies: A Reader*, edited by Susan Manning and Andrew Taylor, 1–13. Baltimore: Johns Hopkins University Press, 2007.

Petri, Inga. *A National Sistema Network in Canada: Feasibility Study and Strategic Plan.* 2013. http:// naccnapdf.s3.amazonaws.com/corporate/SistemaCanada _FeasibilityReport_en.pdf.

Romero Cevallos, Raúl. "Peru." In *The Garland Handbook of Latin American Music*, edited by Dale Olsen and Daniel Sheehy, 352–74. New York: Garland Publishing, 2000.

Scher, Steven Paul. "Literature and Music." In *Essays on Literature and Music (1967–2004)*, edited by Walter Bernhart and Werner Wolf, 173–201. Amsterdam: Rodopi, 2004.

Spaethling, Robert. "Literature and Music." In *Teaching Literature and Other Arts*, edited by Jean-Pierre Barricelli, Joseph Gibaldi, and Estella Lauter, 54–60. New York: The Modern Language Association of America, 1990.

Supičić, Ivo. *Music and Society: A Guide to the Sociology of Music*. New York: Pendragron Press, 1987.

Valdés Miyares, J. Rubén. "Breaking Joy Division's 'Glass': Reading Song Lyrics as Literature." *Atlantis: Journal of the Spanish Association of Anglo-American Studies* 32, no. 2 (2016): 161–80. www.atlantisjournal.org/index.php?journal=atlantis&page =issue&op=view&path%5B%5D=16.

Weisstein, Ulrich. "The Libretto as Literature." *Books Abroad* 35, no. 1 (1961): 16–22. www.jstor.org/stable/40115290.

9 E(xpanded) Dialogues between Literature and Music: Optimizing Synaesthetic Resources for Teaching Language and Literature

MARIA FIGUEREDO

Introduction

In this chapter I highlight the "best practices" that have evolved from the various iterations of teaching a fourth-year seminar course as part of a Spanish-language program: Literature and Music in Spanish America. In particular, three areas are highlighted for providing an overview of the pedagogical tools that may transfer to other teaching settings of language and literature: 1) e-poetry and e-narrative as current ways to consider what it means to "write" and to engage with cultural production and identity-making; 2) song as literature, and the shifting definitions of "literature" and expressive culture over time; and 3) music as a subtext in narrative texts. These serve to expand students' conceptions around what constitutes literature and to ground meaning beyond colonizing binaries. The interplay of the verbal and non-verbal elements in texts are placed in dialogue more expressly. In that signification process, we open the reception of texts to the interplay of artistic genres that contribute to specific ways of interpreting reality. Three theoretical strands are interwoven throughout: a) inter-artistic theory applied to pedagogy for teaching language and literature, and with particular reference to Hispanic studies; b) affect theory and motivational forces for students; and c) performative aspects that teach applicable and transferable skills related to individual communication confidence, autonomy of thinking, and "inter-being" awareness. With regard to structuring the syllabus and designing assignments, this chapter also provides samples of pertinence to advancing students' comprehension skills across the linguistic and literary, arts, humanities, and socio-historical aspects of the materials; several assignment templates and co-curricular activities are described in detail.

Engaging Students in the Paradigm Shift

The syllabus for the sample full-year course Literature and Music in Spanish America[1] fashions a counterpointed selection of textual examples from the genres of poetry, narrative (short story, novella, and novel), short film, video, and song over the course of the academic year. Some of the texts selected as required readings contain all or several of these various media in the same text, such as Laura Esquivel's *La ley del amor* [The Law of Love] that is a novel containing comic strips, musical allusions in the text, a CD with songs to be heard at specific intervals in the text, and song lyrics from popular Hispanic songs.

The first sections of the sample course deal with defining the arts in relation to each other and to the fields of "literature" and language studies. It is essential to chart out historicities and establish a cultural field of reference and a theoretical frame by positing possible ways that the musical and literary arts can find points of contact. As Lois Parkinson Zamora indicates, "[t]o engage in inter-artistic criticism requires a comparison of the signifying capacities of artistic form" (403). Given the course objectives to understand, analyse and place in cultural context the connections between literature and music, the chosen methodology, theoretical paradigms, and terminologies applied in the assigned activities, tasks, and assessments are set out in an overall two-part framework throughout the academic year:

1. The relationship of text and music in Hispanic America, especially in counterpoint to modernity, and re-situating this relationship post-1950 in light of decolonizing the curriculum (all year)
2. Influences of the two arts on each other, and modulations since the Renaissance:
   - music in literature (Sept.–Dec.)
   - literature in music (Jan.–Feb.)
   - the remixing of genre definitions since the invention of the internet, post-1980, as well as since the advent of technologies for reproductions in media (since the 1950s) (Mar.–Apr.)[2]

In the case of the last category above, the reversal of strategies in creative "writing" by Hispanic authors of the Americas studied in the course redefine the exchanges between the visual, aural, and verbal components of a text. In some cases, this reverts our gaze to consider pre-Conquest and pre-Colonization artistic practices and rituals that had previously blended the arts into one event or product. Guadalupe Mejía's "Texto y música en Jalisco" is a useful initial reading to situate learners before the chronology of the subject matter; it discusses the origins of Greco-Roman and Biblical literature, and instruments such as the zither and lyre of the medieval period, which would evolve into the instrument par excellence for the Hispanic world: the guitar. With its Peninsular roots and subsequent rhythmic connections with African and Indigenous musics, it is a synecdoche of cultural fusion. Similarly, the jarchas, and other forms of songs, contribute to this transcultural vein of uniting music and poetry in the voice and song. Beginning with Sor Juana Inés de la Cruz in colonial Mexico, such as in her poetic "Villancico VIII" (1676), that continues into today's popular operas, this moves all the way through the Romantic period with works such as Colombian José Asunción Silva's "Nocturno III" (1908). The corrido and its affiliation with the Mexican Revolution is a type of text whose lyrics are as important, if not more so, than the music. Newer forms like Canto Nuevo across South America with its variations directly unite music and poetic lyrics that speak to a socio-political reality in order to raise consciousness, call to action, or communicate values and beliefs. The blend of classical and popular influences becomes evident as a constant undercurrent of Hispanic cultural production, albeit to varying degrees and in various ways in each era, movement, and/or text.

The separation or division of the arts into hierarchical, distinct categories, thus, is revealed as a European construct, and must be made transparent when studying texts. Latin American modernism took issue with this and sought more authentic ways to encompass lost cultures and civilizations. Modernista writers were to reignite connections with Indigenous ways of seeing the world expressed through their "literature" (scrolls, or graphics, in many cases, such as in Maya-Quiché peoples, or art forms such as the quipú, in Incan Perú, and ritualized song structures that mnemonically preserved some of the history of various pre-Colombian peoples across the northern and southern continents today known as the Americas). As of the dawn of the internet, however, this has reignited word and text as one visual unit. The "illuminated" pages on screens of light, and the possibilities for including sound and music in the same screen, recover some of the synaesthetic qualities that pertained to those older cultures pre-1492. These perceptive containers for expression and for interpreting "reality" as technology shifts allude to the human aspects in contact with waves of technological inventions and with evolving philosophies of ontology.

Other definitions are fundamental for establishing the foundations of the course parameters and content, such as exploring how the terms related to "popular" and other categorizations of performativity through media (Shaw and Dennison; McLuhan; Culler), transforming across centuries, or depending on their acceptance at a societal level, as per categorizations of "high" and "low" cultures. The involves questioning how music can be read as a language (with its own "grammar," as Michael Chanan explains in *Musica Practica*). Moreover, what arises when considering words, music, and the visual in tandem, is a more expanded consideration of what constitutes "literature."

The course syllabus begins with a motivational activity that invites students to bring to class their favourite song in Spanish. By this point in their university career, the students, most of whom are Spanish program major or minors, already have knowledge in this regard. Therefore, they have a chance to draw on their personal preferences regarding music in Spanish, or of songs that are fusions of

Hispanic musical subgenres. The initial activity is meant to ground the course discussion in a personal way for students, acknowledging their previous experiences as valid entry points for listening to this music and for considering their choice. This class-as-a-whole activity provides an essential foundation from which to move into deeper analysis. For this first low-stakes assignment, completed within the first two weeks of classes in a course that meets once a week for three hours, students bring a song to class. They are asked to reflect on what aspects of the lyrics can or cannot be considered poetry (epic, lyric, dramatic, or otherwise a mixture of these), a micro-story, or other type of literary genre. Furthermore, students are asked to identify a main theme and sub-themes in the verbal text, in connection to the ways that the sounds of instrumentation, vocalization, and tone contribute or counterpoint the identified themes.

Each student makes a brief presentation of the song to the class, having brought a recording of the piece as an mp3 file on a USB, or by calling up the song via platforms such as YouTube, Spotify, or iTunes. Once the class has heard at least a portion of the song, to get the gist of its structure (verses, chorus, bridge, instrumentalization, etc.), each student informally talks about the themes they have identified and what musical and sound elements support or contrast with these. The main idea, or general message, is then distilled from the discussion and other students can weigh in on these. In addition, each student is invited to share, to the extent they are comfortable doing so, why they like the song and what effect it has on them personally. The exercise allows us to present the question of how to approach song as literature and to delve into literary analysis. The latter builds upon skills that students began to acquire in the second-year required core course of the program that introduced them to basic skills of literary analysis, interpretation, and cultural reference of texts. The personal connection is motivating, but also ensures that I also have an idea of what musical styles appeal to each cohort of students. These evolve over time, and it is always interesting to make connections for them of canonical poems or experimental forms in Hispanic writing with songs that are popular in the present moment of their favourite repertoire of songs on their phones, tablets, or computers. This allows them greater stake in the course and establishes a place of confidence to share their previous knowledge in forthcoming class discussions. The safe environment created allows classmates to get to know one another early on in the course more readily than otherwise would be the case.

Once this is accomplished, students have a basic analytic framework for examining literary texts in relation to musical concepts and forms. Course readings include primary texts (starting with one short story or various poems per day in the first month of classes). By the second month fragments of novels and a novella are studied. Specific secondary readings accompany (one to two per week) elucidate each variance of inter-artistic connection from various theoretical or cultural angles. Examining why certain connections between these arts appear at particular points in time, vis-à-vis each of the Hispanic American countries studied in relation to the texts (such as during times of political crisis), can also be placed within a larger global context. The second portion of the introductory lectures focuses on the cyclical and dialogical currents in the relationship and terms that associate music and literature. This gives some account of the origins of the relationship, as well as discusses the developments that have unfolded from the eighteenth century to the present (Brown; Chanan; Nattiez; Scher). Branching from the historical overview, the topics lead to presenting various connections:

a) poetry as verbal music and poems that allude to music in their text
b) popular culture, media, and Latin American identities
c) music and literary devices as access to tacit (intuitive) knowledge
d) music as a language and its comparative "grammars" vis-à-vis the Spanish language
e) music and literature that unite during times of political and social crises
f) specific genres of music and their connections to literature over time
g) gender issues and music as a subtext that subverts oppressive marginalization through expressing the non-verbal and the non-normative within the limits of language
h) the relations of music and cultural productions with innovations in literature
i) songs as poetry, such as in salsa, hip hop, and tango
j) spoken word
k) video-poetry, hypertext poems, and other forms of e-poetry
l) each medium's implicit message in the interstices of meaning and sound

Learning outcomes: By the end of course, students who successfully master the course content, approach and assessment milestones, will be able to:

- understand the significant movements and interactions of literature and music that have appeared as authentic expressions of cultural identity in Spanish America, by examining the textual and performative contexts in which musical forms are adopted in literature, and when literature is set to music[3]
- compare and contrast the conditions in which the literary and musical arts find points of convergence in order to discern how these innovations have created responses to collective experience in times of challenging socio-political circumstances and have renewed the reception of literary forms in various historical periods by Spanish American authors
- explore the best means to link literary production (poetry, short story, and the novel) in its ideological, social, and historical context
- critically assess the main issues related to Spanish American cultural production, focusing on issues of literary culture in contact with music,

identity, ethnic/racial, and linguistic aspects and political contexts of the Spanish American societies
- demonstrate improved confidence in utilizing language skills through academic writing, oral presentations, seminar discussions, creative works, and class activities in the target language
- attain higher-order critical skills in the use of various literary theories as applied to the representative works, particularly in the area of the literary in contact with the musical
- collaborate with their peers, with community partners, and other faculty invited to the course discussion periodically to produce position papers and reflective responses, questions, and dialogue about relevant topics applied to current events
- acquire experience working in teams and networking with peers, faculty, staff, authors, and community representatives

Language and Sound, Music and Cultural Identity

Although the course is a literature course taught in Spanish, with all required readings in the target language, it also refers back to lost languages and delves into aspects that transcend language. Music as a way to access lost or unspoken knowledge has much to say here. As Sarah Dowling posits in an interview, the "Americas percolate with languages, from the lost and living languages of those here before the Europeans came, to the many languages of Africa, Asia, and Europe that form our linguistic foundation as poets. I'm inclined to think we need recognize more, not less, lines of resistance and difference" (cited by L'Abbé, 89). The multiply rooted reality of the Hispanic Americas is complex. It involves examining texts in a context of multilingual, multicultural (cultures co-existing), and transcultural (cultures that seep into each other's evolution) dimensions over five centuries in disparate regions, due to geographical and historical circumstances. While retaining a unified language, albeit with variations in power struggles related to each one), and of the substrata of languages, cultural and racial tensions it carries, the study necessitate a "unity-in-diverse" approach, as Ravi Zacharias would say.

To present this aspect of the course, the following assessment aspects are presented in two parts. First are those that pertain more so to language acquisition and development of higher skills in linguistic proficiency, communication, and comprehension of registers. Second, the literary aspects, within the context of cultural studies, humanities, and liberal arts education, focus those dimensions of the course assignments that develop transferable skills in critical thinking, literary and textual analysis (here I use the word *text* broadly to include filmic, narrative, lyrical, and visual works).

Four pillars shape this course work. One is holistic, and by this we understand that music is at the heart of all human communication and understanding, which is closely connected to what Elena Mannes calls the "music instinct."[4] The fact that aspects of "rhythm-as-organizing principle," and sound studies are a reflection of cultural substrata is the key to organizing the materials. The other side of the equation is based upon the formal elements of each art. Therefore, the structural elements of a given Hispanic genre are foregrounded by the transcultural contexts in which they emerged. The specific musical form is the vehicle that carries within it layers of historical experiences, periodizations, and cultural fusions or revisions. Also, the new settings in which each song type appears bear resonances of forms of speech and current connotations that provide more information about its role as a marker of identity. Apart from this latter dimension, questions about what constitutes a literary work, and its relation to cultural categorizations, also come into play.

Categorization of Materials

Most of the pedagogical literature centred on inter-artistic focus on course design – that is, on how to best organize the materials (Baricelli et al.; Brown; Foley; Scher; Spaethling). This is because the sheer amount of sources may seem overwhelming to students to comprehend and for the instructor to deliver. Curricula presented in *Teaching Literature and the Other Arts* (Baricelli et al.) and *Teaching Oral Traditions* (Foley) are focused on panoramic or survey formats. Many cite the origins of the disciplines as inherent to each art. They trace from classical antiquity how the Greek arts were joined, or they cite the Wagnerian concept of the total work of art. While helpful as a first step to gain an overview of the general categories used to organize the crossover study between literature and music, they neither offer detailed sample assignments nor address the particular challenges in employing an inter-artistic approach in teaching.

Sophisticated assessment tools are called for to address the more diverse nature of the multimedia materials in question, as we read texts whose hybridity of genres was essential in the very creation of the primary source itself. These characteristics can be highly motivating to students who have become savvier in engaging with various types of media, although it can also prove challenging. Practice in critical thinking, textual analysis, and communicative skills occur through cues provided by course exercises as they engage with the audio-visual, internet, social media files. I often assign a worksheet to students with discussion questions to consider prior to class, and with organizing contextual data and terminology in tables to map out the various components.

Rhythm, Language, and Identity

In the Hispanic American and Caribbean regions, writers such as Cuban Alejo Carpentier or Argentine Julio Cortázar wrote not only in their fiction works about music and literature as sister arts, but also elaborated deeply in their narrative structures on the profound psychological substrata in the perception of reality that these connections reveal. A sample lesson from the course AP/SP 4650 Literature and Music in Spanish America can be used to explain these tenets in detail. The links between the narrative voice and textual structures (discursive and sequential) with the context personified by the jazz musician/protagonist, expresses the way that music (through its deconstructionist and philosophical use of the techniques of improvisation) offers multilevel views of questions of race, gender, and ethnicity in various urban settings. Cortázar's text, *The Pursuer* (1959), traces the way that jazz music affects the performer's view of life (inspired by the life of Charlie Parker); it also allows the implied hearer to experience reality as metaphysically symbolized in the jazz interpretations of masters such as Parker. What the dialogical nature of *The Pursuer* reveals is a commentary on the arts in society; it teaches students how to engage in a discussion of their life experience in the analysis of the non-verbal in contact with the verbal. The improvisational nature of writing in this case mimics the grasping for words that must occur in learning a language, and in developing one's own sense of self through words.

Discerning the extent to which words can capture what we attempt to say, and become, is the main aim of Cortázar's journey through his main character, Johnny Carter (a play on the initials of Cortázar himself, as improvisor/musician). It also emphasizes "utterance" as an exploratory model for discovering the nature of the (meta)physical self. This reflects the process of being alive whereby we "remix" the elements of language, with its pre-established formal and structural grammars and stylistic norms, to define and express ourselves as individuals. Creating our own speech using these pre-existing signs is an analogy for life and how we engage with its structures to define meaning, purpose and values for ourselves from within and beyond the possible permutations. Cortázar's long story/short novella is a narrative whose discursive style borders on the edge of the lyrical, as do some of the most innovative novels of the twentieth century (James Joyce entire oeuvre, for example, or Carlos Fuentes' *Aura*, 1962). Jazz as an approximation to the ludic in language mirrors structures that move between sound forms and meaning. Poetry as a bridge transitions between sound and narrative as it plays more freely with linguistic laws. Key Hispanic American authors of the post-1950 have traversed these literary frontiers, some opting to use music as integral.

Inter-artistic Theory and Course Materials

The ever-evolving links between rhythm, cultural identity and the two arts is also inherent in many of the texts analysed in the course. It is as important in Cuban writers such as Nicolás Guillén and Alejo Carpentier [5] as it is in Southern Cone expressions such as Cortázar's and Jorge Luis Borges's inclusion of references to tango, classical music, and folkloric traditions. In addition, the study of these techniques applied to literature allows us to delve into the theories of migration, convergence, and contacts between peoples, place, and their cultural expressions. The texts range from poetry set to music to song as poetry (in various musical sub-genres such as salsa, zamba, cielo, milonga, bolero, etc.) and music as a subtext in women's writing (Arrendondo, Ezquivel, and Mastretta). One of the most dynamic and unique developments in this hybrid genre between musical and literary reception is Laura Esquivel's novel *The Law of Love.* It integrates CD-ROM recordings as part of the narrative structure, therefore, teaching it must refer to the experience of the musical in connection to the text. Indeed, the original edition of the book (1995) came with an instruction preface in which the author explained how to read the novel in such a way. Subsequent editions have not contained these specific instructions, which were written in tone-in-cheek, playing with the distinctions between classical music, popular danzones, and those who don't like music at all; the author explains that it will be necessary to engage with music in some way to access meaning and render the full experience of the book.

The polyphonic view is that these novels grapple with irony, false realities, and control mechanisms that subjugate one world view over another. *Arráncame la vida* (1985) [*Take This Heart Out*] by Ángeles Mastretta is an example of the bolerización de la novela that became a trend in the novels of Colombian, Cuban, Mexican, and Puerto Rican authors, and others outside the Caribbean such as Argentinian Manuel Puig. The effects of the lyrics of famous boleros (a musical genre that had its heyday in the 1940s, and shares origins in both Mexican and Cuban cultural histories) impact the way we read novels, on the one hand, and the importance of popular culture and its influence in post-modernity. Other novels such as Luis Rafael Sánchez's *La guaracha del macho Camacho* (1976) exemplify this polyphonic quality, as they dismantle identity crises and reimagine Puerto Rican politics to the beat of the guaracha song form. Themes of displacement and re-writing history are featured themes in which music plays as much a socio-political role, as trope and symbol for alternative world views, as it is a celebration of love, self-discovery, and liberation.

The "musicalization" of the novel is a main component to understanding Hispanic American literature. For example, the inter-artistic approach is akin to what Mary Schwartz sees in her study of Cortázar's novel *Rayuela.* Published in 1963 (and in English in 1966 as *Hopscotch*), it became a canonical novel of so-called "Boom literature." Schwartz based her study on Lois Parkinson Zamora's model of inter-artistic criticism, which "recognizes the intertwining of visual and verbal arts in Latin America as 'modes of communication' [that] have played contemporary roles since the earliest establishments of empire in the Spanish New World" (390). The musical elements could also have been emphasized here, as they are present in many of his fictional writings. Zamora's "comparative semiotic methodology" is useful for interpreting inter-artistic materials in relation to verbal texts. It elucidates how deeply these materials are embedded in the postcolonial unraveling of identity in language, social class, waves of migration, and history of community in Hispano American countries. Sharing over five centuries of experience with empire and nation building, the return to the popular roots of culture is a form of decolonizing the curriculum. Attempts to extricate marginalized and underground voices have been subjugated by various epochs of imperialist forces from Europe (in a trans-Atlantic perspective) and within the Americas (from perspectives of North–South and Global South paradigms of power).

Therefore, the study of the relations between literature and music produced in countries of the region is not only an aesthetic question; it bridges cultural studies, reflects postcolonial aphonias, and problematizes historical accounts, while it also re-envisions the nature of the arts as expressions of individual and collective identities. Students prepare a final research paper in which they synthesize all the prior steps taken in the course. Managing the different sources of information, students are then responsible in their final paper to document and acknowledge these sources, while contributing to the critical dialogue in the fields. As it is a course in language and literature, students become adept at documenting their data through the MLA citation method. More recent poetic works relate to the transformations of literature through the variants in hypertext and expanded forms of reception in digital media. In this last sense, the role of sound and images vis-à-vis the word is at once future-bound yet reverts to an oral tradition as old as the human race. Modernist poets in Spanish America (post-1898) such as Rubén Darío, Leopoldo Lugones, and Juana de Ibarbourou sought synaesthetic expression in poetry as a means of adopting higher levels of attainment in literature while also being more authentic in their Hispanic American expression through the written word. These interests grew also with studies on the psychology of perception, and the expansion of polyphonic and trans-medial artistic expressions.

Affect, Structural Elements, and Student Engagement

To train students in theorizing – that is, for gaining mastery in the abstraction of these terms – the element of reality that appears to exist outside of form, as in the "poetical" or the "musical" as first implied, affect theory should be considered. In the "return to affect" that is outside theory, as suggested in recent critiques such as the following one by Brinkema, we see that the two are intrinsically linked:

> Affect is not the place where something immediate and automatic and resistant takes place outside of language. The turning to affect in the humanities does not obliterate the problem of form and representation. Affect is not where reading is no longer needed. This drive for some magical mysterious intensity X that escapes signification, while durable and even understandable, is a mode of thinking that only defers the more pressing matter: how is critique to keep grappling with affect and affectivity in texts if, indeed, one cannot read for affects to discover anything new about them? (xiv)

Sound as contextual marker is key, as is its relation to poetic and narrative forms that have developed in various cultures.[6]

Another key aspect belongs to the requirement of specificity, related to Latin America in this case. In other words, as Brinkema points out, "close reading," or a sustained interpretation of texts (xv), grounds the meaning. The insistence on the formal dimensions of affect allows not only for specificity but for the wild and many fecundities of specificity: difference, change, the particular, the contingent (and) the essential, the definite, the distinct, all dense details, and the minor, inconsequential, secret, atomic. Combining the structural qualities of each work (poem, short story and long prose, song, or visual dramatic piece) with the affective dimension allows students to identity with the content. Treating affect in such a way deforms any coherence to "affect" in the singular, general, and universal and transforms it into something not given in advance, not apprehensible except through the thickets of formalist analysis (Brinkema, xv). In this way, an analysis that allows the particularities of any individual text can disrupt terms known in advance and serve as a means to explore new questions (Brinkema, xvi). How can musical ideas be conceptualized and developed in collaboration with literature, and vice versa? How can this be transmitted to students of a language in a literature course that includes native speakers, heritage learners, and second or third language learners in the same class setting?

Instructors at other universities have designed courses that study music as text – such as Professor Daniel Chamberlain's work on the Mexican corrido at Queen's University, and more recently Professor Claudio Palomares with his course Hips Don't Lie? Music and Culture in Latin America (LLCU 244), where students approach Latin American history and culture through the study of its musical production. Most recently, Palomares' study of Mexican Nuevo Canto situates one its foremost proponents: Gabino Palomares. His research has turned to the considerations of song as poetry, particularly after Bob Dylan's receipt of a Nobel Prize in Literature in 2016. Yet, beyond the controversies of where to draw the lines between these genres, and of the urge to use music as simply a way of attracting students to the "less hip" study of literature, there are more complex, deeply embedded rationales. Music's inter-relationship to literature, as well as to the other arts, reveals how inherent it is as way to examine the process by which new connections and deeper understandings about ways of being in the world are experienced.

Sample Pedagogical Materials: Assignments and Assessments

Finally, I would like share two assignments that can be used to bring the materials to life for students through highlighting the musical aspects of literature in terms of affect, and language in general.

Response/Reflection Paper: Sound and Cultural Identity

I. "Luciana Souza Sings Neruda." The first is a response paper, which provides a reflective exercise for students. By not requiring research to be conducted in this assigned work, the process can be focused on experiencing the text in relation to its sound components. The three stages of the assignment prepare students to listen actively to each piece – the original poem by Pablo Neruda (one of the most well-known poets in Spanish) of the twentieth century, and a musical setting of his work by a contemporary Brazilian jazz musician and composer, Luciana Souza. The object of study is titled *Neruda*, a compact disc recording of ten songs that Souza recorded with Catalan pianist Mompou in 2004, for the one-hundred-year anniversary of Neruda's birth. Students are assigned to select one of the tracks before reading or listening to the song cycle – that is, based solely on the title of the piece. They then research to establish when and in what context the original poem by Neruda was written and published. Given Pablo Neruda's extensive oeuvre, there are many periods and themes covered by his poetic works. In the second phase of the assignment, students listen to the song by Souza, making note of any allusions they decipher from its soundscape and what instruments or tones they can detect. They are also asked to respond emotionally to the track, indicating their personal experience of the song. Next, they must connect the reading of the poem with the musical aspects they described. The last part of the task is analytical, whereby student engage in sense-making, using all the aforementioned details as their groundwork. Positioning the songs by Souza as an interpretation of the poems originally written by Neruda is also problematized by the language contained in each. Although Neruda wrote his poems in his Spanish mother tongue, either in his native Chile or elsewhere in the world, Souza's first language is Brazilian Portuguese. However, she chose to set the poems to music in English, as she stated that Spanish was too close to her mother tongue to sufficiently differentiate the two. Thus, students are tasked with also engaging with the tensions involved in creating, reading, listening, and interpreting literature from the perspective of translation, and the precise sounds of a language, region, or identity. It is also worth noting that Neruda is the poet in Spanish with the most musical settings of his poetry. Thus, as a choice for study in the course, his work is fundamental. It serves the course objectives well also as his poetry also alludes to musical forms in various stages of his work, such as to the sub-genres of tango, madrigal, sonata, and waltz. So the cycles of poetry reaching out to musical forms, and music reaching out to poetry, are mutual.

E-Textual Analysis: Aurality in Digital and Literary Receptive Practice

II. "E-Poetry: Networks, Blogs, Performance" is a project that takes into account the current state of literature in contact with digital media. This engages students with the way that poets in Hispanic America are mobilizing the internet to reach larger audiences. The media enhancements affect their works in various ways with sound, performance elements and visual amplifications. While opening new access points for authors across huge geographical expanses to reach international audiences more readily, they also preserve their links to local culture(s) and the intimacy of the "ritual" aspect traditionally associated with the performance of literature, especially poetry.

In a 2013 interview for *Revista Bla* (Juan Andrés Ferreira), Machado responded to a question about poetry's contemporary function. Confessing that this question arose for her only after participating in a world cultural event – Poetry Parnassus during the 2012 London Olympics – she posited the oral components of poetry as its greatest strengths:

> It always astounds me that poetry does not sell, that publishing houses do not publish it, or that bookstores place it in the most hidden places on their shelves, and yet poetry is capable of uniting people from across the world, and governments and institutions invest financially in it. It is always continually read in clubs and pubs. There is a flagrant contradiction in this. I think that poetry should return to its initial vehicle: the voice, sound. A return to orality, to the troubadours. It should be spoken, rapped, sung.

Without wishing to discard either side of the generic divide, Machado remains keenly aware of the ability of aural performance to reach audiences.

Furthermore, connections of creative works in "action" is the main thrust of the mobilization of the poetic voices from the page or screen and into interactive arenas. This becomes a main component of the work of art in the digital era. In several projects, the course leads students to identify contemporary Hispano American poets – especially women and people of non-normative sexualities and their relation to sound, rhythm of utterance, and identity. We see how the online platforms allow them to circumvent traditional venues of literature in order to attain greater access to publics and form communities of artists beyond their local and regional settings. They include inter alia, Rocío Cerón in Mexico, Lía Colombino in Paraguay, Melisa Machado in Uruguay, Nelia Prado and Malú Urriola in Chile, Cristina Peri Rossi (originally from Uruguay but now residing in Spain), Belén Gache (Argentina – Spain), Orquesta de Poetas in Chile, and Orientación Poesía youth poets in Uruguay, who engage strongly with internet sites, blogs, video-poems, and online performances to publish their works. The studies of these poets together serve as a corpus to trace common themes as well as divergences among them. It situates poets in relation to digital media within new studies in Latin American cyber literature. It provides students with insight into what is trending in poetry, so that these can be studied in tandem with other literary innovations. Connecting the phenomenon to theories of agency from a gendered consciousness is a second-level aspect of the themes of the e-poetry in relation to identity. The above project ties with the aspect of "reading" defined in the twenty-first century and its relation to digital culture. Also, it homes in on the nature of performance and the rituals of reading in front of others.

The videos are easily uploaded in "gallery" form on any local traffic management system on Moodle and provide a vivid arrangement of visual interaction. The understanding that flows from the interpretations of these "readings as performance" and as an "event" flows well into assignments that involve a social, participatory, and community environment that can extend beyond the classroom. For example, a co-curricular series of events entitled the "Literature and Music in Spanish America: Dialogues" (Fall–Winter 2018–2019) was organized by students of the course Literature and Music in Spanish America, integrating their research and class work into eight events (workshops and lectures) over the twenty-four-week course. The series empowered students to engage with a network of scholars and performers working on musical-literary innovations in Latin American and Caribbean arts. Each event in the series considered the role of music in multi-mediated formats that privilege its performative elements of meaning production, both as a social force and as a link between communities. By examining innovations and new research conducted in traditional formats and through community engagement and art practices, performances and recent publications, the perspectives on Latin American literature and music also highlighted the globalized nature of these relationships in their transnational settings.

Group and individual student projects examine selections of poetry that apply the above theoretical groundwork. Some focus specifically on how e-poetry allows more interaction with texts in relation to the synaesthetic qualities of literature. By incorporating close readings of the language of each text, we can then concentrate students' attention on the oral, performative, and cultural dimensions necessary to make sense of the full meanings of the digital texts. Some belong to the categories of hypertext or gaming (such as in the works of Belén Gache, "Word Toys," and "Electric Moons"). *Digital Poetics* author Loss

Pequeño Glazier posits a "generative" quality of poetry on the Web, describing three forms of electronic textuality: hypertext, visual and kinetic text (that moves on the screen), and works in programmed media, such as Gache's, that generate new versions over specific time stamps (computer-generated works).

The operational definition of e-poetry posited by the Electronic Poetry Center (EPC) and e-poetry literary organization based at the State University of New York, Buffalo, of which Pequeño Glazier is a founding member, specifies it as "digital, visual media arts, sound, and language-based arts." Moreover:

> Its emphasis is on literary practice in an encompassing sense, i.e., the practice of thinking through engagement with the material aspects of media forms, the building of community, and the exchange of ideas across languages, borders, and ideologies. Rather than considering 'new form' in qualifying criterion, it seeks to locate innovative artistic practice in its cultural, conceptual, and media milieu. Hence if digital literature is going to point to emergent artistic processes in a New Media age–inasmuch as they inform the digital-e-poetry can exist in any number of formats, including programmable, performance, visual, sound-based, conceptual, book art, hand held, tablet, immersive environments, game-based, and more.

The use of electronic and other media has complemented how we interpret literary texts, present oral projects, and explore cultural themes. This develops competence in critical analysis and dynamic sociocultural dialogue. In the particular case of Hispanic literature, it invokes colonial threads that are "unwritten" by music or retraced to reveal hidden subtexts such as that of women's and alternative sexualities within traditionally more patriarchal settings and discourses. Furthermore, popular music can be studied alongside canonical literary texts to re-engage with pre-Renaissance categorizations of high and low culture, and musical elements unearthed to decolonize the curriculum and allow other voices to be heard.

Performative/Participatory Praxis: Meaningful Engagement and Comprehensive Assessment

Communicative strategies, such as "poetry art actions," harness the power of creativity through literature, and highlight its contacts with the other arts. Judith Butler and Athena Athanasiou, Julia Kristeva, Luce Irigaray, and other poststructuralist and feminist philosophers and theorists maintain that these trans-artistic movements have an impact on social and political imaginaries. The performative aspects of literature say more than just what appears on the surface.

Music in contact with literature offers different ways for students to become more motivated and empowered in their learning process. Yet, despite the overall appeal of music to young people, its nuances are far more subtle than the popularity of some of the most internationally known genres (salsa, merengue, tango, marcha, reggaeton, bolero, corrido); others such as zamba (from the Southern Cone, not to be confused with the Brazilian samba), milonga (as a forerunner of the tango and its variations), cielo, cuenca, and fusions of newer forms, are also relevant and they transcend national borders. As Pablo Vila writes in *Music and Youth Culture: Identity Construction Processes from New York to Buenos Aries*, the musics of the region that affect its youth are much more diverse, such as those that reveal the grappling with "post-Communist Subjectivies in Cuba" (Vila, chapter 4). As he states:

> Music is a privileged cultural artifact that offers us the real experience of our narratives, imagined identities. Therefore, part of the understanding of our identity (which is always imaginary) would occur when we submit ourselves to the bodily pleasure of the performance or music listening. It is precisely here [that] the connection between interpellation and desire, between the identitarian offer and the actual identification, occurs. (35)

One way to achieve this is by designing course work and assignments that incorporate community event planning and networking with media contacts (print, television, radio, and online), as discussed earlier. Each week students complete one of the steps of the task-based final projects that involve community and media engagement, while practising oral, written, and time management skills. Individual research and preparation times are balanced with group work. What James Beane termed "integrative learning" or "unforgettable learning experiences" (616) is built into the community engagement and experiential components of the course. These have taken several forms over the trajectory of its offerings since 2008 at York University. Most recently, a lecture and performance series in 2018–19 entitled Literature and Music in Dialogue featured spoken word, candombe drumming and tango demonstrations in relation to primary and critical readings on literature that alludes to musical structure. Researchers in the field were invited to discuss their work on salsa as poetry, issues of migration and immigration.

Additionally, the aforementioned attributes of the course cultivate an environment of autonomous learning. The course empowers students to engage more actively with the readings and sound files. Undergraduate students can readily appreciate this connection. Priya Parmar and Bryonn Bain discuss how spoken word, hip hop, and rap are important contemporary cultural expressions in the Americas that link literature and music. These forms contain markers of identity and resonance that cannot and should not be discarded in the academic curriculum of university courses in literature. Parmar and Bain suggest working in and with the various mediums that speak loudest to their students. Excluding the various forms of hip hop texts from the curriculum excludes voices from being heard, denying the valid existence of life experiences, languages, and cultural expressions of many students. The refusal to incorporate such pedagogy supports the belief that the culture that students bring to the schools is not legitimate of valued. The inclusion of students' views (subjugated knowledge) creates an awareness that all individuals can claim an identity on their own rather than one forced on them (156).

By studying literature and music as related fields, and not just contrasted disciplines, students are made aware that these inter-artistic approaches offer them complex strategies to express their life experiences: "As testimonials of educators already integrating hip hop texts and spoken word poetry into their classrooms prove, both art forms are one kind of cultural literacy whose addition to the classroom curriculum renders positive benefits that include the legitimation of student knowledge, student voices, and student agency" (Parmar and Bain, 156). In the sample course examined here, students have opportunities to engage with representative media outlets (in the local community and in Latin America and the Caribbean) as well as with other scholars, artists, NGOs, community centres, and consular representatives in relation to the course themes and texts (sound files, texts, videos, performances, lectures, workshops, interviews). Student writing can then be informed by scholarly and popular texts in print, hypertext, video, and sound files, which provide ample resources to analyse effectively through reading, researching, and preparing articles for print in academic settings and for community newspapers and online forums. In consultation with their group members, they create interview questions for author, artist, scholar, or community member visits to the class sessions (open to the community).

Conclusion

Therefore, inter-artistically based assignments in the course sampled above offer students various ways of developing communication and interpersonal skills to master higher orders of critical thinking to succeed academically, professionally, and personally beyond the classroom. The research abilities that students gain with close reading skills complement their capacity to place centuries of cultural productions of the Hispanic world into context, while thinking critically about how cultural products dialogue with the world. The ability to focus on what is most relevant within a wealth of materials, efficiently, methodically, and in meaningful ways for them personally and professionally, is meant to give students greater confidence and authority over their own thought process and place of being in the world. Although geared mainly towards upper-level undergraduate Hispanic studies, culture, and literature classes, this pedagogical research is also transferable to graduate courses in the field, as well as language courses of other literary and cultural traditions that seek to incorporate music and multimedia sound files to expand ways for interactive and community-engaged learning of language and culture. Through an interwoven set of assignments – that is, class presentations, dialogues with community, in-class group activities, events to present their research findings and writing and reading assignments – a comprehensive balance of skills is reached. In addition, students are able to experiment with different presentation formats for communicating their research results, performing task-based activities related to course themes, and receiving continuous feedback from the instructor and peers. The main attributes of courses such as these – focusing on the ability to navigate across disciplines, historical periods and media – train students to challenge themselves intellectually and teach them to be more aware of how they perceive the world around them.

NOTES

1 The course framework presented in this chapter is one that I have developed at York University. The new course was proposed in 2006–7 and first taught by me in 2007. Its design was based on previous courses that I designed and created, such as "Poetry and Popular Music in Latin America and Spain" in 2003–4, which flowed from my doctoral research completed in 1999, and subsequent research since then such as on gendered and "networked poetries," and New Song movements. I have taught "Literature and Music in Spanish America" five times: 2007–8, 2010–11, 2011–12, 2015–16, and 2018–19.

2 In these categories, representative texts (short stories, poems, video-poems, songs, novels, novellas, films, visual poems, hypertext poems, and performance poems) are selected. In total, this includes one novella in the Fall semester, a longer novel in the Winter term, and excerpts of two to three novels across terms. Poems by such canonical writers as Juana de Ibarbourou, Pablo Neruda, Gabriela Mistral, Mario Benedetti, and Jorge Luis Borges, among others, are blended with lesser-known writers.

3 In my doctoral thesis, I presented empirical evidence of "movements" of poetry set to music coinciding with dictatorship years in Argentina, Brazil, Chile, and Uruguay in the 1960s and 1970s and part of the 1980s; later, similar trends appeared in Central America (1980s–90s) and other parts of the world, such as Iran – see for example Farzaneh Hemmasi's work.

4 One of the best texts to assign in the early part of the course is a 1965 short story by Mexican author Inés Arredondo: "Canción de cuna" [Lullaby] contains "gaps" in the text that allude to the effects of trauma, due to repressed memory. Integrating German and Mexican Spanish dialogues, it is the music played on guitar, together with songs deciphered in adulthood, that will connect the dots, freeing the matrilineal characters from the effects of patriarchal societal taboos and censorship of linguistic freedom.

5 See the work by Antonio Benítez Rojo, for example, whereby he defines keys to understanding Cuban identity through the links between historical context, musical structures, and literary forms.

6 For a discussion of the relation of poetry to sound, and to sound in poetry, see Marjorie Perloff's work, such as her edited volume with Craig Dworkin. This was one of the first to attempt a systematic theoretical approach that surpasses cultures. However, there is a definite foregrounding of North American works in the English language in the aforementioned volume.

WORKS CITED

Barricelli, Jean-Pierre, Joseph Garibaldi, and Estella Lauter, editors. *Teaching Literature and the Other Arts*. New York: The Modern Language Association of America, 2015.

Beane, James A. "Curriculum Integration and the Disciplines of Knowledge." *The Phi Delta Kappan* 76, no. 8 (1995): 616–22.

Benítez-Rojo, Antonio. "Cuba in Three Keys: Rhythm, music, and literature." *Literature and Arts of the Americas* 34, no. 63 (2001): 17–22. https://doi.org/10.1080/08905760108594667.

Brinkema, Eugenie. *The Forms of the Affects*. Durham, North Carolina: Duke University Press, 2014.

Brown, Calvin. "The Relations between Music and Literature as a Field of Study." *Comparative Literature* 22, no. 2 (1970): 97–107.

Butler, Judith, and Athena Athanasiou. *Dispossession: The Performative in the Political*. Cambridge: Polity, 2014.

Chamberlain, Daniel. Courses in 20th-century Spanish American narrative, Mexican corrido, Literary History and oral narrative traditions, contemporary literary theory, narrative perspective, Queen's University, 1990. www.queensu.ca/llcu/spanish/people/daniel-chamberlain.

Chanan, Michael. *Musica Practica: The Social Practice of Western Music from Gregorian Chant to Postmodernism*. London: Verso, 1994.

Culler, Jonathan. *Literary Theory: A Very Short Introduction*. Oxford: Oxford University Press, 2011.

Electronic Poetry Center. 1994–2020. writing.upenn.edu/epc/.

Figueredo, Maria. "Latin American Song as an Alternative Voice in the New World Order." In *The New World Order: Corporate Agenda and Parallel Reality*, edited by Gordana Yovanovich, 178–200. Montreal, QC: McGill-Queen's University Press, 2003.

– *Poetry and Popular Song: Their Convergence in the Twentieth Century. The Case of Uruguay, 1960–1985*. Montevideo: Linardi y Risso, 2005.

– "From Pablo Neruda to Luciana Souza: Latin America as Poetic-Musical Space." In *Latin American Identities after 1980*, edited by Gordana Yovanovich and Amy Huras, 167–95. Waterloo, Canada: Wilfrid Laurier University Press, 2010.

– "The Rhythm of Values: Poets and Musicians in Ekphrasis and the Case of Uruguay, 1960–85." In *The Militant Song Movement in Latin America: Chile, Uruguay and Argentina*, edited by Pablo Vila, 143–64. Lanham: Lexington (RLPG), 2014.

– "Networked Poetries: Two Latin American Perspectives." *The International Journal of Communication and Media Studies: New Media, Technology, and the Arts* 1, no. 1 (2016): 23–9. https://doi.org/10.18848/2470-9247/CGP/v01i01/23-29.
– *Creation Sounds: Latin American Literature, Music and Performativity.* Champaign, IL: Common Ground, University of Illinois, 2018.
Foley, John Miles, editor. *Teaching Oral Traditions.* New York: The Modern Language Association of America, 1998.
Gaché, Belén. "The Language of Birds." English version of *El idioma de los pájaros.* Interactive poetry. Fin del mundo.com, 2001. findelmundo.com.ar/pajaros/indexeng.htm.
– El libro del fin del mundo: Poesía, hipertextos [The Book About the End of the World: Poetry, Hyptertexts]. Fin del mundo Ediciones, 2002. findelmundo.com.ar/belengache/ElLibroDelFinDelMundo.pdf.
– *Lunas eléctricas para las noches sin luna. [Electric Moons for the Nights without a Moon].* Argentina: Sudamericana, 2004.
– "Escribir y leer el mundo" [Writing and Reading the World]. In *Poesía y poéticas digitales / electrónicas/ tecnos /new-media en América Latina: definiciones y exploraciones*, edited by Luis Correa-Díaz and Scott Weintraub, 473–90. Colombia: Universidad Central, 2006. www.ucentral.edu.co/editorial/catalogo/poesia-poeticas-digitales.
– *WordToys (1996–2006): Poesía interactiva digital* [Interactive digital poetry]. *An Anthology of Electronic Literature.* Belengache.net. 2006. www.findelmundo.com.ar/wordtoys/index.htm.
– *Word Market. Belengache.net*, 2012. archive.turbulence.org/Works/word-market/.
– "Augmented Reality Poetry Readings + DIY Books" (Spanish Version). Downloadable, interactive book. Belengache.net, 2016. belengache.net/arpoetry/index.htm.
Hemmasi, Farzaneh. "Intimating Dissent: Popular Song, Poetry, and Politics in Pre-Revolutionary Iran." *Ethnomusicology* 57, no. 1 (2013): 57–87. www.jstor.org/stable/10.5406/ethnomusicology.57.1.0057.
Irigaray, Luce. *To Speak Is Never Neutral.* Translated by Gail Schwab. Milton Park: Routledge, 2002.
Kerr, Lucille and Alejandro Herrero-Olaizola, editors, *Teaching the Latin American Boom.* New York: The Modern Language Association of America, 2015.
Kristeva, Julia. *Revolt, She Said*, edited by Sylvere Lotringer. Translated by Brian O'Keefe, New York: Semitotext(e), 2002.
Machado, Melisa. "Melisa Machado." Blog. 29 Jul. 2012, melisamachado.blogspot.ca.
– In an interview by Juan Andrés Ferreira. "Machado, Melisa." Revista Bla, June 2013. issuu.com/lapielroja/docs/poetas.
– "Canto Rojo." YouTube. Efectos visuales por Cristóbal Severín Garcés. Música de Pablo Bonilla (DJ y productor: Boni). Centro Cultural de España, Montevideo. 11 Nov. 2013, www.youtu.be/R8YX4LRr2bI.

– *El canto rojo* [The Red Song]. Mexico: Sediento Ediciones, 2015.

Mannes, Elena. "The Music Instinct: Science and Song." PBS. 27 Feb. 2011. www.youtube.com/watch?v=QnTkHeBn_wY.

McLuhan, Marshall. *Understanding Media*, edited by W. Terence Gordon. Berkeley, CA: Gingko Press, 2003.

Mejías, Guadalupe. "Texto y música en Jalisco." *Sincronía Primavera*, 2000. http://sincronia.cucsh.udg.mx/mejia.htm

Nattiez, Jean-Jacques. "Musical Meaning: The Symbolic Web." In *Music and Discourse: Toward a Semiology of Music*, translated by Carolyn Abbate. Princeton: Princeton University Press, 1990.

Palomares, Claudio. "Gabino Palomares: A History of Canto Nuevo in Mexico," translated by Silvio J. Dos Santos. *Music & Politics* 12, no. 1 (2018): 1–25. doi: dx.doi.org/10.3998/mp.9460447.0012.104.

Parkinson Zamora, Lois. "Interartistic Approaches to Contemporary Latin American Literature," *Hispanic Issue* 114, no. 2 (1999): 389–415.

Parmar, Priya, and Bryonn Bain. "Spoken Word and Hip Hop: The Power of Urban Art and Culture." *Counterpoints* 306 (2007): 131–56. www.jstor.org/stable/42979453.

Pequeño Glazier, Loss. *Digital Poetics: The Making of e-Poetries*. Tuscaloosa: University of Alabama Press, 2001.

Perloff, Marjorie, and Craig Dworkin, editors. *The Sound of Poetry/The Poetry of Sound*. Chicago, IL: University of Chicago Press, 2007.

Scher, Steven Paul. "Literature and Music." In *Essays on Literature and Music (1967–2004)*, edited by Walter Bernhart and Werner Wolf, 173–201. Amsterdam: Rodopi, 2004.

Schwartz, Mary. "Instructions for How to Teach the Boom in Julio Cortázar's Rayuela." In *Teaching the Latin American Boom*, edited by Lucille Kerr and Alejandro Herrero-Olaizola, 83–95. New York: Modern Language Association, 2015.

Shaw, Lisa, and Stephanie Dennison, editors. *Pop Culture Latin America!: Media, Arts, and Lifestyle*. Santa Barbara, CA: ABC-CLIO, 2005.

Spaethling, Robert. "Literature and Music." In *Teaching Literature and Other Arts*, edited by Jean-Pierre Barricelli, Joseph Gibaldi, and Estella Lauter, 54–60. New York: Modern Language Association, 1990.

Vila, Pablo, editor. *Music and Youth Culture in Latin America: Identity Construction Processes from New York to Buenos Aires*. Oxford: Oxford University Press, 2014.

Zacharias, Ravi. "Passion 2020." 6 Jan. 2020, www.youtube.com/watch?v=8WOHS-OGAlY.

10 When Art and English Language Instructors Collaborate

TAMARA WARHOL AND KATHERINE RHODES FIELDS

Introduction

Scholars in applied linguistics and higher education have explored co-teaching and collaboration in a variety of educational contexts. Within applied linguistics, researchers have primarily investigated teacher collaboration as a means of facilitating content and language learning for English-language learners in elementary and secondary schools. These studies examine different models of teacher collaboration (Dove and Honigsfeld, 7–8; Honigsfeld and Dove, *Strategies*, 74–5; *A Leader's Guide*, 36–7; Stewart, 4), as well as the processes involved in co-planning and co-teaching with different pedagogical discourses (Creese, 29; Davison, 467–8). Additional studies have investigated how collaborating L1 and L2 teachers balance each other's strengths and weaknesses in English-language classrooms (e.g., Carless, 328; Carless and Walker, 463; Gunning et al., 72). Within higher education contexts, scholars have similarly examined how discipline and English-language specialists can work together through collaborative teaching to support learning in a linguistically diverse classroom (e.g., Evans et al., 597). Furthermore, they have interrogated whether and how collaborating teachers shared expertise (e.g., Hanusch et al., 66) and improved their pedagogy (e.g., Lester and Evans, 273). Together these studies present an array of models and incarnations of collaboration, but in every study of co-teaching involving an English-language instructor, the instructor plays a supporting role. These studies do not consider how collaboration between a disciplinary specialist and English-language specialist may promote English-language learning and multimodal literacies. This case study directly explores this latter possibility.

Specifically, this case study discusses the benefits that arose from the collaboration between the first author, an English-language teacher (ELT), and the second author, an art teacher, in an Intensive English Program (IEP) at a public university in the south-eastern United States. Together, we constructed and implemented a curriculum that required students to create visual arts projects and write a blog about the cultural differences among the students. In implementing the curriculum, we based instruction on expertise: Tamara, the ELT, taught English, with an emphasis on second-language writing; Katherine, the art instructor, taught techniques from the visual arts. However, as the course was based in an IEP, Tamara was not teaching English to help students successfully participate in a university art course. Instead, Katherine taught art techniques to support English-language learning and multi-modal literacies. This case study describes one project in order to illustrate how the authors' collaboration and co-teaching provided students with creative tools that could potentially help them improve their academic and multimodal English skills. The chapter first defines collaboration and describes the collaborative approach Tamara and Katherine adopted. It then describes the context, curriculum, and project. Finally, it concludes by discussing the benefits and challenges of English-language instructors collaborating with visual arts instructors to promote English-language learning and multimodal literacies.

Collaboration

Collaboration among instructors represents a broad category of practices that may include minimal interaction, such as consultation, to maximum interaction, as in the case of co-teaching. Honigsfeld and Dove suggest that, despite the diversity in practices, collaboration among instructors is marked by voluntary participation, shared goals, interdisciplinarity, and creativity (*Strategies*, 6). Furthermore, they note that co-teaching is a unique collaborative practice in that it requires partners to not only share traditional pedagogical responsibilities, but also to establish trust, openly communicate, and handle conflict in constructive ways (*Strategies*, 6–7). Originally established as a practice between general-education and special-education teachers, co-teaching has increasingly become a norm between general-education and English-language instructors (Creese, 29). As collaborative teaching has become more widespread, different models of co-teaching have emerged. Based on their personal observations of general-education and English-language instructors, Honigsfeld and Dove list seven models of co-teaching, including "One Group: Two teachers teach same content" (*Strategies*, 75) in which both teachers teach course content, specialized lexis, and linguistic structures to the entire group – the model we adopted.

Honigsfeld and Dove describe this model as "[t]wo teachers are directing a whole class of students. Both teachers are working cooperatively and teaching the same lesson at the same time" (*Strategies*, 76). The advantages of this model include more authentic course materials and extensive modelling of communicative practices, collegial observation among instructors and students, and immediate reinforcement of appropriate practices or remediation of errors.

Challenges include becoming familiar with one another's material for the course, as well as finding time for collaborative lesson planning and practising co-teaching. Co-teaching presents significant challenges for instructors accustomed to teaching alone and controlling the floor. Practice allows instructors to establish rules for turn-taking and smooth delivery of course content. As illustrated below, the instructors experienced these advantages and challenges as they created and implemented the curriculum.

Context and Curriculum

Although ultimately successful, this collaboration came together by happenstance. In June 2009, a high school in Venezuela requested a custom program for a group of twelve students in late July and early August. The high school was flexible about what would be taught; however, they were inflexible about the dates. Unfortunately, the dates of the program fell during the August intercession, when most of the IEP instructors take vacation. Tamara, then IEP director, needed to come to a solution quickly. When Tamara first discussed the problem with Katherine, she did not plan on asking her to help, let alone collaborate and co-teach. However, during the course of a casual conversation, they brainstormed a tentative plan for a cross-cultural awareness course with an arts-based curriculum. Tamara lacked the ability, training, and expertise to teach the visual arts, while Katherine had never taught any additional language class. Once conceived, the course was offered successively in 2009, 2010, and 2011 during the intensive English program's summer sessions. This case study focuses on a project from the first incarnation of the course taught in 2009 as it illustrates how the course was originally collaboratively conceived. Furthermore, a discussion of this initial course offers particular insight into the challenges and benefits of collaboration and co-teaching.

During the first iteration of the course, twelve students were enrolled. The students either matriculated to a university in the subsequent semester or entered the advanced-plus level of the Intensive English Program in preparation to eventually matriculate. Because the students would soon be participating in a demanding academic program comprised of a diverse student body, we had three primary objectives for the students: 1) to improve students' academic English skills, 2) to promote cross-cultural awareness, and 3) to introduce students to multimodal literacy. Thus, we collaborated to create a curriculum in which students completed multimodal projects that explored issues related to cross-cultural contact. This paper specifically discusses the project titled *Perception and Projection*, created for the 2009 summer course (Warhol and Fields, *Perceptual Prose)*. Additional projects include *Movie Magic* (Fields and Warhol, 175–6), book art, photomontage, and video. Drawing on research about the efficacy of using multimodal and digital literacy practices in L2 settings (see

Lotherington and Jenson, Warner and Dupuy, for reviews of the literature), these projects were based on the philosophy and agenda originally presented by the New London Group in their seminal essay, "A Pedagogy of Multiliteracies."

In "A Pedagogy of Multiliteracies," the New London Group argued that literacy pedagogy could no longer only consist of teaching reading and writing traditional texts in one language. Because of technological advancements and increasing cultural and linguistic diversity due to globalization, literacy pedagogy now had to account for teaching comprehension and design of multiple modes of communication – print, gesture, sound, colour, and other forms of meaning making – in multiple languages (64). Furthermore, they outlined a teaching approach that included: a) situated practice, where instructors draw on students' personal experiences; b) overt instruction; c) critical framing, where students explore power relationships; and d) transformed practice, where students redesign traditional texts (85–7). Inherent in the New London Group's proposal for literacy pedagogy is interdisciplinarity: a pedagogy of multiliteracies requires expertise not only in monolingual written communication, but also in multilingual intercultural communication, imaging arts, and science, and technology. Yet few individuals possess equal expertise across disciplines. One solution to teachers' varying levels of disciplinary expertise is collaboration and/or co-teaching (Stevens, "Multiliteracies" and "Revisiting Multiliteracies"). This case study demonstrates how an English-language instructor collaborated and co-taught with a visual arts instructor to promote multiliteracies.

Tamara and Katherine first asked students to complete the *Perception and Projection* project to introduce them to multimodal literacies and practise English composition. In this project, students are required to create a series of blog postings in which they post text entries and digital photographs comparing and contrasting stereotypes of the USA and their own country. Similar to a studio art class, students then present each blog entry to the class for oral critique about how they could make their entry more linguistically and visually appealing. There are two main objectives for this project. The first is for students to learn organizational strategies for compositions across several media: traditional essays, digital photographs, and blogs. The second is for students to practise their oral language skills and critical thinking by describing their own stereotypes and approach to creating their blog entries about stereotypes. Throughout the unit, students engage in traditional reading, writing, speaking, and listening tasks to promote academic English proficiency. However, by learning and practising digital photography and engaging in critique similar to a studio art class, students also acquire additional tools that may promote multicultural and multimodal literacies.

Throughout the *Perception and Projection* project, we collaborated to plan, implement, and assess each task. We first modelled how to discuss personal stereotypes about different cultures so that the students could then engage in situated practice. As Katherine is from the southeastern United States and Tamara is from the northeastern United States, we engaged in a conversation about regional stereotypes. Because of her expertise as a language teacher, Tamara took the lead by describing how many people in the northern United States are stereotyped as taciturn, cold, and workaholics when compared to their southern counterparts. As she modelled describing stereotypes, she also explicitly highlighted more advanced vocabulary and grammatical structures needed for comparative discourse (i.e., comparative adjectives and transitions words, such as "similarly," "in contrast," etc.). Katherine repeated the model, describing how people in the southern United States are often portrayed as very friendly people, who move at a slower pace than their northern counterparts. We then facilitated a discussion in which the students shared their own stereotypes about the United States and their own culture. Throughout the course of the discussion, we both monitored student language and made corrections when communication was impeded by lack of language proficiency. Following in-class discussion, students wrote a traditional blog post about their cultural stereotypes as part of their situated practice.

Overt instruction included readings and lectures about traditional composition and the diversity of cultures in the USA (by Tamara), and about digital photography and visual language (by Katherine). Following the overt instruction modules, students were asked to post a second version of their blogs by revising the text from their initial blogs and supplementing them with digital images that illustrated their argument. The digital images had to be photographs that the students took themselves using compositional techniques from studio art (Warhol and Fields). As part of critical framing, the students orally presented their revised blogs and received feedback on their writing and photographs from their peers and both instructors. While Katherine primarily commented on photographs and Tamara focused on the text, we critiqued the blogs as multimodal texts together. Transforming traditional descriptive essays, students then posted their third and final blog entries of revised text and photographs based on their own engagement with the subject matter and constructive criticism from the feedback session. Neither Tamara nor Katherine has the expertise to teach all of the required material described above, but, as co- teachers, they scaffold one another's abilities so that they could introduce the students to multimodal literacies and promote English-language learning.

Benefits and Challenges

As noted above, the instructors in this case study follow the model of collaboration, "One Group: Two teachers teach the same content," and experienced many of the same benefits and challenges discussed by Honigsfeld and Dove.

There they describe this model as "[t]wo teachers are directing a whole class of students. Both teachers are working cooperatively and teaching the same lesson at the same time" (*Strategies*, 76). They suggest that the advantages of this model include more authentic and extensive modelling, collegial observation, and immediate reinforcement or remediation. We experienced similar benefits. Through collaboration, we were able to model authentic interactions, which are important for promoting English-language learning, cross-cultural awareness, and multimodal literacies. Additionally, as instructors with differing expertise, we could provide immediate reinforcement and error correction when students struggle with either English language or multimodal tasks. For us, sharing expertise represents the most important benefit of the collaboration. Through the multiple iterations of the course, we scaffolded one another through activities where one is not as proficient as the other. Thus, rather than teach only traditional English-language skills or studio arts with English support, we believe we teach a more holistic curriculum that promotes both English-language learning and multimodal literacies.

Nevertheless, we did face several challenges in creating and delivering the course curriculum. Honigfeld and Dove identify the main challenges to this model of co-teaching: time for planning, becoming familiar with one another's material for the course, and time to practise co-teaching for smooth delivery of course content (*Strategies*, 76). Because we had additional administrative, research, and teaching responsibilities, we often had difficulty finding time for planning and almost never practised co-teaching prior to class. Thus, we sometimes had difficulty allocating and sharing the floor, not only with one another but also with the students. While sharing the floor improved as the course was taught over successive summers, when and how to speak remained a significant challenge in co-teaching. The method of assessing student work was also a continual work in progress. Since we were co-teaching an English-language course, we did not want to assess the students' artistic talent; however, since we were teaching not only English but also multimodal literacies, we did want to assess student visual and spatial literacies along with their linguistic literacy. Although some assessment occurs during the critique sessions, the rubric for the overall assessment of the projects was never finalized. Finally, while the collaboration allowed for the instructors to build on each other's expertise, it also sometimes limits the instructors from fully utilizing their pedagogical knowledge. For example, in sharing the floor, sometimes Katherine would engage in what Tamara considered too much "teacher talk." Similarly, Tamara often focused on negotiating the meaning of instructions rather than taking a hands-on approach and demonstrating how to complete the project as Katherine did. Despite these ongoing challenges, we believe the benefits of the collaboration outweigh the possible drawbacks.

Conclusion

This case study described the collaboration between art and English-language instructors in an Intensive English Program (IEP) at a public university in the south-eastern United States. Unlike previous research, which primarily demonstrated how English language instructors supported disciplinary specialists through co-teaching, this study focused on how an English-language instructor could collaborate with an art instructor to collectively promote English-language learning and multimodal literacies. Drawing on their individual expertise, they constructed and implemented a curriculum that required students to incorporate fine art projects in blogs about cultural diversity. Although not without its challenges, the collaborative curriculum and pedagogy offered students new tools and strategies for learning academic and multimodal English skills. This case illustrates how collaboration between English-language and discipline specialists need not only be designed to support content learning through additive language instruction, but also may be designed to enhance English-language learning by teaching disciplinary skills.

WORKS CITED

Carless, David. "Collaborative EFL Teaching in Primary Schools." *ELT Journal* 60, no. 4 (2006): 328–35. https://doi.org/10.1093/elt/ccl023.

Carless, David, and Elizabeth Walker. "Effective Team Teaching between Local and Native-Speaking English Teachers." *Language and Education* 20, no. 6 (2006): 463–77. https://doi.org/10.2167/le627.0.

Creese, Angela. *Teacher Collaboration and Talk in Multilingual Classrooms*. Bristol: Multilingual Matters, 2005.

Davison, Chris. "Collaboration between ESL and Content Teachers: How Do We Know When We Are Doing It Right?" *The International Journal of Bilingual Education and Bilingualism* 9, no. 4 (2006): 454–75. https://doi.org/10.2167/beb339.0.

Dove, Maria, and Andrea Honigsfeld. "ESL Coteaching and Collaboration: Opportunities to Develop Teacher Leadership and Enhance Student Learning. *TESOL Journal* 1, no. 1 (2010): 322. https://doi.org/10.5054/tj.2010.214879.

Evans, Elaine, et al. "Collaborative Teaching in a Linguistically and Culturally Diverse Higher Education Setting: A Case Study of a Postgraduate Accounting Program." *Higher Education Research & Development* 28, no. 6 (2009): 597–613. https://doi.org/10.1080/07294360903226403.

Fields, Katherine Rhodes, and Tamara Warhol. "Movie Magic Collages." In *New Ways of Teaching Speaking*, 2nd ed., edited by Julie Vorholt, 175–6. Alexandria, VA: TESOL Press, 2019.

Gunning, Pamela, et al. "Raising Learners' Awareness through L1-L2 Teacher Collaboration." *Language Awareness* 25 nos. 1–2 (2015): 72–88. https://doi.org/10.1080/09658416.2015.1122022.

Hanusch, Folker, et al. "Theoretical and Practical Issues in Team-Teaching a Large Undergraduate Class." *International Journal of Teaching and Learning in Higher Education* 21 (2009): 66–74.

Honigsfeld, Andrea, and Maria Dove. *Collaboration and Co-Teaching: Strategies for English Learners*. Thousand Oaks, CA: Corwin, 2010.

– *Collaboration and Co-Teaching for English Learners: A Leader's Guide*. Thousand Oaks, CA: Corwin, 2014.

Lester, Jessica N., and Katherine R. Evans. "Instructors' Experiences of Collaboratively Teaching: Building Something Bigger." *International Journal of Teaching and Learning in Higher Education* 20, no. 3 (2009): 373–82.

Lotherington, Heather, and Jennifer Jenson. "Teaching Multimodal and Digital Literacy in L2 Settings: New Literacies, New Basics, New Pedagogies." *Annual Review of Applied Linguistics* 31 (2011): 226–46. https://doi.org/10.1017/S0267190511000110.

New London Group. "A Pedagogy of Multiliteracies: Designing Social Futures." *Harvard Educational Review* 66, no. 1 (1996): 60–92. https://doi.org/10.17763/haer.66.1.17370n67v22j160u.

Stevens, Vance. "Multiliteracies for Collaborative Learning Environments." *TESL-EJ* 9, no. 2 (2005). www.tesl-ej.org/wordpress/issues/volume9/ej34/ej34int/.

– "Revisiting Multiliteracies in Collaborative Learning Environments: Impact on Teacher Professional Development." *TESL-EJ* 10, no. 2 (2006). www.tesl-ej.org/wordpress/issues/volume10/ej38/ej38int/.

Stewart, Tim. "Introduction: Situating Collaboration, Team Teaching, Team Learning and Innovation in ELT Practice." In *Team Teaching and Team Learning in the Language Classroom: Collaboration for Innovation in ELT*, edited by Akira Tajino, et al., 3–10. Milton Park: Routledge, 2016.

Warhol, Tamara, and Katherine Rhodes Fields. "Perception and Projection." *Perceptual Prose*. Unpublished pedagogical materials. Intensive English Program, University of Mississippi, 2010.

– "Organizing Blogs in an ESL/EFL Class using the Rule of Thirds." *TESOL Journal* 3, no. 4 (2012): 735–44.

Warner, Chantelle, and Beatrice Dupuy. "Moving Toward Multiliteracies in Foreign Language Teaching: Past and Present Perspectives … and Beyond." *Foreign Language Annals* 51 (2018): 116–28. https://doi.org/10.1111/flan.12316.

SECTION IV

Experiential Education in Language Teaching and Learning

The vigour of experiential education as a pedagogical focus in current language teaching reveals itself in this section through manifold expressions. The three chapters included here position language at the helm of methodologies that, by their very nature, require continuous interaction with the learning materials at hand. Namely, this involves direct communication and engagement with language within its cultural context. It also places great emphasis on the need to foster student motivation, intercultural awareness, and sensibility, while addressing the critical-thinking skills inherent in "doing" rather than just "thinking about" a language and its cultural sphere of origin and influence. The following chapters reflect upon how experiential education can build bridges between students' comfort zone while learning about a new one. In addition, it engages practices that enable students to find a greater purpose in engaging with the communities represented by those languages, locally and globally. The various methods presented strive to highlight the notion of "otherness" from within and without language.

These multidisciplinary ways of raising linguistic questions that harbour cultural identities and belonging also reach into the benefits for students' future endeavours. Taking their cue from primary materials and active methodologies in their work with subjectivities, theories, and tools, the authors in the next section present their time-tested materials to propose new directions to continue to hone this dimension of our pedagogy.

In chapter 11, "Communicating and Understanding the 'Other' through Experiential Education: Portuguese Language and Culture in Toronto," Maria João Dodman, Inês Cardoso, and Vander Tavares address the purpose and significance of experiential education within the curriculum of a foreign-language university program. The authors draw on theory and their experiences from teaching Portuguese in a fourth-year undergraduate course. Aside from describing this pedagogical method through specific examples, they explain how fostering students' engagement with members of the Portuguese-speaking community in the Greater Toronto Area (GTA) furthers their development at the linguistic, professional, and subjective levels. The authors tackle their subject through the lens of social interactionism. Sociolinguistic and literary empathy research informs their discussion of the significant aspects and effects of utilizing experiential methods. These are rooted in empirical data gathered through various stages of implementing curricular activities that provide "real-life and personalized learning experiences and continuous opportunities for personal reflection." As they suggest, students in these cases "not only test and develop their linguistic skills, but also challenge pre-existing cultural and linguistic assumptions." Various examples are drawn from Luso-Brazilian language and culture courses that linked the teaching materials and themes to community activism, cultural exhibits, and workplace immersions. These topics cover issues of ethnicity, (im)migration, and cultural identity, as well as mental illness and homelessness. The chapter argues against a purely "utilitarian role" for the humanities, one that focuses only on development for tasks or specific employment skill sets, while not denying the importance of these. Beyond those specific skills, the benefits they consider rest on deeper issues related to tolerance and understanding of different cultures.

In similar ways, chapter 12, "Using Experiential Learning Theory as a Framework for Undergraduate Academic Communication Development" is founded on pedagogical theory and experiences to debate the practices of the experiential learning approach. It bases its findings, however, on a discipline-specific academic communications course. Delivery methods, teaching and learning activities, and assessment tasks are presented in relation to the manner in which this student-centred approach to learning addresses students' multidisciplinary needs. The chapter examines these courses using a consistent approach and design. The different disciplinary foci, as Maria Herke, Deanna Wong, and Susan Hoadley explain, are connected in a course on academic communication at Australian universities that brings together students from different disciplines to ease their transition into university. Drawing from their study of this trio of courses, their data gathered since 2010 represents a total of over 5,000 students, three convenors – one for each course (i.e., academic communication in arts and social sciences, business and economics, and science) – and up to twelve tutors. Some of the teaching materials include the e-portfolio, involving online formatting and design, text choices, and creating audience-specific texts. The outcomes feature preparing students to create "a new learning cycle beginning with the concrete experiences of foregrounding their communication skills as part of their professional identity." This student-centred approach, as also discussed in the first chapter of this section, reveals the cutting-edge innovation and success in pedagogies that are "supportive, responsive, and sustainable" to equip students for both employability and essential communication skills.

Chapter 13, "Words at Play: Language Learning at Work," stresses the significance of interactions and the exposure to humour as key components in the second language learning process. Agustina Tocalli-Beller delivers the results of a recent study that involves a series of authentic materials from newspapers – such as jokes, cartoons, and riddles. The author also considers possible methods and choices of delivery to enhance students' learning outcomes and to make recommendations for future pedagogical work. Teaching through humour is an effective way to point out cultural differences while also bridging aspects that link to our common experiences in the world. Humour and teaching in higher education can promote understanding, while also lessening student anxiety, and motivate each learner. As Tocalli-Beller shows in her research on this topic, the relationship between humour and cultural awareness is a key component in learning a language. She cites research that attests to humour as "a highly valued art and practice across societies. In western societies, humour is an essential element of everyday interaction and of socialization" (Boxer and Cortés-Conde). Tocalli-Beller also theorizes her work in opposition to the structure of cognitive-perceptual theory (Vizmuller-Zocco). This work identifies different types of humour and proposes ways to ameliorate difficulties posed to second-language learners in grasping the dimensions of those meaning constructions in new cultural settings. She rounds out her chapter by discussing conversation as performance in situations that can usher in new levels of knowledge acquisition and communicative competence through an active engagement with humour.

Overall, the chapters in this section provide starting points for renewed discussions on experiential education as it applies to language teaching and learning. Each provides examples on how to develop successful teaching and learning across the three Ls of pedagogy – languages, literatures, and linguistics – as well as across cultures and geographical spaces. While sharing techniques that are unique to their fields, they could also be transferable to other cultural and linguistic areas.

11 Communicating and Understanding the "Other" through Experiential Education: Portuguese Language and Culture in Toronto

MARIA JOÃO DODMAN, INÊS CARDOSO, AND VANDER TAVARES

Introduction

In this chapter, we draw on the teaching and learning of Portuguese language (PL) and Portuguese-speaking (PS) cultures to address the purpose and value of experiential education (EE) within the curriculum of a foreign language university program. We rely on a social-interactionist approach to language teaching to examine the re-construction of students' personal relationships with the language. We explore the cultural and linguistic benefits of immersion in the language in and outside the classroom by focusing on a pioneering fourth-level Portuguese undergraduate course. Subsequently, in light of current sociolinguistic and literary empathy research, we discuss how curricular activities lead students to experientially access matters of ethnicity, (im)migration, and cultural identity that characterize the diverse PS communities of the Greater Toronto Area (GTA). We argue that, through this pedagogically innovative curriculum that provides real-life and personalized learning experiences and continuous opportunities for personal reflection, students not only test and develop their linguistic skills, but also challenge pre-existing cultural and linguistic assumptions. We highlight key pedagogical devices that have fostered student engagement and understanding of the ethnic other.

Theoretical Frameworks

Social-Interactionist Approaches to Language Teaching and Learning

The guiding principles of the Portuguese and Luso-Brazilian Studies program and of its pedagogical devices draw on Vygotskian sociocultural theory, namely in the socio-discursive interactionist (SDI) approach to language education, as proposed by Bronckart. SDI emphasizes learning through social interaction, and language practices are seen as instruments of human development given that each person becomes familiarized with and learns through specific textual genres as means of both communication and action. Of particular interest in a university program, then, is the role of language as both a mediator and a powerful tool of personal (linguistic and cultural) development. Therefore, learning either a heritage or a foreign language, and enabling students to manoeuvre through complex cultural references, demands interactional experiences of a linguistically diverse, (in)formal, communicative, and reflexive nature. The need for meaningful interaction becomes even more crucial as we teach a non-official, yet significant, language within Canada's varied cultural and linguistic mosaic.[1]

As such, we are challenged to design and implement mediatory pedagogical tools for authentic and engaging interactions in Portuguese amongst students, instructors, and the community at large. These mediated activities signal a dialectical relationship between the subjects through new linguistic practices. In fact, whereas previous language interaction was always of an informal character, following this intervention students are able to engage in more formal contexts. These (co-) (extra-)curricular tools form the basis of not only communicative, cross-cultural, and critical-skills development, but also a holistic form of growth, strengthening the individuals' ties with the language and the PS communities. In other words, we strive to foster the development of a solid, continuous, and fruitful relationship with the language. When individuals come together in a specific socio-historic environment, they bring into play their linguistic and social representations of the PL and its speakers. These images do not necessarily prevent students from learning, but might, eventually, prove to be uncritical and anchored in stereotypes. As scholars have noted,[2] however, these images can ultimately influence students' commitment and progress. Consequently, it is crucial for us to critically engage with these images and with students' relationships with the PL while planning and evaluating pedagogical practices.

We draw on the notion of "relationship with the language" – as proposed by Barré-De Miniac, Cardoso, and Charlot – to understand the process through which each student deals with diverse elements that dynamically and continuously shape their relationship with the language. Within these elements we find student-formed representations of the other, which allow educators to invite the social and affective dimensions of learning into the acquisition of knowledge, moving beyond the traditionally cognitive view of learning to a more holistic assessment of the student. For us, the notion of "relationship with the language" effectively includes the aforementioned representations and opinions, as well as different language practices and their regularity. In addition, as Cardoso and others discuss, this relationship also comprises attitudes of greater or less detachment and engagement towards the language, values (or a lack thereof) attributed to the language, feelings, conceptions about language learning, and ultimately, the manner by which individuals talk about the language itself. Portuguese, in our case, is indeed more than an object of learning; in multicultural Toronto, it is or becomes part of the subjects' trajectory in and outside the university, enhancing their human development.

Understanding Others through Empathic Fiction

In addition to language, the program emphasizes the teaching of literature with a focus on fiction reading and enhanced empathy. Fiction, as Blackey Vermeule reminds us, provides sites of social information upon which we are invited to sort out and reflect on a number of moral issues. Katja Mellman adds that the pleasure we derive from fiction is in fact "due to its eliciting [of] our social predispositions (cognitive as well as emotional ones)" (426). Jeanette Winterson also notes that literature, and any art for that matter, is far removed from what she calls our "money culture" (179). Instead, art speaks to us as it "gives us a sense of ourselves" (175).[3]

Research that links the reading of fiction and enhanced empathy serves us in a timely manner as we live in an age of social media, online inter-connectivity, and a perceived devaluation of the humanities. Several scholars believe that reading fiction teaches readers to identify and empathize with other people. This is the so-called "empathy-altruism hypothesis," a term dubbed by psychologists and applicable to a wide range of disciplines and studies.[4] Suzanne Keen has been the leading voice for empathic studies in literature. In her revealing work entitled *Empathy and the Novel*, Keen proposes that narrative empathy is the sharing of feeling and perspective-taking induced by reading, viewing, hearing, or imagining narratives of another's situation and condition. In some of their studies, York University psychologist Raymond Mar and his team concluded that readers of fiction tend to a have better ability of empathy: the ability to figure out what someone is thinking or feeling from their expressions, behaviour, or circumstances.[5] In the classroom, Keen's definition of broadcast empathy[6] has been particularly useful in the selection of readings. In Fall 2017, students in AP/POR/HUMA 3600/3616 read a recent and acclaimed novel, *The Shelf Life of Happiness* by Portuguese writer David Machado, and later had the opportunity to meet the writer himself. This particular work was chosen not only because of the EE opportunity, but also due to the work's theme: the seeking of happiness and the complexity of human nature in an apparently more connected world. The students' responses revealed their empathic relationship with the characters and the theme. Despite cultural differences, students came together within the human commonalities as exposed by Keen. Yet, in their discussions, they also seemed prone to understanding those characters who presented no obvious cultural similarities to them, but suffered from mental illness or experienced homelessness.[7]

In 2017–18 students from the intermediate language course wrote books of short stories for children in East Timor. Using online platforms – that is, *Storybird* and *Storyjumper* – students collaborated to craft stories that were culturally and age sensitive, as well as inspiring. In addition to the instructor, students received guidance and praise from a panel of judges and educators regarding the value of such work with underprivileged children. The photos and video that captured the delivery of the books to the children particularly moved students.[8]

Experiential Education

According to Fleming and Walter, the ideas of educators John Dewey and Paulo Freire have had a remarkable influence on present-day conceptions of experiential education. Both Dewey and Freire emphasized real-world-based and problem-solving-based education for their transformative potential in the construction and acquisition of knowledge, and in the improvement of the conditions of the self. Today, as Fleming and Walter have put it, experiential learning is generally understood to be "*learning by doing* and is often associated with learning that is based on personal experiences outside the institutional setting of schools" (60).

Critical reflection is a key component of EE. Knutson proposes that meaningful learning occurs through a systematic process characterized by reflection, understanding, and re-application. In this view, critical reflection is what draws learning out of an experience; in other words, it is the "missing link" of this experience-learning relationship (53). By reflecting on an experience, we come to assess it in relation to past experiences. This assessment involves considering how and whether the experience met previously set expectations, goals, and needs – that is, what worked and what needs to be changed moving forward. This reflection leads to an understanding of the value of the experience, thus generating new insights and discoveries that enable us to go through the same experience in the future with enhanced awareness of our personal roles in the experience and the expected outcomes.

Activities based on an EE approach in the second-or foreign-language (L2) classroom aim to develop learners' linguistic skills by working with and on all dimensions of learners. Rather than simply receiving discrete and fragmented linguistic information, as Knutson's article reveals, experiential education-based L2 teaching invites learners' affective and socio-cognitive domains into learning. It often does so through experience-, project-, and task-based learning with a reflective component in which learners collaboratively discuss and draw on previous knowledge and experiences to devise a plan for solving problems that will lead them to the acquisition of new linguistic information.

Research on experiential education and L2 acquisition outside the classroom has traditionally examined students' L2-related experiences in contexts of study abroad (SA) programs. Yet, linguistic development in the L2 through EE may also occur through community-based and work placement opportunities. Lear defines L2-focused EE within community and professional settings as "a type of experiential learning that blends specific course content with real-world applications and ties them together through structured reflection" (158). Through these hands-on experiences, students acquire linguistic skills in the target language in addition to interpersonal and workplace-specific ones. Unlike SA programs, which require students to leave their countries, community-based and work placement opportunities afford learners the possibility to develop L2-related skills at home.

Experience-Based and Empathic Devices

In a university situated within the largest demographic concentration of Lusophone peoples, 70 per cent of the student population in our program, on average, comes from PS backgrounds. From data analysis of our online language placement test and other curricular activities, we have been able to better understand students' individual relationships with the PL and its cultures. Generally speaking, our analyses reveal that this relationship tends to be defined by several tensions among and within different varieties of the language – European and Brazilian – and the dialectal diversity within the same variant, as in the case of Portuguese as spoken in diverse regions of Portugal as well as its island variants. In addition, we diagnose strains between the so-called "broken Portuguese," as students characterize their performance in comparison to native speakers. Students show awareness of contrastive ways of perceiving and stereotyping Lusophone peoples. For instance, whereas immigrants fall under hardworking, blue-collar, and less educated individuals, those who remained in their home countries tend to be viewed as more relaxed, wiser, and healthier in terms of lifestyle, attractive to those seeking an alternative to fast-paced, capitalist societies. As such, these sunny nations boast creativity and engagement as a means to face an array of challenges. Students also acknowledge the presence of Lusophone cultural manifestations in Canada, although their perceptions suggest a tension between innovation and tradition as discussed by Cardoso and Tavares in their book on teaching and learning Portuguese in Canada.

Students of non-Lusophone backgrounds note mainly Brazilian cultural references, such as those referring to music and dance. Surprisingly, this group demonstrates an awareness of the enormous linguistic diversity within the different PS territories. While this group remarks on the difference between Portuguese and English, they also note Portuguese's similarity to Spanish. This understanding of students' relationship with the PL and cultures, as in Canada or in Lusophone countries, directly informs our curricular planning.[9] Through this continuous process of data collection and analysis, we integrate students' contributions into the enhancement of teaching, learning, and evaluation devices through a collaborative approach.

A curriculum that pursues these goals does not neglect established programming, but makes room for unforeseen, yet meaningful, circumstances designed by and negotiated with the students, challenging all involved to a "willingness to tune ourselves to others, to commit to a common cause, and to engage in manner that is other-oriented" (Roth and Radford, 305). Here, enhancing the students' zone of proximal development follows Roth and Radford's ideas: acknowledging students', teachers', and community members' complex and evolving relationships with language and cultures. All participants partake in a non-transmissive and non-individualistic learning process, sharing different expertise, representations, knowledge, strengths, and weaknesses.

In-class and outside-class activities, designed according to different levels of proficiency and promoting autonomy, afford a number of opportunities to debate the above-mentioned representations through different inputs (oral, written, visual), while developing a sense of belonging aligned with an improvement of listening, speaking, reading, and writing skills. Students bring the need to polish their grammar to speak a "proper Portuguese." To alter this view of language performance, we promote grammar analysis focused on contexts of use, which are aimed at promoting self-awareness as a means of progression and building self-confidence.

Consequently, we design writing activities to enhance performance by promoting collaboration and language awareness, as within in-class compositions using computer and linguistic resources. These written pieces receive formative feedback by the instructor, guiding students to reflectively improve their draft. The final grade takes into consideration the quality and level of improvement in language skills from the last version submitted. Under the supervision of the instructor, senior students also offer guidance to a pair at a lower level. Students cooperate, develop a heightened awareness of their own linguistic development, and see it reflected in their final grade.

The assistance of volunteers, York students fluent in Portuguese, has been tremendously beneficial in fostering linguistic and cultural development. These volunteers are from different Lusophone backgrounds, with varying levels of proficiency, thus exposing students to diverse varieties of the language, while attending PL classes regularly. In addition to motivating students, volunteers also enhance class discussions by sharing cross-cultural perspectives and exposing students to new linguistic material, particularly new vocabulary and pronunciation. As a result, students get to experience the diversity of the language in the classroom and revisit their own preconceived notions of difficulties regarding other variants.

Students are called upon to become free agents of their own learning. They advance at their own pace while having the freedom to explore topics of their own interest. However, students must assume a variety of roles, thus positioning themselves as legitimate language users on different online platforms (forums,

YouTube channels, blogs, our social media channels) or live contexts – on campus, in-class, at the "Portuguese Speaking Hour" – or outside the university. These practices provide the students material for reflection in the classroom and online, and with PL speakers with whom they interact at Lusophone events, through pen-pal correspondence, or face-to-face conversations using the technological software of their choice.

Students report their interests and experiences with the language and its cultures, while building learning portfolios, reading and writing both academically and in a more reflective personal manner. Of particular importance are the free writing assignments where, as the title suggests, students can explore and pursue writing in an unstructured manner, following their instinctual approach to the language. The goal of this activity is to learn from previous errors, as well as build fluency and awareness of linguistic proprieties. They often report positive and non-judgmental feelings about this task. Some students even publish in a multitude of media outlets and in a wide range of genres.

A Pioneering Experiential Education Course: AP/POR 4010 3.0 Language in Context: Portuguese in the GTA

Created in 2013, Language in Context: Portuguese in the GTA has been offered twice since 2014. This course was developed as a result of the faculty's encouragement for programs to create and include more EE opportunities for students. However, there were also a series of contextual circumstances particular to the case of PL and cultures in Toronto that influenced the development of the course – namely, the presence of one of the largest PS communities in the world. Therefore, and in the absence of an immersion experience in a PS country,[10] students have access to diverse PS environments including established businesses that use the language professionally. In fact, Teixeira has noted the high level of institutional completeness of the appreciable number of Portuguese businesses in the GTA (215–16).

Second, the program had an established relationship with the local Portuguese community, whose members voiced a strong desire to develop placement opportunities for students. Through these opportunities, we aimed to provide our students chances to experience hands-on learning in authentic and dynamic ways. There was the natural exposure to context-specific registers of language, but also cultural behaviours unique to Lusophone cultures, especially those that relate to business environments.[11] Third, and in order to better understand this specific cultural group, we wanted students to recognize the reasons and trends behind Lusophone immigration so that their perceived images and stereotypes could be critically challenged. Our goal has been to lead students to not only explore the remains of the culture left behind, but also to grasp and reflect upon this community's contributions to Canada, the connections to their family's homeland, and the current challenges posited by the persistent (yet uneven) negotiation and interaction between two often disparate cultures and languages.

Therefore, POR4010, an advanced language course, was founded in EE in order to engage students in a learning process that blends theory and coursework with practical, real-life experience. Through EE, students refine their language skills, especially those necessary for communication in professional environments. In addition to advanced grammar and composition, the course includes readings on the cultural and linguistic heritage of the PS communities in Toronto, which involve topics on culture and language retention, and immigrant and gender issues. Students learn authentic business terminology and procedures employed in professional communication, such as in writing business letters and engaging in oral interaction in Portuguese. The EE component enables students to apply the course content to a variety of community-based projects assigned by the community partner in consultation with the instructor.

The 10-hour EE component provides an opportunity for immersion into workplace-specific cultural practices. The final project in the course is a community-based publication. This project aims at combining the students' reflections, hands-on experiences, and course materials into a publishable piece, often in the form of a newspaper article. Although students in both offerings of the course were placed within the Portuguese community, there are other emerging Lusophone communities in the GTA, such as the Angolan and the Brazilian communities.

Both offerings of the course promoted a cross-disciplinary approach to teaching and learning. Thus, in addition to grammar and writing skills, students engaged with texts from history, sociology, and literature journals, as well as magazine articles. For instance, while students read and discussed the reasons for immigration as outlined by sociologists, they also read accounts by immigrants themselves or short stories on this topic. The inclusion of fiction is designed to foster students' empathic reaction to immigration, as discussed earlier. Since most immigration to Canada occurred during the Portuguese dictatorship (pre-1974), it was critical to stress the value and role of fiction within oppressive regimes. Issues of youth community involvement and integration, especially those of academic underachievement, were included. These readings played an important role in fostering critical reflection and empathic responses as all students in both iterations were of immigrant backgrounds, particularly Portuguese and Hispanic youth, who have been consistently stigmatized and marginalized.[12] Another key topic relevant to our contextual circumstances is the role of women in the immigration saga, as well as their ongoing role within the Portuguese family and community. Readings concerning immigrant women, such as those included in anthologies, were analysed and discussed as marginal to official discourses, yet women's role has proven invaluable in domestic, professional, and diasporic spheres.[13]

Other important factors to consider are the needs of both students and community partners. As such, previous consultation with the partners must occur and communication between instructor and community partners must be ongoing throughout the placement. Prior to their placements, students need to be prepared accordingly. In the first class, students are introduced to the community partners and fill out a questionnaire that outlines their interests and preferred placement. For instance, students interested in teaching are placed with Camões Toronto, while those interested in social and/or community work are placed with the Working Women Community Centre. In preparation for their placements and prior to making contact with the assigned partner, students learned to draft a curriculum vitae and a cover letter in Portuguese, in addition to professional address.[14] Students were expected to visit their partners on at least three separate occasions in order to establish a more substantial rapport.

Whenever possible, other site visits were organized. In both iterations, visits to the special archive on the Portuguese-Canadian History Project were suggested. Our approach allowed students to interact directly with materials regarding the Portuguese-Canadian immigrant experience in Canada.[15] In the 2016 iteration, students explored immigration issues in the Gallery of Portuguese Pioneers, a museum that documents Portuguese immigration with a special focus on the pioneers.[16] This visit was significant for the students as they engaged with artefacts from the homeland brought by immigrants that served as evidence of the scarcity and poverty from which most of them fled. As Portuguese immigration was first a male-led movement, the lack of women-related objects in the gallery led to important discussions on the need to address their (later) pioneering efforts.

Students were asked to reflect continuously on their experiences, especially on the placements with the partners. In 2014, for instance, one student wrote that upon meeting two Brazilian immigrants and learning of their fascination with Canada and its "cleanliness," he recalled the reading of Aida Batista and the ironic observation of an orderly, rule-prone Canada, different from the homeland. In 2016, a student of Korean background found inspiration in both readings and placement to further investigate his own immigration story. Immigration, youth, and women were topics of great interest to students in both iterations of the course.

One of the most heartfelt pieces was written by a student in 2014, who reflected on the life experiences of the elderly women she met with during her placement at the Working Women Community Centre. These experiences ranged from matters of sexual health to loneliness and financial difficulties. These were real-life accounts of the lived experiences of immigrant women similar to those highlighted by several scholars in *A Mulher nos Açores e nas Comunidades/Women in the Azores and in the Immigrant Communities*, as the student wrote in her portfolio. Another student in 2016 attended a conference at the University of Toronto where matters of gender and civic integration were discussed. As the student elaborated in her portfolio, this was a decisive moment for her as she met scholars and community activists. Another student commented on his participation in a book launch. In the learning portfolio, the student made reference to the value of knowing a second language and of experiencing biculturalism and bilingualism.

Conclusion

Taking into account the sociocultural and experiential milieus, as well as the active role of students as free agents of learning, we have explored students' relationship with the language and culture as well the program's vast array of multidisciplinary and pedagogical tools that promote holistic development. We have stressed the essential role of reading fiction and of producing free, creative, and reflective assignments allowing for self-expression and building transferable knowledge about life experiences. The promotion of empathic connections continues to be vital in the understanding of the self and others.

EE opportunities within the community have been successful due to the community's size and our decade-long relationship. EE and emphatic devices reveal the vitality of the language and its speakers in both local and global communities. They also highlight the value of the humanities in the formation of a new generation of students who are more aware, tolerant, and understanding of others. Contrary to a merely utilitarian role, a university education that emphasizes the study of foreign languages, cultures, and literatures pushes students to confront uncritical and stereotypical images, their own humanity, and global citizenship.

NOTES

1 According to Statistics Canada, at least 237,000 people of Lusophone origins have reported Portuguese as their mother tongue. The majority of Portuguese speakers are in Ontario, specifically in the GTA.

2 See for instance the findings of Castellotti and Moore, and Melo-Pfeifer and Simões.

3 In her defence of realist literature, Ngozi Adichie claims the human stories we read don't just speak of our humanity, but rather tell profound truths about ourselves. For instance, when we read about a once proud man, now abused and exploited by the colonizer, we are coming to terms with dignity and the loss of it. Adichie's 2012 Commonwealth lecture is available at: www.youtube.com /watch?v=vmsYJDP8g2U.

4 The Changing Lives Through Literature program, established in 1991 by Robert Waxler and Jean Trounstine, encourage convicts to explore empathy through

fiction. The program has promoted a 20 per cent decrease in recidivism: https://cltlblog.wordpress.com/about/.

5 See www.yorku.ca/mar/papers.html.

6 "… calls upon the reader to empathize with others, by emphasizing common vulnerabilities and hopes through universalizing representations" (xiv).

7 This is the so-called difficult empathy that pushes the limits of our understanding in reaching out to those we might not otherwise wish to contact or associate with (Leake, 176).

8 The same project took place in 2018–19, and the stories were destined for children in Guinea Bissau.

9 See the article of Cardoso and others for a fuller discussion on this topic.

10 Only 11 per cent of Canadian undergraduate students study abroad, and 70 per cent cite cost as a barrier to doing so: https://www.univcan.ca/universities/facts-and-stats/.

11 For a full list of community partners, see course description of 4010: https://www.yorku.ca/laps/dlll/por/4010-language-in-context/.

12 Students read Da Silva's "Heroes or Zeros? Portuguese-Canadian Youth and the Cost of Mobilizing different Sociolinguistic resources" and Oliveira's *Jovens Portugueses e Luso-Descendentes no Canadá: Trajectórias De Inserção Em Espaços Multiculturais*, along with reports from the Toronto Public School Board, and mainstream newspaper articles on this topic.

13 For instance, in the 2016 iteration a guest speaker came to York to address the role of grandmothers in the retention and linkage to Portuguese culture and values.

14 The EE office within our faculty offers assistance to instructors, students, and partners: https://www.yorku.ca/laps/get-experience/.

15 The Portuguese-Canadian History Project is held at York University and led by York's visiting professor Gilberto Fernando: archives.library.yorku.ca/exhibits/show/pchp.

16 See pioneersgallery.ca.

WORKS CITED

Barré-De Miniac, Christine. "Le Rapport à L'écriture: Une Notion à Valeur Euristique." In *Diptyque 12. Le Rapport à L'écrit: Un Outil pour Enseigner de L'école à L'université*, edited by Suzanne-G. Chartrand and Christiane Blaser, 11–23. Villeneuve d'Ascq: Presses universitaires du Septentrion, 2008.

Bronckart, Jean-Paul. *Activité Langagière, Textes et Discours. Pour un Interactionisme Socio-Discursif.* Paris: Delachaux et Niestlé, 1997.

Cardoso, Inês. "Experiências Didáticas Com a Escrita Em PLNM: Questionando Vias de Promoção de (Des)Envolvimento." In *O Mundo Do Português e o Português No Mundo Afora: Especificidades, Implicações e Ações*, edited by Maria Luisa Ortiz Alvarez and Luís Gonçalves, 427–71. São Paulo: Pontes, 2016.

Cardoso, Inês, et al. "Desenvolvimento de competências de escrita em contextos de PLNM: abordagem adotada em duas gramáticas pedagógicas." In *Geopolítica Do Português: História, Políticas e Ensino*, edited by Kleber Silva and Cátia Martins. São Paulo: Mercado de Letras. 2020.

Cardoso, Inês, and Vander Tavares, editors. *Teaching and Learning Portuguese in Canada: Multidisciplinary Contributions to SLA Research and Practice*. Roosevelt, NJ: Boa Vista Press, 2020.

Castellotti, Veronique, and Daniele Moore. *Social Representations of Languages and Teaching. Reference Study*. Strasbourg: Council of Europe, 2002.

Charlot, Bernard. *Da Relação Com o Saber Às Práticas Educativas*. São Paulo: Cortez Editora, 2013.

Cross, Russell. "A Sociocultural Framework for Language Policy and Planning [Socikultura Kadro Por Lingvaj Politiko Kaj Planado]." *Language Problems & Language Planning* (2009). doi: 10.1075/LPLP.33.1.02CRO.

Fleming, Douglas, and Pierre Walter. "Linking Teacher Professionalism and Learner Autonomy through Experiential Learning and Task Design." *TESL Canada Journal* 4 (2004): 58–72. https://doi.org/10.18806/tesl.v0i0.1040.

Keen, Suzanne. *Empathy and the Novel*. Oxford: Oxford University Press, 2007.

Knutson, Sonja. "Experiential Learning in Second-Language Classrooms." *TESL Canada Journal* 20, no. 2 (2003): 52–64. https://doi.org/10.18806/tesl.v20i2.948.

Kolb, David A., and Roger Fry. "Toward an Applied Theory of Experiential Learning." In *Theories of Group Process*, edited by Carl L. Cooper, 33–57. New York: John Wiley & Sons, 1975.

Leake, Eric. "Humanizing the Inhumane. The Value of Difficult Empathy." In *Rethinking Empathy through Literature*, edited by Meghan Marie Hammond and Sue J. Kim, 175–85. Milton Park: Routledge, 2018.

Lear, Darcy. "Languages for Specific Purposes Curriculum Creation and Implementation in Service to the US Community." *The Modern Language Journal* 96 (2012): 158–72. https://doi.org/10.2307/41478795.

Mellmann, Katja. "Objects of Empathy." In *Characters in Fictional Worlds: Understanding Imaginary Beings in Literature*, edited by Jens Eder, Fotis Jannidis, and Raft Schneider, 416–41. Berlin: De Gruyter, 2011.

Melo-Pfeifer, Sílvia, and Ana Raquel Simões, editors. *Plurilinguismo Vivido, Plurilinguismo Desenhado: Estudos Sobre a Relação Dos Sujeitos Com as Línguas*. Portugal: Instituto Politécnico de Santarém / Escola Superior de Educação, 2017.

Roth, Wolff-Michael, and Luis Radford. "Re/Thinking the Zone of Proximal Development (Symmetrically)." *Mind, Culture, and Activity* 17, no. 4 (2010): 299–307. https://doi.org/10.1007/978-94-6091-564-2_5.

Teixeira, Carlos. "On the Move: Portuguese in Toronto." In *The Portuguese in Canada: From the Sea to the City*, edited by Carlos Teixeira and Victor M.P. Da Rosa, 207–20. Toronto: University of Toronto Press, 2000.

Vermeule, Blakey. *Why Do We Care about Fictional Characters?* Baltimore: Johns Hopkins University Press, 2010.

Vygotsky, Lev Semenovich. *Pensamento e Linguagem. 3 Edição*. Translated by Jefferson Luiz Camargo and José Cipolla, revised by José Cipolla Neto. São Paulo: Martins Fontes, 2005.

Winterson, Jeanette. "What Is Art For?" In *The World Split Open. Great Authors on How and Why we Write, A Literary Arts Readers*, 173–88. Portland: Tin House Books, 2014.

12 Using Experiential Learning Theory as a Framework for Undergraduate Academic Communication Development

MARIA HERKE, SUSAN HOADLEY, AND DEANNA WONG

Introduction

In order to support students' transition to university our institution offers a suite of three first year undergraduate courses in academic communication: academic communication in arts and social sciences, business and economics, and science. While the overall approach and design is consistent across the three courses, the different disciplinary foci mean that each course is more relevant to the needs and interests of students, as well as to the learning demands of the different disciplinary fields (Kolb). The academic communication teaching team consists of three convenors, one for each course, and up to twelve tutors, who often teach multiple classes on more than one of the courses. The arts and social sciences course has the largest student cohort with up to 400 students per session, not least because the course is a requirement for some programmes. The business and economics course has up to 175 students and science course up to 100 students per session. The number of students taking the courses has steadily increased since they were first offered in 2010, and in total over 5000 students have completed the courses within the university, with many more completing versions of the same courses in the university's international pathways college.

Overall, the courses have proven to be an effective and sustainable way to support students in developing the language and communication skills needed at university, in their disciplines, and, in turn, in their professions, by allowing students (and increasingly programme directors) to choose to integrate them into their programmes (Hoadley and Hunter). Interest in including the academic communication courses in programmes has risen as Australian universities have been increasingly called upon to account for graduate outcomes through national and vocational accreditation frameworks, as well as in response to employer criticisms. Further, including the courses in programmes aligns with the university's requirements that graduates are capable of communicating effectively. All these requirements and pressures highlight the importance of communication as a fundamental skill for employability, which enables students' successful entry into their chosen careers.

In the next section, we discuss the overall design of the three courses in relation to experiential learning theory (ELT), with reference to the course descriptions (as per the university handbook) and the learning outcomes. The rest of the chapter is organized into three main sections – learning outcomes, assessment tasks, and learning and teaching activities – and in each section we explain and provide examples of how ELT informs our approaches, practices, and methods, followed by a short conclusion.

Course Design

The design of the courses is broadly underpinned by experiential learning theory (ELT), which sees learning as "a continuous process grounded in experience" where "everyone enters every learning situation with more or less articulate ideas about the topic at hand" (Kolb, ch. 2). This focus on learning as a process is central to the courses. Most university-level academic communication courses prioritize the product or outcome of learning, whereby marks are awarded only for assignments such as essays, reports, and presentations, but the learning process is not explicitly rewarded. This practice tends to lead strategic learners to focus reductively only on course material that they judge as being directly relevant to the next assessment task, and thereby disengaging from other course material and their own learning. Overlooking the learning process in this way denies students the opportunity to learn to recognize, value, and relate their own prior learning or beliefs to new ideas and future applications (Kolb). Viewing learning as a process as well as product (Kolb and Kolb) enables students to develop insights into both the centrality of communication and the value of sustained engagement in leading successful lives, both within and beyond university.

The orientation of the courses to ELT is evident in the course description(s) and the learning outcomes shown in tables 12.1 and 12.2 respectively. The courses are designed to draw on students' previous experience and learning, and therefore expectations (Kolb, ch. 2), in relation to academic practices, behaviours and values, by examining and testing these in independent and collaborative learning activities that reiteratively cover all stages of the experiential learning cycle (ELC) (Kolb, ch. 2). Following Kolb and Kolb (2018), students' learning is motivated by the dialogue between their contemporaneous concrete experience of academic communication (both within the course and their programme more broadly) and their abstract conceptualization of academic communication. This dialogue helps students understand their experience. Further, the dialogue between reflecting on their concrete experience of academic communication and acting on these reflections transforms student understanding.

Also, as advocated in ELT, the courses take a developmental approach that recognizes the progressive transitions to university, then to specific disciplines and on to professions (Taylor Millwater and Nash; Wood and Solomonides) specifically in relation to language development (Arkoudis et al.). To do this, as articulated in the learning outcomes, students engage with and create texts that are appropriate to their discipline and profession, backed by learning activities that are informed by linguistic theory (namely genre pedagogy, see for example Rothery; Martin; Dreyfus et al.). These learning activities involve reading, thinking, and expressing ideas effectively and critically, using discipline-specific language and perspectives to address issues in contemporary society. As such, the courses facilitate learning by examining and testing the student beliefs and theories about disciplinary and professional communication, as well as academic communication enabling students to learn new ways of understanding, classifying, and formulating meanings (Coffin and Donohue). These insights lead them to develop their own new knowledge and more refined ideas that allow them to adapt to and transact with academic, discipline, and, in turn, professional environments (Kolb). Thus, the courses aim to enable students to progress through all three development stages identified in ELT – that is, acquisition, specialization, and integration – rather than focusing primarily on the acquisition stage (Kolb).

Learning Outcomes

Just as the courses have essentially the same unit description (table 12.1), there is considerable overlap between the learning outcomes (table 12.2). Overall, the learning outcomes focus on the following skills: reading, interpreting, and evaluating sources; producing texts; and academic practices including referencing. Differences in the order, expression, and, to a lesser degree, content of the learning outcomes across the three courses are the result of frequent liaison with the respective faculties, which is a key aspect of the continuous (re)development and ongoing delivery of the courses. For example, in terms of the order and number of learning outcomes, for the business and economics course the outcomes are condensed into four outcomes in accordance with preferred faculty practice, and academic integrity is emphasized as the first outcome because this is felt to be of particular importance for this very large and diverse faculty. In terms of the arts and social sciences course, grammar is included to satisfy the accreditation requirements for education programs. The science learning outcomes are more diffuse, in order to better align with faculty requirements for more specific statements of student attainment.

Table 12.1. Course description(s)

Arts and Human Sciences	Business and Economics	Science
This unit is designed to support students in their transition to university by enabling them to understand and achieve standards of performance required in an academic environment.		
The unit provides a three-level focus, which is initiated by facilitating the development of academic practices, behaviours, and values.		
Secondly, it fosters a level of familiarity with the disciplinary language, texts, and conventions used when studying in programs offered by the Faculty of Arts and Faculty of Human Sciences.	Secondly, it fosters a level of familiarity with the disciplinary language, texts, and conventions used when studying in programs offered by the Faculty of Business and Economics.	Secondly, it fosters a level of familiarity with the disciplinary language, texts, and conventions used when studying in programs offered by the Faculty of Science.
Finally, it raises an awareness of the diverse perspectives offered by disciplines and the different contributions they can make to solving problems and addressing issues of concern in contemporary society.	Finally, it raises awareness of the impact of business and economics principles when they are applied to solving problems and addressing issues in contemporary society.	Finally, it raises an awareness of the impact of scientific knowledge and the role of scientists when they act to solve problems and implement innovations affecting contemporary society.
Learning and assessment activities are designed to build the capacity for independent and collaborative approaches to learning.		
Students are guided to develop their capacity for reading, thinking, and expressing ideas effectively and critically.		

Note: Courses are referred to as “units” in our institution.

Assessment Tasks

The focus of the courses on learning as a *process* is evident in the assessment strategy, as shown in table 12.3. There are two types of assessments: a series of reflections with an e-portfolio and discipline-specific texts. The arts and social sciences course also has a grammar assessment task in accordance with accreditation requirements of education programmes. The first reflection is the initial assessment task, further reflections are interspersed with the other discipline-specific assessment tasks throughout the teaching session, and the e-portfolio is the final assessment activity. Thus, through this strategy, students are constantly reflecting on their learning process and this reflection contributes to their overall grade.

A process approach is also key to the discipline-specific assessment tasks that are embedded in the learning activities in the courses in accordance with the four stages of genre pedagogy – that is, building the field (e.g., reading), deconstruction of model texts, joint construction, and independent construction of texts (Rothery and Stenglin). Further, the texts the students produce for their formal assessment tasks (see table 12.3) build on one another, revisiting the same topic field yet re-contextualizing the information, progressing from basic information summaries to persuasive academic and/or professional texts (Martin and Rose) as appropriate to the discipline. For example, the science course assessments (see table 12.3) begin with an information synthesis that provides students with a basic introduction to the conventions of academic writing, which forms the core of a literature review. The skills acquired here are developed further by students working in groups to deliver an oral information report with a more elaborate structure (introduction, body, and conclusion) requiring more sophisticated evaluation synthesis and a change of modality (i.e., written to multimodal). Having produced two texts on the same topic using different modalities, the focus is then shifted to different audiences. This is achieved by asking students to create a formal scientific research report, which follows the typical structure (IMRD – introduction, method, results, discussion) written for a professional scientific audience. The students then transform the scientific report to create a brochure exploring the same field, intended for a non-expert audience. In contrast, the progression in the business and economics assessments focuses more on a change of purpose, with a less distinct change of audience.

The iterative reflection and recontextualization required by the assessment strategy mean that the ELC is repeatedly revisited for each task and at various levels, leading to the recurring cycle or spiral identified by Kolb, and represented horizontally for the academic communication courses in figure 12.1. While a full description of the practices and methodologies at each stage and level of the

Table 12.2. Learning outcomes

Arts and Human Sciences	Business and Economics	Science
1. Read efficiently to gather, interpret, synthesize, and apply concepts from discipline-specific sources.	1. Demonstrate acceptable academic practices, behaviours, and values (academic integrity) in the completion of assessment tasks and other learning activities.	1. Read efficiently to gather specific information and ideas from discipline-specific sources.
2. Critically evaluate information and ideas relevant to social science and arts related disciplines.	2. Critically gather, read, interpret, evaluate, and synthesize information and ideas from appropriate sources.	2. Demonstrate an ability to interpret and apply concepts from sources used in the discipline.
3. Analyse the purpose and language strategies of disciplinary and professional texts.	3. Produce written, oral and, multimodal texts appropriate to the purpose and audience in accordance with academic, disciplinary, and professional communication conventions.	3. Analyse the purpose, language, and features of academic, disciplinary, and professional genres.
4. Apply the knowledge gained through critical evaluation and analysis of other writers to the production of each student's own texts in both written and oral contexts.	4. Reflect on learning experience to inform future academic, disciplinary and professional practice.	4. Critically evaluate information and ideas from academic, disciplinary, and professional sources.
5. Understand the basic grammatical foundations of clear academic and professional communication.		5. Express ideas using appropriate language and structure for academic and professional purposes in written and/or oral texts.
6. Carry out directed reflection on the learning experience of the unit.		6. Apply academic referencing conventions accurately and appropriately.
7. Apply academic referencing conventions accurately and appropriately.		7. Apply reasoning to formulate and support a position or argument.
		8. Plan and produce texts to reflect academic and disciplinary standards.
		9. Engage in independent and collaborative learning activities.

Table 12.3. Assessment tasks

Arts and Social Sciences	Business and Economics	Science
e-portfolio and online tasks 30% Weeks 1–13	Reflections and e-portfolio 20% Weeks 2–13	e-portfolio and reflections 20% Weeks 1–13
Integrative summary 20% Week 6	Information synthesis 20% Week 6	Information synthesis 20% Week 5
Persuasive texts A and B 35% Weeks 11/13	Business report 40% Week 9	Persuasive texts 40% Week 12
Grammar quiz 15% Week 8	Persuasive presentation 20% Weeks 12/13	Group presentation 20% Week 8

spiral is beyond the scope of this paper, we describe the integrative summary assessment task in the arts and social sciences course below as an example.

In the arts and social sciences course, the integrative summary is the first discipline-specific assessment task, and it is also one of the first formal university assessments many of the students encounter. In preparing the students for this assessment, we take them around the learning cycle twice. First, students complete a practice task as part of the first assessment task. On a macro level, this practice task provides students with the opportunity to gain concrete experience (CE) in all aspects of the assessment preparation and submission process without risking marks. This practice assessment task enables students to both have a concrete experience (CE) of, and reflectively observe (RO), the overall university assessment preparation and submission process before they move to conceptualizing (AC) the first formal assessment and then actively experimenting (AE) as they submit their final version of the integrative summary. On a micro level, as with all the other discipline-specific assessment tasks in the courses, the students are taken around the learning cycle in relation to the practice task. We ask the students to engage in the following tasks: prepare a draft of the assessment (CE); bring that draft into class so that it forms part of the in-class peer review activity and discussion (RO); use the feedback from the peer review to revisit relevant lecture and textbook material; and, finally, conceptualize (AC) an improved, newly considered version of the assessment for final submission (AE). As with all assessment tasks, the final submission generates "consequences" (Kolb and Kolb, 10) in the form of tutor feedback, which triggers the cycle to begin anew, as students experience the feedback (CE) and reflect on it (RO) to conceptualize (AC) how this feedback can be used to shape the next assessment (AE).

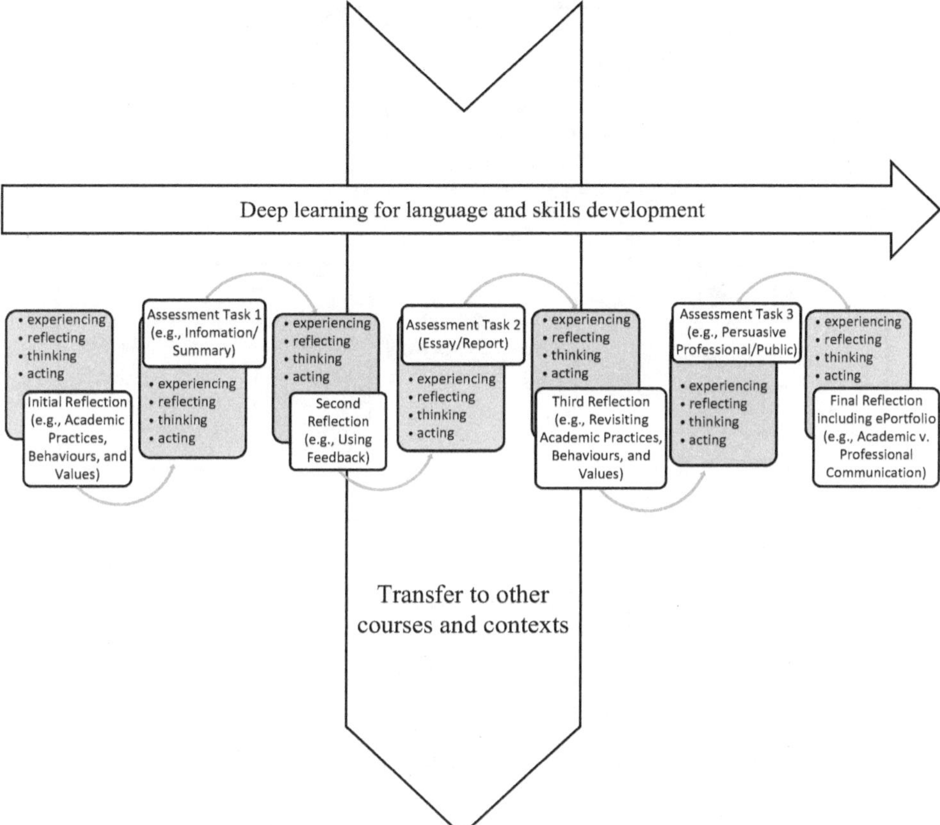

Figure 12.1. Academic communication courses experiential learning spiral

Learning and Teaching Activities: Full Cycle Teaching

In this section, we map the key learning and teaching activities used in the courses to the ELC, in order to demonstrate how we use the cycle to support the students through the different stages of the learning process (see figure 12.2 below). One of the strengths of the ELC is that it makes each of the four stages of learning explicit, scaffolding educators in the design and delivery of learning and teaching activities. Although ideally all learning and teaching activities follow the cycle, incorporating each of the four stages, albeit at different levels, in this section we focus on the key practices and methodologies, discussing each stage of the ELC in turn. An important implication of the focus on process and

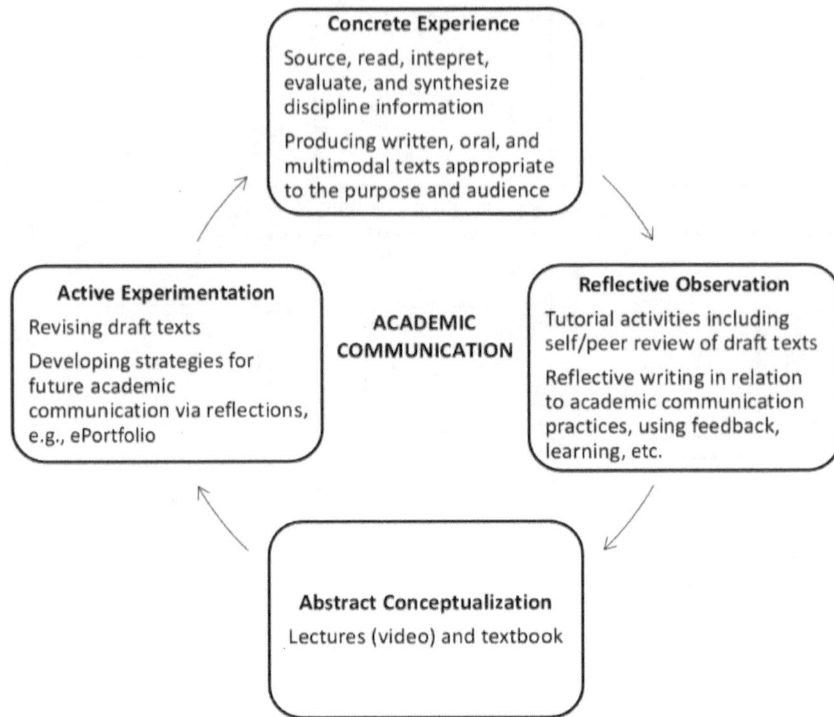

Figure 12.2. Academic communication unit experiential learning cycle (adapted from Kolb, 32)

the assessment strategy in the courses is that assessment tasks are included as (and in) learning activities at different stages of the ELC.

Concrete Experience

Kolb has consistently emphasized the necessity of experience for learning; however, what is also discussed is the difficulty of differentiating concrete "pure" experience that "violates the expectations of previous convictions and habits of thought" from everyday experience, which incidentally occurs at all stages of the cycle (Kolb and Kolb, 9). This distinction is even more nuanced for academic communication courses, since the concrete experience *is* academic communication that arguably occurs in other stages of the ELC in other learning contexts. For example, the courses aim to develop students' readings skills so that they can read discipline-specific texts as part of the abstract conceptualization stage of the learning process in other courses. Thus, in the context of the academic communication courses, the concrete experiences we focus on are 1) sourcing, reading, interpreting, evaluating, and synthesizing disciplinary information and 2) producing written, oral, and multimodal texts as appropriate to the academic (and by extension disciplinary and professional) purpose and audience. These two types of concrete experiences can be seen as the "building the field" and "text construction" aspects of genre pedagogy, which are discussed in turn below.

Building the field activities are a significant part of studying at university, however students have different expectations, based on their experience and knowledge, of what this involves. To give students concrete experience in building the field activities, the courses incorporate sourcing, reading, interpreting, evaluating, and synthesizing discipline-specific texts in the learning and teaching activities. For example, students read discipline-specific texts in class using scaffolds based on the 4-S reading strategy articulated by Boddington and Clanchy, which is also presented in the course textbook (Brick, Herke, and Wong) and lectures (videos) (AC). Similarly, there are further in-class learning activities that involve students sourcing, reading, and discussing other source texts in preparation for the discipline-specific assessment tasks.

Following from the building the field learning and teaching activities, the courses involve a staged approach to producing written, oral, and multimodal texts. In broad terms, the initial stages of the approach are in-class joint and independent construction and writing activities, leading to students independently producing the discipline-specific assessment task texts. For most students the process of writing in-class is an experience that produces a shock "that violates the expectations of previous convictions and habits of thought" (Kolb and Kolb, 9) of what is involved in academic writing. At all stages, the students' concrete experiences are in dialogue with the features of academic writing and the model texts presented in the lectures and textbook (AC), thereby enabling the students to understand their experience (Kolb and Kolb, 9).

Reflective Observation. Opportunities for students to reflect on their concrete experiences of academic communication are embedded in the courses in the reflection assessment tasks (as discussed previously) and the in-class activities in tutorials. A key in-class reflective activity is the review of draft versions of the texts students have prepared for their discipline-specific assessment tasks. For each discipline-specific assessment task an entire two-hour class is allocated to self and peer review of the draft versions prior to submission. Self and peer review is used not only for practical purposes, but also to allow students to take charge of their own learning through considering their own texts, which enables conversational learning (Kolb) as students discuss their experiences of creating the texts with one another. Key to the conversation is the physical presence of a paper copy of the draft texts (an electronic copy also works, but not as well). The reflective observation is scaffolded by using the rubrics, which will be used to formally assess the tasks to structure the discussion. The students are already familiar with these rubrics from previous tutorial activities, which may have involved applying them to a sample text, drafting the standards, or deciding on the weighting of the criteria. In keeping the learning outcomes of the courses, the rubrics are designed to focus on the structure, language and (academic and professional) presentation of the text as appropriate to the purpose and audience (Brick et al., 225), with less emphasis on "content." Students work in pairs according to the following process:

1. As detailed in the 4S reading method, skim and search your partner's text.
2. Agree which criteria you both want to focus on first with your partner.
3. Re-read your partner's text, selecting (refer to 4S) evidence of that criteria.
4. Discuss with your partner (allowing 3–5 minutes per text as a guide).
5. Repeat steps 2–4 until you have worked through all the criteria.

Students are encouraged to ask questions during the process, and the tutor moves around the room speaking to students individually, answering questions, making connections across the questions and discussion points between groups, and providing other general support. The tutor also notes key points on the whiteboard (or similar) for a whole-class debrief (approximately ten minutes) at the end of the class.

Abstract Conceptualization

Students engage with the abstract conceptualization stage of the learning cycle as they prepare subsequent discipline-specific assessment tasks. Typically, they find the requirement to reformulate their arguments for a new audience or purpose very challenging. The learning cycle is a helpful means of leading the students over this hurdle. In particular, we scaffold the students through the components of the AC stage, including choosing, planning, problem solving, and making decisions to accomplish a goal (Kolb and Kolb). For example, when students are required to reformulate a previously submitted persuasive academic argument into a persuasive public audience text, the change in audience demands that students make new and appropriate language choices for a public audience through lecture and textbook engagement. Two key aims of the courses include: 1) understanding the way in which the intended audience of a text influences language choices, and 2) illuminating the relevance of academic communication learning for the students' professional communication requirements in their future careers. It is important that students see that the learning in these courses is valuable beyond just the university context. The steps students move through are as follows:

1. Review your last assessment and choose the argument(s) you think are most appropriate for the purpose and audience of your next assignment.
2. Refer to your model text deconstructed in the lectures and jointly constructed in tutorial groups.
3. Review other relevant information from your lectures, model texts, and the course textbook, focusing on making suitable language choices for your public audience.

Once the above steps are complete, students move to the AE stage of the learning cycle where they prepare their draft of the next assessment. This stage also prepares students for active experimentation when constructing the professionally oriented e-portfolio discussed below.

Active Experimentation

Active experimentation sits between abstract conceptualization and concrete experience and is opposite to reflective observation on the ELC. It functions to "close the learning cycle" by generating "consequences that create new experiences that begin the cycle anew" (Kolb and Kolb, 10). It is at this point in the ELC cycle that students become ready to draw together the ideas and knowledge developed through the preceding stages of the cycle. A key active experimentation activity in all three forms of academic communication is the e-portfolio task. The aim of the e-portfolio is to enable students to bring together their prior learning in the academic communication courses and to begin the transition from student to professional life by applying academic, disciplinary, and professional communication strategies, thus creating an entirely new experience.

For the e-portfolio, students are asked to select a collection of extracts from their work completed throughout the teaching session (in any course they are enrolled in, not just the academic communication courses) that they feel best represents their current identity as academic writers, as well as sets the foundation for their future professional selves. The challenge inherent in this task is that the selected texts are not being curated for academic scrutiny, but instead for prospective employers. In other words, students need to consider the needs and perspectives of a professional audience rather than the academic one they are accustomed to. However, the creation of the e-portfolio permits experimentation that extends beyond a change in audience and encourages students to engage with an online medium. Once students have identified which extracts they want to use for their e-portfolios, they are provided with instructions on how to create an online blog to house their e-portfolios. The formatting and presentation of these blogs are determined solely by the students, allowing them to explore how they want their work to be presented to their chosen audience. In addition, students are asked to write a short commentary for each extract highlighting why the text was chosen. These commentaries need to identify which features they consider salient to their professional audience. This process of shaping the e-portfolio–in terms of text choices, online formatting and design, and of creating audience-specific texts – prepares students for the creation of a new learning cycle beginning with the concrete experience of foregrounding their communication skills as a part of their professional identity.

Conclusion

In this chapter, we have described the ways in which ELT underpins the practices and methodologies in academic communication courses and enables a student-centred approach that is supportive, responsive, and sustainable. Using ELT has resulted in innovative courses that are oriented to assessments of both individual student learning processes and the products or outcomes of their learning. Attesting to the flexibility of ELT and our approach is its application to a broad range of disciplines (arts and social sciences, science, and business and economics) across different institutional contexts (the university faculties and the international pathways college). The systematic character of ELC enables us to respond with agility to the changing demands of the course stakeholders, thus ensuring the sustainability of these valuable communication courses within the university. Importantly, we have been able to better meet the needs and expectations of students, employers, and the community more generally in relation to equipping students with essential communication skills for employability.

WORKS CITED

Arkoudis, Sophie, Chi Baik, and Sarah Richardson. *English Language Standards in Higher Education: From Entry to Exit*. Camberwell: ACER Press, 2012.

Boddington, Paula, and John Clanchy. *Reading for Study & Research*. Queensland: Longman Australia, 1999.

Brick, Jean, Maria Herke, and Deanna Wong. *Academic Culture: A Student's Guide to Study at University*, 3rd ed. South Yarra: Red Globe Press, 2016.

Coffin, Caroline, and Jim Donohue. "A Language as Social Semiotic-Based Approach to Teaching and Learning in Higher Education." *Language Learning* 64, no. 1 (2014): i–x. https://doi.org/10.1080/1554480X.2016.1128142.

Dreyfus, Shoshana, et al. *Genre Pedagogy in Higher Education: The SLATE Project*. London: Palgrave Macmillan, 2016.

Hoadley, Susan, and Kerry Hunter. "Whole of Institution Academic Language and Learning Practice: Systemic Implications." *Journal of Academic Language & Learning* 12, no. 1 (2018): 48–63.

Kolb, David A. *Experiential Learning: Experience as the Source of Learning and Development*, 2nd ed. London: Pearson Education, 2015. www.safaribooksonline.com/api/v1/dashboard/continue9780133892512/

Kolb, Alice Y., and David A. Kolb. "Learning Styles and Learning Spaces: Enhancing Experiential Learning in Higher Education." *Academy of Management Learning & Education* 4, no. 2 (2005): 193–212. doi:10.5465/ AMLE.2005.17268566.

– "Eight Important Things to Know about the Experiential Learning Cycle." *Australian Educational Leader* 40, no. 3 (2018): 8–14.

Martin, James R. "Mentoring Semogenesis: 'Genre-Based' Literacy Pedagogy." In *Pedagogy and the Shaping of Consciousness: Linguistic and Social Processes*, edited by Frances Christie, 123–55. London, UK: Cassell, 2000.

Martin, James. R., and David Rose. *Genre Relations: Mapping Culture*. Sheffield: Equinox Publishing Ltd., 2008.

Rothery, Joan, "Making Changes: Developing an Educational Linguistics." In *Literacy in Society*, edited by Ruqaiya Hasan and Geoffrey Williams. New York: Longman, 1996.

Rothery, Joan, and Maree Stenglin. "Writing a book review: A unit of work for junior secondary English (Write it Right Resources for Literacy and Learning)." Sydney: Metropolitan East Disadvantaged Schools Program, 1994.

Taylor, Peter G., et al. "Talking about Transitions: The Value of a Conceptual Approach." *Enhancing Higher Education, Theory and Scholarship*, Proceedings of the 30th HERDSA Annual Conference, Adelaide, 2007.

Wood, Leigh N., and Ian Solomonides. "Different Disciplines, Different Transitions." *Mathematics Education Research Journal* 20, no. 2 (2008): 117–34. doi: 10.1007/BF03217481.

13 Words at Play: Language Learning at Work

AGUSTINA TOCALLI-BELLER

Introduction

Classroom interaction is unquestionably considered a key part of the second-language (L2) learning process because it can become a fruitful site for L2 development. With this in mind, since 2004 I have investigated ways to make classroom interactions more lively, motivating, and conducive to language learning through language play (LP). I define LP as the use of words, phrases, and expressions in a clever or funny way that breaks grammatical or semantic conventions in order the bring language into focus. So far, a few researchers like Bell, Tarone, Lantolf, and others have examined instances of spontaneous LP, which may or may not be humorous. Only a few applied linguists, such as Pomerantz and Bell in the 2000s, had begun to draw attention to humour, LP, and creativity in everyday contexts and interactions and their links to language learning. Therefore, I decided to document and measure the actual impact that humour, LP, and linguistic creativity have on learning, following Bell's assertion that "[i]n order to determine further to what extent LP may aid in L2 acquisition, observation of a learner hearing L2 structures introduced or reformulated in a playful context and later using the vocabulary or structure would be ideal" (214). (See Reddington for a review on humour and L2 pedagogy).

The first part of the data in this paper comes from an in-depth study with ESL university students. The second part of the data comes from a recent replication study carried out with 72 Grade 4 students in an English immersion program in Mexico City. Both studies involved the selection and implementation of authentic material from national newspapers – including jokes, cartoons, and riddles – in the second-language classroom. These pieces of LP embedded certain words and idiomatic expressions that inevitably came into focus as the students tried to understand the linguistic creativity, humour, and language involved. Through a focus on one of the jokes, I will demonstrate that dialogues about the language of the joke allowed ESL adult students to understand L2 humour and learn new vocabulary from it. Through a focus on vocabulary testing, I will also demonstrate that the LP material implemented in four regular immersion classes was useful and memorable.

Theoretical Framework

Understanding and Using L2 Humour

> [I]f you can learn the humor of a people and really control it you know that you are also in control of nearly everything else.
>
> – Hall, *The Silent Language*, p. 52

Humour is a highly valued art and practice across societies. In the West, humour is an essential element of everyday interactions and of socialization. Friendly joking is a salient element in social discourse among English speakers. The theory of humour most commonly linked to classroom pedagogy is the cognitive-perceptual theory. This theory assumes that humour results from playful situations – that is, when "the perceiver meets with an incongruity (usually in the form of a punch line or a cartoon) and then is motivated to resolve the incongruity either by retrieval of information in the joke or from his/her own storehouse of information" (Suls, 42). Out of such situations, two characteristics of the rational human being arise: amusement and problem-solving. The former is precisely the enjoyment of becoming aware of incongruity, that is, of noticing "something which clashes with our mental patterns and expectations" (Morreall, 1).

There are three types of humour according to Schmitz: 1) universal or reality-based humour, 2) culture-based humour, and 3) linguistic or word-based humour. Linguistic humour is a recurrent type of humour and, more often than not, difficult for L2 speakers to comprehend, even when their proficiency in the language is high (as is culture-based humour, which is beyond the scope of this paper). The difficulty in understanding linguistic humour usually lies in the use of a word or expression referred to as "the semantic script-switch trigger" (Raskin), or simply "the trigger." The semantic trigger (ST) is the key element because it is the "centre of energy, some word or phrase in which the whole matter of the joke is fused, and from which its powers radiate" (Nash, 7).

Unquestionably, the use and understanding of L2 humour constitute two of the greatest challenges for L2 learners, as it often requires sophisticated linguistic, social, and cultural competence. For many L2 learners both the forms and functions of humour differ from those of their language, which makes the understanding and use of humour all the more problematic for them. L2 humour has therefore earned the reputation of being "unteachable," prompting L2 teachers to shun its inclusion in the curriculum.

L2 Communicative Performance and the Importance of Being Humorous

Linguistic competence is known as the mental representations of linguistic rules that constitute the speaker-hearer's internal grammar, whereas communicative competence is the "knowledge that the speaker-hearer has of what constitutes appropriate as well as correct language behaviour and also of what constitutes effective language behaviour in relation to particular communicative goals" (Ellis, 13).

As important as the distinction between linguistic competence and communicative competence has always been in the field of L2 teaching and learning, the distinction between the latter and communicative *performance* is equally significant. Because communicative competence constitutes mental knowledge, it is therefore not open to direct inspection. One can only explore and describe the learners' communicative competence by examining samples of their performance. Thus, communicative performance is regarded as the actual use of linguistic, sociolinguistic, strategic, and pragmatic knowledge in understanding and producing discourse. As Block rightly observes, there is still a limited view of language, which has become evident in the literature and research on L2 tasks. Therefore, tasks that prompt student involvement through dialogues are considered to be the backbone of the Input-Interaction-Output model (hereafter, IIO).

The IIO model has its origins in the shift from linguistic competence as the sole object of acquisition to communicative performance as a broader view of language that includes the ability of students to engage in conversations. This ability is to be taught by carrying out tasks that, according to Long, reflect real-world activities: "the hundred and one things people *do* in everyday life, at work, ***at play***, and in between" (89, emphasis added). A good deal of current L2 pedagogy, however, seems to focus more or less exclusively on the simulation of the conversations in which students might engage when doing more transactional and goal-oriented activities, such as making an airline or hotel reservation, giving directions, etc. That is, while L2 learning is embedded in a contextually rich and content-based curriculum, certain tasks lead students to focus on meaning and on getting things done, as if it were a real-life situation outside the confines of the classroom. However, Cook argues that a great deal of adult speech is form-oriented:

> Many conversations between friends and intimates contain little information, and may be regarded as instances of play and banter. These discourses are not ... "task-based." They are language for enjoyment, for the self, for its own sake. And they are

> often fantasies – not about the real world, but about a fictional one in which there are no practical outcomes. (231)

Carter and McCarthy, for the CANCODE[1] corpus, as well as Nerlich and Clarke, who collected data from various adult native speech genres and social contexts, argue that in everyday life people play with language forms and that much interaction is structured by playing with multiple meanings. Therefore, the ubiquity of LP in native speech indicates that playing with language is indeed part of what Hymes coined a long time ago as communicative competence, because it is what would normally be held to be part of a native speaker's competence.

When students leave the safety of the classroom, the odds of encountering pedagogical texts are low. Most likely, students will get access to authentic material and participate in real-life conversations in which, as argued above, playful and humorous language is a daily occurrence. Therefore, for the studies reported here, the goal was to integrate LP tasks into the curriculum in which students encounter the authentic use of linguistic creativity to measure their learning effect.

The Studies

The Research Sites

The first data reported in this chapter is from a 2004 study that was conducted during my teaching of a non-credit course of the English Conversation Program (ECP) at a Canadian university. I conducted the study throughout the ten-week course. The focus of the ECP lied primarily in developing fluency and accuracy in oral English communication. The students were mostly international graduate students seeking opportunities to speak English outside of academic environments. The proficiency levels varied, and their backgrounds and interests were also different. On average, their TOEFL score was 592 and they had ten years of ESL instruction prior to coming to Canada.

The second part of the data in this chapter is from a 2016 study that was carried out as part of a special activity in four Grade 4 classes (seventy-two students in total) in an English immersion school in Mexico. As part of their math unit, students were required to gather and analyse data statistically; little did they know that while doing so, they would focus on language.

Methodology

Both studies addressed the following question: What impact does the discussion of humorous and creative language have on students' learning? Can this allow learning to better take place and be more memorable?

Table 13.1. VKS scoring categories: Meaning of scores

Possible score	Meaning of scores
0	No answer
X	Wrong answer
1	The word is not familiar at all
2	The word is familiar, but the meaning is unknown
3	A correct synonym and/or definition is given
4	The word is used with semantic appropriateness and grammatical accuracy in a sentence

Data Collection Procedure

- **Pre-test**: The same for all pairs, it included all the words and expressions that were key to understand all the LP pieces.
- **LP task**: Students worked in pairs on jokes, riddles, and cartoons taken from the media, which were selected for the nature and richness of the semantic trigger (ST) such as homonyms, vocabulary, idiomatic expressions, and morphology. Dictionary usage was permitted to help them solve the LP task and, hopefully, aid their learning and assist them in their awareness of various functions of the English lexicon.
- **Post-test**: The same as the pre-test. The 2004 group also had a delayed post-test about 4 weeks after the LP.

All tests were based on Wesche and Paribakht's Vocabulary Knowledge Scale (VKS). However, because the VKS does not tap knowledge of different meanings of the same word, I adjusted the test to incorporate knowledge about more than one meaning of the ST. Table 13.1 presents the adaptation of the original VKS and its scoring categories.

Unlike the original VKS, my scoring includes no answers and wrong answers as possible scores. For Wesche and Paribakht, a category (c) may lead to a score 2 if the synonym and/or definition are wrong. In the same way, if knowledge of the meaning of the word is shown in category (d) but the word is not appropriately used in a sentence, a score of 3 (instead of 4) is given. I understand the rationale for this scoring, however, for my study, once a wrong answer was given (no matter at what stage), it was counted as wrong because I wanted to be able to count and trace where there was still a gap in the knowledge of my students. It should also be noted that for category (d) and its corresponding score 4, I sought to find semantic and grammatical accuracy for the target word or expression. That is, a score of 4 would also be given to sentences in which other parts or aspects of the sentence that did not involve the target word were not grammatically correct and/or had spelling mistakes, as in the following example (for the STs "ajar"): *The door was ajar so the thief come* in.*

Unit of Analysis: Language-Related Episodes

Student dialogues were audio and video recorded only for the 2014 study in order to operationalize the students' dialogues through the identification of language-related episodes (LREs). As defined by Swain and Lapkin, an LRE is any part of the dialogue where learners discuss language, question or reflect on their language use (and/or knowledge), or correct themselves or others. The following LREs have been identified:

Meaning LRE: Students attempted to understand the STs or the new meaning(s) of a word/expression they already knew.

Form LRE: Students focused on formal features of the STs (or other linguistic items) or singled out a particular feature of such items (e.g., suffix, prefix, spelling, etc.) to understand the ST or other words involved.

Metatalk LRE: Students used meta-linguistic terms (e.g., noun, adjective, verb, etc.) to understand and/or explain to others the reasoning behind the joke, cartoon, or riddle.

Data Analysis and Findings

For the sake of brevity and yet deeper understanding, I will present the results of the learning process for one word from the 2004 study. For the 2016 study, I will present the results of all of the words tested.

2004 Study

The playfulness of the joke in question resides in the morphology of words, which generated a great deal of conversation about language. To illustrate this point, I present three of the most illustrative excerpts of the student dialogues about one of the STs.

Harry and John:

302. H: OK. We need to know two things. What is the meaning of bar and what is **ST**. And clergymen defrocked. I don't know none of these words.
303. J: I think the bar, the bar where the lawyers come to defend their customers. That's the bar. **ST** means you are disqualified to (be) lawyer.
304. H: Is that the court? Is a court?
305. J: No, just a place in the court.

Tim and Lisa:

326. T: If a lawyer, lawyers are **ST**. What this means?
327. L: **ST**? It's when he is not allowed to be a lawyer anymore? If he committed a crime or something very unethical, he might be **ST**. And then he would not be permitted to the court anymore.
328. T: Defrocked, defrocked. Defrocked is, means remove the clergymen from church like the lawyer –
329. L: – from the courtroom. Yeah. [checks the dictionary]
330. T: [after reading] The lawyer is **ST** in the bar. Leave the bar.
331. L: The legal profession.
332. T: Not, lose job.
333. L: xx losing the job. If you are the lawyer and you have to leave the bar, you have to leave the profession.

Helen and Kim:

326. H: What is leave the bar? That means leave profession [checks the dictionary. "A group of lawyers."
327. K: The bar?
328. H: "A group of people who are barristers."
329. K: Ah, bar, bar. Lawyer, lawyer.
330. H: Group of lawyers. I still don't understand what is bar. It didn't say clear what is **ST** … **ST**. This one means "to officially remove something."
331. K: Yeah.

By now, it should be evident that the ST was *disbarred*. None of the students knew the word and therefore struggled to understand it by engaging in a problem-solving and knowledge-building dialogue. Such a collaborative dialogue, conceptualized as "languaging" (Swain), indicates that language is not an object or product but an activity or process that produces language that has key functions in externalizing cognition, manipulating it, and internalizing it. The excerpts reveal how the students interact and become agents in their own learning. They also show how discussion mediates thinking and learning. Indeed, these dialogues enabled the students to understand the word and co-construct knowledge, as well as to enjoy the playfulness and the humour of the joke.

Table 13.2 shows that, except for Lisa, the students did not know the word prior to the LP task. The LP post-tests show that the dialogues did have an impact on the learning of the students, who were able to define and/or illustrate the meaning of "disbarred" in a sentence (see the appendix to this chapter).

Table 13.2. VKS scores for "disbarred"

Disbarred			Student name							
Cycle 2 Data collection schedule			Tim	Lisa	Helen	Kim	Don	Eric	Harry	John
Stage 1	Week 1	Pre-test	1	4	1	1	1	2	1	1
Stage 2	3–5 days	LP task	↓	↓	↓	↓	↓	↓	↓	↓
Stage 3	later	LP post	3	4	4	4	4	4	4	4
Stage 4	Week 6	D-Post	3	4	4	4	4	4	3	3

Table 13.2 presents the number and type of LREs that the joke prompted. What is fascinating to consider is how a joke could stimulate so much thought and talk about language. This joke was, by far, the longest LP piece. But it is likely to be much shorter than most texts that teachers usually choose for students to discuss in pairs, hoping that they will focus and learn from the language in use.

The average number of LREs that the joke prompted is 23.5. I had originally targeted two words that would be put to the VKS test: *disbarred* and *defrocked*. Yet, students focused on a total of eighteen words throughout their dialogues. Some of these words were also learned or reinforced and, together with the whole context of the joke, they helped the students understand and remember the STs. Figure 13.1 illustrates an overview of the learning that took place for the joke. Whereas prior to the LP task students knew approximately 30 per cent of the words they focused on and talked about in the LP task, after the LP task students were able to define and/or illustrate in a sentence 70 per cent of the words. Interestingly, this learning was not only maintained but also increased by the time of the delayed post-test, which points to the fact that further discussion of the words after the LP task must have had an impact on learning.[2]

2016 Study

Four classes, comprising a total of seventy-two students ten years old on average, participated in a special activity linked to the math curriculum of their English immersion program in Mexico. The goal was to gather data for statistical analysis. The activity they participated in became the data; little did they know that, by taking part in it, they would be focusing on learning language. Students had been pre-tested on all of the ST (which total eighty-five meanings) prior to LP tasks, and they were then post-tested the next day. Students were told that they would be discussing some jokes, riddles, and cartoons that would help them complete the second test, which was the same as the first test they

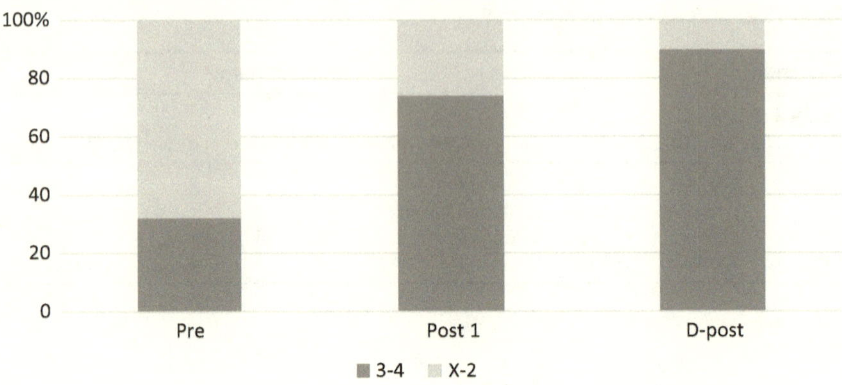

Figure 13.1. Pre-test and post-test results (in percentage) for the joke

had submitted already and would provide data for them to compare and contrast. Figure 13.2 shows the impact of the LP task on the learning of all targeted words. Clearly, learning took place in every class. In this study, even when the students were not focused on completing the task for language purposes but on gathering data for math purposes, they found themselves caught in good "language traps" that "pushed" the learners to analyse it, and thereby increasing their "depth" of memory.

Though this issue is beyond the scope of this paper, it is important to note that, when we plotted the results on the tables, the students were pleasantly surprised at their learning and reported that indeed they had learned new language in their math class. And they were not the only ones. One of the class teachers wrote to me: "Thank you for all the hard work, the kids have learned quite a lot, I certainly have."

Conclusion

This chapter has argued that a comprehensive view of L2 communicative performance should incorporate the playful (i.e., ludic) and humorous functions of language. Making jokes and being witty and creative with language presupposes a reasonably high level of L2 performance. Yet, many L2 learners, despite their high proficiency, do not feel comfortable or capable of understanding and using the genres of LP and humour.

The students in my studies were asked to discuss examples of humour and, in so doing, learned new language and gained insights into how L2 and culture

Table 13.3. LRE count and type for “disbarred” joke

LP Input	If lawyers are **disbarred** and clergymen **defrocked**, doesn’t it follow that electricians can be delighted, cowboys deranged, organ donors delivered, teachers declassified and dry cleaners depressed? On a more positive note, though, perhaps we can hope that politicians are devoted.																							
LRE	Harry and John						Tim and Lisa						Don and Eric						Helen and Kim					
	Form		Meaning		Meta-Talk		Form		Meaning		Meta-Talk		Form		Meaning		Meta-Talk		Form		Meaning		Meta-Talk	
	#	T*	#	T	#	T	#	T	#	T	#	T	#	T	#	T	#	T	#	T	#	T	#	T
Totals	9	25	12	62	4	8	6	12	17	90	5	10	6	14	10	83	19	14	2	3	7	54	1	2
LP/Pair Total	25						28						35						10					
Ave. LREs	23.5																							

*T stands for Turn

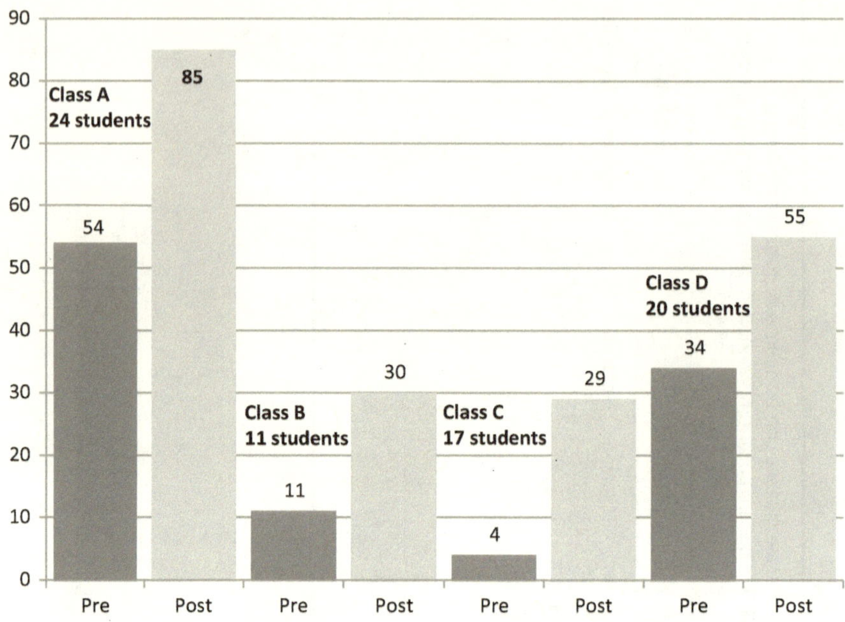

Figure 13.2. Pre-test and post-test results (in ST meanings) for the joke

work. Furthermore, they became equipped with the ability to tell jokes, riddles or cartoons to others if they wish to do so. As one of the students in the 2004 study reported: "I told the jock [joke] to my fellow student and he laughed so I think that I am not so bad jocks [joke] teller." This demonstrates that he felt pleased with himself for being able to engage in real-life humorous discourse.

The cognitive effort involved in solving the incongruity inherent in humour not only prompted a great deal of discussion but made the learning that took place during this talk more memorable. As Ellis notes, "what learners can find out for themselves is better remembered than what they are simply told" (163) because learning is more significant when it involves greater depth of processing. Therefore, one strategy that teachers can use is to challenge student knowledge by providing examples of linguistic creativity for them to discuss and understand. This kind of input can prompt interesting, insightful, and enjoyable discussions that will, in turn, create feelings of uncertainty and curiosity and promote the students' transitions from one level of understanding and reasoning to another.

The inclusion of humour in the L2 curriculum can indeed be a daunting and intimidating task for both L2 teachers and students. However, since humour is deeply embedded in language, "[w]e can use the language to make humour accessible for students and, conversely, use humour to make language accessible" (Medgyes, 5). The greatest challenge lies in finding material exemplifying LP that would suit the specific needs of students. At the same time, however, it is sometimes difficult for language teachers to find or create materials that continue to promote the learning of advanced students. Word-based or linguistic humour itself can be fully exploited, however, at the advanced stage.

Creating a friendly and harmonious learning atmosphere is a priority in every academic context, because humour triggers and maintains students' attention and increases retention while fostering a constructive attitude towards mistakes and stimulating both critical and creative thinking during classroom interactions. Indeed, the social and cognitive benefits that playful and humorous language afford in classroom discourse and learning must not be neglected.

More than a decade separated the two studies reported in this chapter, and yet both reached the same conclusion: words at play put language to work. There is no doubt in my mind that the school world without LP is alien and counterproductive to literacy and the development of language skills. Nevertheless, a tendency to equate play with leisure and school with work still prevails. Therefore, it seems fitting to conclude this paper by saying that the word *school* derives from the Greek for *leisure*, and this is not a play on words.

Appendix

2004 Study LP Post-Test Answers

- Tim: Law lose his job.
- Lisa: To loose* lawyer license – The lawyer was disbarred after committing a crime.
- Helen: Dismiss, get rid of the duty – The lawyer was disbarred.
- Kim: Loose one's own right. – The lawyer is disbarred.
- Don: To be without license (lose license). – This lawyer was disbarred last year.
- Eric: The lawer was disbarred for the tried to corrupt the judge.
- Harry: Preventing from attending the court/trial. – He was disbarred last year.
- John: Disqualified as a lawer. – The lawer is disbarred.

*Note: Answers were reported from students' texts with grammatical/ spelling errors.

NOTES

1 CANCODE stands for Cambridge and Nottingham Corpus of Discourse in English.
2 Exposure and/or use of such words outside the classroom is a factor that is impossible to assess.

WORKS CITED

Attardo, Salvatore. "The Semantic Foundations of Cognitive Theories of Humor." *Humor* 10 (1997): 395–420. https://doi.org/10.1515/humr.1997.10.4.395.

Azizinezhad, Masoud, and Masoud Hashemi. "Humour: A Pedagogical Tool for Language Learners." *Procedia – Social and Behavioral Sciences* 30 (2011): 2093–8. https://doi.org/10.1016/j.sbspro.2011.10.407.

Bell, Nancy. *Using and Understanding Humour in a Second Language: A Case Study*. Unpublished doctoral dissertation, University of Pennsylvania, 2002.

– "Exploring L2 Language Play as an Aid to SLL: A Case Study of Humour in NS-NNS Interaction." *Applied Linguistics* 26, no. 2 (2005): 192–218. https://doi.org/10.1093/applin/amh043.

Bell, Nancy, and Ann Pomerantz. *Humour in the Classroom: A Guide for Language Teachers and Educational Researchers*. Milton Park: Routledge, 2016.

Beltz, Julie A. "Second Language as a Representation of the Multicompetent Self in Foreign Language Study." *Journal of Language, Identity, and Education* 1, no. 1 (2002): 13–39. https://doi.org/10.1207/S15327701JLIE0101_3.

Block, David. *The Social Turn in Second Language Acquisition*. Edinburgh: Edinburgh University Press, 2003.

Broner, Maggie, and Elaine Tarone. "Is It Fun? Language Play in a Fifth-Grade Spanish Immersion Classroom." *Canadian Modern Language Review* 58, no. 4 (2002): 493–525. https://doi.org/10.1111/0026-7902.00114.

Carter, Ronald. *Language and Creativity: The Art of Common Talk*. Milton Park: Routledge, 2004.

Cekaite, Asta, and Karin Aronsson. "Language Play, A Collaborative Resource in Children's L2 Learning." *Applied Linguistics* 26, no. 2 (2005): 169–91.

Cook, Guy, "Language Play, Language Learning." *ELT Journal* 51, no. 3 (1997): 224–31.

– *Language Play, Language Learning*. Oxford; Oxford University Press, 2000.

Crystal, David. *Language Play*. Australia: Penguin Books Ltd., 1998.

Ellis, Rod. *The Study of Second Language Acquisition*. Oxford: Oxford University Press, 1994.

– *Task-Based Language Learning and Teaching*. Oxford: Oxford University Press, 2003.

Hall, Edward. *The Silent Language*. New York: Anchor Press/Doubleday, 1973.

Hymes, Dell. *Foundations of Sociolinguistics: An Ethnographic Approach*. Philadelphia: University of Pennsylvania Press, 1974.

Lantolf, James P. "The Function of Language Play in the Acquisition of L2 Spanish." In *Contemporary Perspectives on the Acquisition of Spanish*, edited by Ana Teresa Perez Leroux and William R. Glass, 3–24. Somerville, MA: Cascadilla Press, 1997.

– *Sociocultural Theory and Second Language Learning*. Oxford: Oxford University Press, 2000.

Medgyes, Peter. *Laughing Matters: Humour in the Language Classroom*. Cambridge: Cambridge University Press, 2002.

Morreall, John. "Enjoying Incongruity." *Humor* 2, no. 1 (1989): 1–18.

Nash, Walter. *The Language of Humour*. New York: Longman, 1985.

Nerlich, Brigitte, and David Clarke. "Ambiguities We Live By: Towards a Pragmatics of Polysemy." *Journal of Pragmatics* 33 (2001): 1–20. https://doi.org/10.1016/S0378-2166(99)00132-0.

Pomerantz, Anne, and Nancy Bell. "Learning to Play, Playing to Learn: FL Learners as Multicompetent Language Users." *Applied Linguistics* 28, no. 4 (2007): 556–78. https://doi.org/10.1093/applin/amm044.

Raskin, Victor. *Semantic Mechanisms of Humor*. Dordrecht, Holland: D. Reidel Pub. Company, 1985.

Reddington, Elizabeth. "Humor and Play in Language Classroom Interaction: A Review." *TESOL & Applied Linguistics* 15, no. 2 (2015): 22–8.

Schmitz, John Robert. "Humor as a Pedagogical Tool in Foreign Language and Translation Courses." *Humor* 15, no. 1 (2002): 89–113. https://doi.org/10.1515/humr.2002.007.

Stevick, Earl W. *Memory, Meaning and Method*. Rowley, MA: Newbury House, 1976.

Sullivan, Patricia N. "Language Play and Communicative Language Teaching in a Vietnamese Classroom." In *Sociocultural Theory and Second Language Learning*, edited by James P. Lantolf, 115–31. Oxford: Oxford University Press, 2000.

Suls, Jerry. "Cognitive Processes in Humour Appreciation." In *Handbook of Humour Research*, edited by Paul E. McGhee and Jeffrey H. Goldstein, 39–57. Berlin: Springer-Verlag, 1983.

Swain, Merrill. "The Output Hypothesis and Beyond: Mediating Acquisition through Collaborative Dialogue." In *Sociocultural Theory and Second Language Learning*, edited by James P. Lantolf, 97–114. Oxford: Oxford University Press, 2000.

– "Integrating Language and Content Teaching through Collaborative Tasks." *Canadian Modern Language Review* 58, no. 1 (2001): 44–63. https://doi.org/10.3138/cmlr.58.1.44.

– "Languaging, Agency and Collaboration in Advanced Language Proficiency." In *Advanced Language Learning: The Contribution of Halliday and Vygotsky*, edited by Heidi Byrnes. London: Continuum, 2007.

Swain, Merrill, and Sharon Lapkin. "Task-Based Second Language Learning: The Uses of the First Language." *Language Teaching Research* 4, no. 3 (2000): 251–74. https://doi.org/10.1177/136216880000400304.

Vizmuller-Zocco, Jana. "Critical Thinking and Verbal Humour in Textbooks of Italian as a Second Language." In *Problem-Solving in Second-Language Teaching*, edited by Caterina Cicogna, Marcel Danesi, and Antony Mollica, 130–40. Welland: Éditions Soleil Pub, 1992.

SECTIONS V AND VI

From Technology-Enhanced Teaching to Fully Online and Blended Learning Platforms

As technology has become increasingly ubiquitous, there have been widespread efforts to take advantage of technology within education, including the fields of language, literatures, and linguistics. Technology has played a significant role in enabling new types of learning experiences, as well as enriching existing ones. Sections V and VI discuss educational technology in the subject area of language education. This profound transformation in language education has been brought about by the development of information and communication technology (Lawrence in this volume). Educational technology offers diverse teaching and learning modalities by complementing in-class learning with technology tools and resources through creating various learning environments.

Broadly defined, technology-enhanced learning (TEL) refers to learning through the use of educational technology. Under the umbrella of TEL, there are different course delivery modalities ranging from Type A (no reduction in face-to-face contact time, accompanied by technology enhanced elements), to Type B (blended learning with some reduction in face-to-face contact time), to Type C (completely online without any face-to-face components).[1] While chapter 14 provides an overall introduction to TEL and teacher development, chapters 15 and 16 (both about incorporating digital storytelling in a language class), chapter 17 (about e-Tandem language learning), and chapter 19 (about project-based learning) belong to Type A. Chapter 18 (about fully online language courses) and chapter 20 (about synchronous online language teaching) belong to Type C. All seven chapters in these sections emphasize and demonstrate how technology can enhance language education in general and collaborative learning in particular. The cases of digital storytelling, e-Tandem learning, and the use of Google Docs for student group projects in these sections exemplify how a specific application of technology facilitates teaching and learning experience and enhances collaboration among learners. Some tackling of the challenges of these TEL components are also included.

Chapter 14, "Building Capacity for Twenty-First-Century Digital Language Teaching Practices" by Geoff Lawrence, not only highlights the various potentials of TEL and the profound transformation by TEL, but also insightfully points out how technology disrupts the norms in educational environments, including teacher and learner roles, requiring teachers to leverage the benefit of specific technologies in given educational contexts. Lawrence offers three key areas to build teaching capacity to integrate appropriate technologies into a language teaching practice. First, he emphasizes the need to critically assess technology tools and approaches in terms of their affordances (defined as a teacher's ideas regarding the perceived benefits of technology). He suggests that time experimenting with technology and critically reflecting on the use of it can help develop teachers' sense of affordances. Second, Lawrence discusses the importance of rethinking TEL curriculum and pedagogy in practice. He presents some useful points to consider in designing and teaching tech-mediated courses. Lastly, he outlines strategies for ongoing teacher development, including peer mentoring and communities of practice. Lawrence points out how teachers prefer peer mentoring for TEL training, which can build professional communities of practice. He concludes his chapter with a list of additional readings and resources.

By focusing on digital storytelling, chapter 15, "Digital Storytelling in the L2 Classroom: Enhanced Writing Skills" by Yujeong Choi and Na-Young Ryu, highlights how education technology can be utilized in designing activities where learners are actively engaged by providing students with more opportunities to experiment with self-expression. After defining digital storytelling as the creation of digitized narratives through video, sound, and image, Choi and Ryu provide an overview of digital storytelling in terms of its history as an educational tool. They discuss research findings that demonstrate the benefits of using digital storytelling to increase language fluency and accuracy, provide access to a variety of cultures, develop critical thinking, and provide personalized learning experiences. They also highlight how digital storytelling promotes multiple types of literacy including digital, multicultural, technological, visual, and information literacies, which are relevant to twenty-first-century communication skills. Choi and Ryu's empirical study demonstrates how digital storytelling is employed in the classroom. Their study shows how a digital storytelling project helped the students learn the target language, and that the students perceived the instructor feedback as helpful for rewriting scripts. Their study is especially valuable in that it addresses the emotional and motivational experiences students have during computer-supported learning projects. This chapter demonstrates that digital storytelling not only helps learners to develop language proficiency but also motivates them to become more responsible for their own learning.

The next chapter by Angela Lee-Smith, "A Pedagogical Module for a Place-Based and Multiliteracies-Based Digital Storytelling Project for Language Learning," also exemplifies how technology can be incorporated in language education through a collaborative digital storytelling project. Lee-Smith showcases a digital storytelling project as an example of standards-based learning projects to promote learners' multiliteracies. Lee-Smith demonstrates how the storytelling project provided the learners with meaningful applications of the target language to improve communicative competence and to develop multiliteracies by integrating a variety of language skills. The digital storytelling project as an authentic and meaningful task also promoted students' interests and motivations, as well as helped students to make personal connections to their local community. Lee-Smith highlights how project-based learning environments that include activities such as a digital storytelling project can compensate for the limitations of language textbooks by more flexibly corresponding to the learners' needs.

Another successful practice of TEL and computer-supported collaborative learning is e-Tandem language, which is examined by Christine Schallmoser and Pia Resnik in chapter 17, "Using Facebook as a Resource for e-Tandem Language Learning in Higher Education." E-Tandem language learning involves two language learners of different first languages serving as each other's language partner via digital tools such as Skype and Facebook. The case study presents how to implement e-Tandem in language education by utilizing Facebook as a communication tool to bring together learners from Austria, the UK, and the USA. After providing an overview of e-Tandem language learning, Schallmoser and Pesnik outline the core principles of e-Tandem learning: reciprocity and autonomy. This chapter demonstrates that the participants in the e-Tandem project found a positive relationship between the e-Tandem language learning and their learner autonomy. Schallmoser and Pesnik recognize, however, that dropping out and the lack of participation represents one of the main challenges to this approach. To prevent students' dropping out, they suggest the introduction of an official learning contract with specified goals, obligations, and meeting schedules.

Section VI focuses on fully online and blended learning platforms in language education. The first chapter of this section, "Students' Insights on a Fully Online Language Course" by Mihyon Jeon and Ahrong Lee, addresses student responses to a fully online language course offered at a Canadian university. This chapter starts with the introduction of the development of the online course and the course itself. Drawing on surveys and interviews with students, Jeon and Lee present the students' evaluation of and response to the course as a whole, as well as to different elements of the course such as online lectures, animations, weekly virtual meetings via Adobe Connect, and conversation recording submissions. The study shows that students appreciate the flexibility and convenience of the online format, while expressing some dissatisfaction regarding the low level of synchronous interaction with the instructor and the classmates, as well as some technical issues. Jeon and Lee suggest some potential ways to encourage more interaction through computer mediated communication and to help learners deal with technical difficulties. They also provide a discussion about the issues surrounding online (and blended) education along with the possible solutions via utilizing AI-powered education tools.

In chapter 19, "Preparing Future Global Professionals: Technology-Enhanced Group PBL Pedagogy," Monica Broido and Daniel Portman demonstrate how to utilize Google Docs in managing and monitoring project-based learning projects in their advanced-level English for economics course at a postsecondary institute in Israel. Their case study highlights how project-based learning pedagogy facilitates learners' development of the 4Cs (creativity, communication, critical thinking, and collaboration), as well as information, media and technology skills, and life and career skills. In their case study, Google Docs as a platform is adopted to organize group projects, which leads to class-wide collaboration by encouraging students to help other groups and by enabling them to learn from each other. In addition, Google Docs serves as an ideal platform for providing students with informative feedback, while allowing instructors to closely monitor student progress and to immediately access all of their work. Overall, the adaptation of Google Docs contributes to the high quality of group projects.

The last chapter in this section, "A Guide to Synchronous Online Language Teaching" provides an overview of online classroom settings and offers guidelines and hands-on strategies for designing online language teaching by utilizing Adobe Connect, a widely used software to create virtual classrooms in academic institutions. Seung-Eun Chang shows how to effectively utilize multimodal tools such as breakout rooms, Power Point, video file sharing, and chat boxes. Chang also addresses the benefits and changing character of virtual classrooms. This chapter demonstrates how synchronous online language courses can be effective in providing more focused and individualized learning environments.

In sum, sections V and VI demonstrate how educational technology can enhance and extend teaching and learning experiences. The chapters in these sections exemplify how technology has changed the ways to collaborate and to construct knowledge for learning and teaching in various learning environments, including within in-class, blended, and online learning spaces. These two sections that focus on the interlacing of new digital pedagogies also show that technology has brought new types of challenges for learners and educators. The authors in these chapters shed light on how to leverage technology to enhance learning experiences and to improve the quality of education that is critical to students' success.

SECTION V

Technology-Enhanced Teaching

14 Building Capacity for Twenty-First-Century Digital Language Teaching Practices

GEOFF LAWRENCE

Introduction: Our Tech-mediated Communication Shift

Communication in today's societies is increasingly digital. Twitter, texting, social networks, and information and communication technologies (ICTs) are transforming the way we use language, the way we collaborate, and the way we can teach and learn languages. We are living in a time when we can communicate with unlimited global audiences, and when we can access authentic resources in a range of languages and modalities. We can use virtual or augmented environments through a mobile device to plunge ourselves into a cultural and linguistic immersion, all from the comfort of home.

Technology is changing the frequency, nature, and genre of communication. The physical and virtual worlds are increasingly fused. ICTs are changing the way we connect to others, negotiate identities, build relationships, and make meaning. Technology-mediated literacy practices involve new forms of language use, new forms of social interaction, and new understandings of agency and community (Kessler). Social media is being used by three billion users around the world (Kessler, 206). In short, we are living in the middle of the most profound communication shift in human history (Van Camp), and this transformation is changing the way we need to think about language and how we teach it (Sykes et al.).

The Potential and Challenge of Educational Technology Use

ICTs offer immense potential for language teaching and learning that would have been unimaginable a decade ago. Web 2.0[2] tools like wikis, Google Docs, and social networks are intensely collaborative and redefine authorship, notions of genre, and relationships between the communicator and their audience. Artificial intelligence can provide learning feedback while virtual reality can offer culturally immersive environments (Kessler; Lawrence and Ahmed; Ranalli; Xi). For example, instructors can leverage aspects of artificial intelligence through automated writing evaluation that can provide students with initial guidance on language areas needing further support (Ranalli; Xi). Using digital images, sound, and video clips, students can produce and share multimodal identity texts with classmates and the instructor to present a more personalized, nuanced portrayal of their background and experiences that can contribute to the classroom community (Bonham). A student can share a document with an instructor, who can then provide this student with personalized interactive audio *and* visual corrective feedback, highlighting successes and areas of growth in efficient detail with a screen casting tool.

A core French-language teacher can lead students through a simulation projected on a classroom screen, where the instructor interacts with a French-language-speaking colleague in a virtual world looking for a holiday home to rent in a French town. Students watch this virtual world simulation, responding to questions the speakers ask, guiding the speakers in their simulation and writing notes. Then, in small groups, students prepare a verbal report on what they have seen (Lawrence and Ahmed, 9).

Creating opportunities for students to co-construct knowledge through community interaction helps develop learner autonomy, motivation, and engagement (Kessler, 206). Studies have revealed improvements in writing production, confidence, and overall writing abilities by using the self-paced benefits of specific technologies (Armstrong and Retterer; Kessler et al.). In research exploring the use of blogging in an college-level intermediate Spanish class, students reported enjoying the blog writing environments, exhibiting increased confidence using the target language and producing an average of 3000 words per term in Spanish, sometimes ten times more than students at the equivalent level in non-blogging classes (Armstrong and Retterer, 243).

Technologies offer educators diverse teaching and learning modalities to facilitate language acquisition and learning about technology-mediated language use. Classes can be tech-enhanced, where an instructor complements in-class learning with tech tools and resources. Classes can be delivered through a blended approach where there is a strategic division of traditional class and online learning time. Teachers can set up a flipped learning environment where they strategically assign self-paced and/or collaborative work for students to do outside of class online and then use the classroom to apply this learning. Alternatively, teachers can teach students around the world through a fully online program, exploiting asynchronous (self-paced) tools like discussion boards and blogs along with synchronous (same time) activities like videoconferencing or chatting.

Disruption in Teaching and Learning

While these communication tools and teaching modalities have rich potential, the rapidly evolving range of tools and approaches can paralyze even the most well-intentioned educator. Technologies disrupt the norms that have characterized teaching and learning environments for centuries. Technology use dramatically alters teacher and learner roles, requiring advanced planning and a *mindful explicitness* in teaching. That is, teachers have to methodically curate and facilitate teaching, cognitive, and social presence in online learning environments. Approaches to pedagogy and curriculum design need rethinking and must leverage the affordances (the perceived benefits and uses) of specific technologies for use in specific educational contexts. Teachers also need to orient learners to online language learning approaches, supporting critical digital literacies and scaffolding twenty-first-century skills that prioritize autonomy, as well as collaborative, technology-mediated communication skills (Dede).

This chapter will discuss three key areas that can help build teaching capacity to appropriately integrate relevant technologies into a language teaching practice. First, the need to critically assess the affordances of tech tools and approaches within specific teaching and learning contexts will be examined. The chapter will then discuss the importance of rethinking technology-mediated language teaching curricula and pedagogy in practices, as this is an area often overlooked in professional development. Finally, strategies for ongoing teacher development will be outlined that include peer mentoring and communities of practice. The chapter will conclude with a list of additional readings and resources.

The Need to Critically Assess Affordances

As noted above, keeping up to date with relevant new language teaching technologies is often an overwhelming challenge. A key to critically assessing new tools and developing techno-pedagogical competence (Guichon and Hauck) is to identify the affordances and the limitations of a specific technology to see how it can (or cannot) support learning outcomes within a teaching and learning environment (Haines, 165). Affordances can be described as a teacher's perceived benefits of a specific technology to support specific aspects of teaching and learning (Haines, 166). In other words, affordances are the perceived advantages a tool can offer teachers and students within a practice. Developing the ability to critically assess the affordances and limitations of educational technologies is crucial to not being deceived by the "wow" factor of new technologies. Sometimes new technology can initially appear promising but after greater analysis may lack the educational benefits to facilitate effective learning (Bax).

The challenge with assessing affordances is that, when initially using a new technology, we may "see" specific benefits, but then after using a tool over time with different classes, our perceptions of the tool's benefits are likely to expand and become more complex. For example, when analysing the affordances of using a Zoom videoconferencing tool, most teachers would be familiar with the functions of launching the video conference, connecting with a group using video, audio, and chat. However, fewer instructors would be aware of the ability to record the video conference for students to watch later or to offer breakout rooms so small groups can hold separate discussions outside of the main videoconference. These additional affordances can be particularly useful for language learners. As a result, teachers with different experiences and time using a tool may well perceive different affordances that inform unique and sometimes more effective approaches with the same technology (Stockwell).

In addition, an educator's priorities in teaching, along with familiarity with related technologies, can influence perceptions of a tool's affordances. Haines studied the perceived affordances of blogs and wikis with two Italian teachers over a two-year timespan. These instructors initially used blogs in their classes, identifying a range of blog affordances, before trying out wikis. This study found that these teachers' perceived affordances of wikis were initially strongly influenced by their familiarity with blogs and the affordances they saw from blog use in their practices. Findings also revealed that these teachers' priorities in teaching and learning predisposed them to specific affordances. For example, one of the instructors, Lucy, focused her classes on language and cultural proficiency development, whereas the other instructor, Elena, prioritized the affective dimensions of learning, including motivation, engagement, and confidence in the language-learning process (168). As a result, Lucy tended to focus on affordances that could help students develop linguistic and cultural competence. Elena, on the other hand, identified affordances related to communication, interaction, and the social presence these tools offered learners (175). As Haines writes, "teachers' perceptions of affordances will relate to their approaches to learning and teaching and the processes they value in the language classroom" (175).

As a result, time experimenting with and critically reflecting on the use of a technology with a range of students can help broaden one's sense of affordances. Being aware of one's use of related technologies and how these experiences may be influencing perceptions is key. In addition, actively working with colleagues who may think differently about a technology can be helpful. Below are some guiding questions that can be used to critically reflect on the affordances and limitations of a specific technology.

1. What seem to be the initial affordances and constraints created by this tool?
2. Does this tool and the associated approach effectively facilitate specific learning outcomes?
3. What may be influencing my perceptions of these affordances (i.e., previous technologies used, classroom contexts, students' use, and digital literacies)?
4. How does time and use change my perceptions of this tool's affordances and constraints?
5. Does the students' use of this tool inform my perceptions?

Curricular and Pedagogical Rethinking

A key challenge for teachers is not simply navigating new technologies but the methodological changes required to effectively use such tools. As scholars have warned, we must not simply "computerize" what we do in classroom practice; we must think of *new* ways of doing *new* things with *new* tools (Garrett; Kessler). However, such curricular innovation can be difficult as teachers have often undergone years of apprenticeship in face-to-face classroom environments (Borg) and clearly understand the procedures of classroom teaching that are often implicit but *not* always transferable to digital language teaching practices. When integrating technologies, both curriculum design and pedagogy need to be rethought so teachers can effectively leverage relevant affordances identified in any digital tools.

For example, in a study examining the feasibility of integrating e-learning into community-based ESL programs (Lawrence et al.), researchers interviewed one curriculum-development team who worked on consecutively designing three technology-mediated English-for-specific-purpose programs. The first program was to be blended and was designed from an existing classroom-based curriculum where the team moved about 20 per cent of the classroom activities online, as they worked well as self-paced, homework-like activities. Responses from piloting students were lacklustre, however, as students felt there was too much online "alone" work. The next two programs, a blended and a fully distance program, were each designed from scratch, where the team strategically chose tech tools and delivery modalities to meet specific learning outcomes. In these program designs, the team worked to identify how specific outcomes could be supported by the affordances of various tools, activities, and types of interaction. The third course, which was delivered completely online, had a listening and speaking skills focus and used a mix of asynchronous tools (audio recordings; Vocaroo, a Web-based audio recording tool; and Voicethread, an interactive presentation tool) and synchronous communication tools (videoconferencing and chat) to engage learners in listening and speaking skills practice. Students in both of these later course pilots felt these courses maximized their learning efficiency in highly interactive and engaging ways. Students in the final online listening and speaking course were "evangelical" in their enthusiasm about this course, appreciating the highly individualized, flexible and interactive nature of the learning (Lawrence et al., 225). As this example illustrates, matching the affordances of specific technologies to help students meet specific learning outcomes is key in effective curriculum design and pedagogy.

Changing Roles and Needs

An important curricular and pedagogical consideration is that technology introduces an often dominant third player into the teaching and learning environment that can dramatically alter classroom roles and the organization of teaching practices. Teachers often need to adopt more of a facilitator, planning role in teaching and lesson planning, putting explicit thought into structuring the learning environment(s), planning learning pathways, explicitly stating teaching approaches, and anticipating challenges before a course begins. For example, in a blended course, a teacher needs to plan the number of classes online versus face-to-face; then in those online classes, teachers need to plan how students are going to interact, with whom, with what, and when. This is where a course outline can be helpful in defining and establishing routines around class schedules and expectations regarding online communication. If teachers are using an online discussion tool, communication protocols need to be clearly defined for students – that is, the number of messages per week, the maximum length of a message, and the number of times students should check into the discussion. Teachers need to build in time and strategies to support varied digital literacies or establish a peer tech mentoring system to support students. Online peer mentoring and support can help teachers manage the workload of online teaching and can enhance student connections, thereby building a cohesive learning community. Given the learning curve involved in online environments, online learning must be adequately chunked so as not to overwhelm students, as digital learning can sometimes take much more time than anticipated.

If integrating Web 2.0 tools like a wiki, discussion tool, or a social network, pedagogy should ideally leverage the collective, interactive nature of these tools and focus on task-based approaches, where students work in small groups to collectively complete a task using an online tool. Such tasks must be well structured, outlining steps and outcomes with a corresponding schedule to keep students on task and to establish online accountability. While students work in groups on these tasks, the instructor can assess progress and remind students of timelines and completion goals. Scheduled check-ins with students to assess online approaches should be built into a course to gauge student progress and comfort, as well as to gather feedback that can help revise approaches.

In order to be successful in online language learning, students often need to adopt autonomous learning strategies while teachers need to support this autonomy, explicitly discussing strategies and providing guidance. With enhanced autonomy, teachers need to pay attention to social and teaching presence in online environments, so students feel "connected" to others. While online learning can offer incredible flexibility and self-paced options, if there is little interaction, some students can feel disengaged. This is where video introductions, instructions for videoconferencing, and synchronous communication, along with online office hours can be useful to help build a "human feel" into online learning (Lawrence, "A Call for the Human").

To assess learner engagement, user analytics provided by an LMS (learning management system) or an online tool can be a useful affordance, allowing

Table 14.1. A statistical impact report of student participation in an online discussion tool

Student	Time online	Notes written	Replies	Words written	Notes read
1	20:49:41	26	21 (80.8%)	1756	377 (59.3%)
2	28:23:08	37	22 (59.5%)	3795	617 (97.0%)
3	41:10:20	32	31 (63.3%)	3043	537 (84.4%)
4	**36:33:40**	**49**	**30 (73.2%)**	**4380**	**619 (97.3%)**
5	**21:09:18**	**41**	**19 (73.2%)**	**4556**	**613 (96.4%)**
6	15:08:24	24	19 (79.2%)	2080	385 (60.5%)
7	6:49:52	3	2 (66.7%)	526	360 (56.6%)

Source: An anonymous excerpt from an online discussion workspace, Pepper (http://integrate.act.utoronto.ca/pepper/), developed and used at the University of Toronto.

teachers to get a quick snapshot of student participation, and sometimes the degree of interaction, in an online space. For instance, table 14.1 below is an example of analytics from an online discussion tool that gives a quick overview of student participation. Rows bolded (students 4 and 5) are 1 to 2 standard deviations above the class participation mean, while student 7 in the shaded row is 1 or more standard deviations below the class mean.

Such analytics can help teachers quickly identify students not participating online, allowing teachers to check in with these students and discuss strategies and support. This quantitative data can be combined with qualitative data – that is, searching for and reviewing individual students' discussion notes, analysing content, syntax, and vocabulary use – to provide students with individualized, ongoing feedback. One of the benefits of online approaches is that, while students are engaged in online learning, teachers have some time to use analytics to track the individual progress of students. This can help teachers differentiate teaching practices and offer guidance at points throughout a course.

Below are some points to consider when designing or teaching a tech-mediated course.

- When planning digital teaching, work to maximize the affordances of specific technologies to help students meet specific learning outcomes.
- Remain critical of technology's "wow" factor and ensure teaching with technology is informed by strong pedagogy, targeting specific learning outcomes.
- Allot time at the beginning of a course to help orient learners to online routines, learning environments, and communication protocols, in order to support diverse digital literacies and to allow "play" with new technologies; consider these orientation "activities" as language practice work, offering learners authentic communicative interaction.

- Mix synchronous (particularly video) and asynchronous communication tools to offer varied genres of communication, to encourage safe, self-paced expression while encouraging students to interact spontaneously to develop language skills and build interpersonal interaction.
- Offer learners a choice in activities to enhance autonomy and engagement; support learners with explicit discussions of autonomous learning strategies.
- Provide a supportive teaching presence in online environments that encourages student-student interaction to help build social presence and a cohesive community.

Conclusion: Mentored Professional Development

Given the rapidly evolving nature of educational technology, ongoing professional development is key. Unfortunately, training in language teaching educational technology has often been haphazard and superficially addressed (Lawrence, "The Role of"). Training often consists of decontextualized one-off workshops on specific technologies, where the focus is on the technologies rather than on how to use them in language teaching practices. Research findings indicate that teachers tend to favour informal learning about technology integration from peers and from personal explorations (del Rosal et al.; Kessler). Teachers have expressed a desire for job-embedded, mentored training for instructors to learn from experienced peers as they teach with a technology (Lawrence et al.). This allows teachers to methodically examine the integration of educational technology in context, where affordances and limitations can be discussed with a colleague. Some institutions have created a Continual Contribution System where instructors share educational technology practices at PD meetings to introduce innovative practices and to gain feedback from peers (Lawrence et al., 35). Such mentoring can build professional communities of practice that can critically inform technology integration within specific teaching contexts.

One of the best ways to develop a personalized understanding of online teaching and learning is for educators to take an online or blended course, ideally with a PD focus. This can help build techno-pedagogical competence and an understanding of affordances, limitations and online learning empathy from a learner's perspective. Such a perspective is more relevant than ever as language teachers are increasingly teaching students who expect to use social technologies in ways that align with their established social practices. This is where a critical reflective practice should actively consider student perspectives, leveraging students' suggestions about technology use and strategies, and using student skills to support teacher and class digital literacy.

Such an approach not only supports the instructor and class, but also shifts classroom power dynamics and engages students as active participants in the design and teaching of their course. Critical input from students and mentors as well as a flexible, creative, and mindful approach around teaching practices can help prepare language teachers to meet the needs of today's twenty-first-century learners.

Additional Readings and Resources

Language Learning and Technology: www.lltjournal.org
A peer-reviewed open-source journal reporting on research and practices in language teaching technologies.

Kessler G. "Technology and the Future of Language Teaching." *Foreign Language Annals*, vol. 51 (2018): 205–18. doi.org/10.1111/flan.12318.
A timely discussion of the current state of educational technology, its impact on language education, and professional development needs for teachers.

Teacher Training Videos: www.teachertrainingvideos.com
A continually updated list of webinars, videos, and tutorials that offer teacher education on a range of language technology use and integration in teaching contexts.

LearnIT2Teach: learnit2teach.ca/wpnew
A website to support English-language educators with educational technology; offers free publications on blended learning, best practices, and a certificate in online teaching for community-based ESL teachers.

NOTES

1 Although TEL has also been used to refer to Type A when it is narrowly defined, in this volume TEL is used in its broad definition.

2 Web 2.0 refers to today's social Web that emphasizes user-generated content and a participatory, interactive culture.

WORKS CITED

Armstrong, Kimberly, and Oscar Retterer. "Blogging as L2 Writing: A Case Study." *AACE Journal* 16, no. 3 (2008): 233–51.

Bax, Stephen. "Digital Education: Beyond the "Wow" Factor." In *Digital Education. Palgrave Macmillan's Digital Education and Learning*, edited by Michael Thomas, 239–56. New York: Palgrave Macmillan, 2011.

Bonham, Susan. *Multimodal Identity Texts: Pictures of Engagement for Adult Immigrant Language Learners*. Dissertation, University of British Columbia, 2013.

Borg, Michaela. "The Apprenticeship of Observation." *ELT Journal* 58, no. 3 (2004): 274–6. https://doi.org/10.1093/elt/58.3.274.

Dede, Chris. "Comparing Frameworks for 21st Century Skills." In *21st Century Skills: Rethinking How Students Learn*, edited by James Bellanca and Ron Brandt, 51–75. Bloomington, IN: Solution Tree Press, 2010.

Del Rosal, Karla, et al. "Mentoring Teachers of English Learners in an Online Community of Practice." *International Journal of Computer-Assisted Language Learning and Teaching* 6, no. 3 (2016): 1–17. https://doi.org/10.4018/IJCALLT.2016070101.

Garrett, Nina. "Computer-Assisted Language Learning Trends and Issues Revisited: Integrating Innovation." *The Modern Language Journal* 93 (2009): 719–40. https://doi.org/10.1111/j.1540-4781.2009.00969.x.

Guichon, Nicolas, and Miriam Hauck. "Teacher Education Research in CALL and CMC: More in Demand Than Ever." *ReCALL* 23, no. 3 (2011): 187–99. https://doi.org/10.1017/S0958344011000139.

Haines, Karen. J. "Learning to Identify and Actualize Affordances in a New Tool." *Language Learning & Technology* 19, no. 1 (2015): 165–80.

Kessler, Greg. "Technology and the Future of Language Teaching." *Foreign Language Annals* 55 (2018): 201–18.

Kessler, Greg, et al. "Collaborative Writing among Second Language Learners in Academic Web-Based Projects." *Language Learning & Technology* 16, no. 1 (2012): 91–108.

Lawrence, Geoff. "A Call for the Human Feel in Today's Increasingly Blended World." *Contact Research Symposium* 40, no. 2 (2014): 128–41.

Lawrence, Geoff. "The Role of Language Teacher Beliefs in an Increasingly Digitalized World." In *Integrating Technology into Contemporary Language Learning and Teaching*, edited by Bin Zou and Michael Thomas, 140–60, Pennsylvania: IGI Global, 2018.

Lawrence, Geoff, et al. *Rationale and Recommendations for Implementing E-Learning in Ontario NonCredit Adult ESL Programs: A Feasibility Report*. The Toronto Catholic District School Board, 2013.

Lawrence, Geoff, and Farhana Ahmed. "Pedagogical Insights into Hyper-immersive Virtual World Language Learning Environments." *IJCALLT* 8, no. 4 (2018): 1–14. https://doi.org/10.4018/IJCALLT.2018010101.

Ranalli, Jim. "Automated Written Corrective Feedback: How Well can Students Make Use of It?" *Computer assisted Language Learning* 31, no. 7 (2018): 653–74. https://doi.org/10.1080/09588221.2018.1428994.

Stockwell, Glen. *Computer-Assisted Language Learning: Diversity in Research and Practice*. Cambridge: Cambridge University Press, 2012.

Sykes, Julie. M., et al. "Web 2.0, Synthetic Immersive Environments, and MobileResources for Language Education." In *Landmarks in CALL research*, edited by Greg Kessler, 160–83. CALICO Book Series: Equinox, 2016.

Van Camp, Jeffrey. "Tech is Upending the Ways We Write, Speak and Even Think." *Digital Trends*. 2017, www.digitaltrends.com/features/dt10-language-and-tech/. Accessed 12 Feb. 2017.

Xi, Xiaoming. "Automated Scoring and Feedback Systems: Where are We and Where Are We Heading?" *Language Testing* 27, no. 3 (2010): 291–300. https://doi.org/10.1177/0265532210364643.

15 Digital Storytelling in the L2 Classroom: Enhancing Writing Skills

YUJEONG CHOI AND NA-YOUNG RYU

Introduction

As one of the oldest forms of human communication, storytelling has been widely used for various educational purposes. Particularly in the second-language (L2) classroom, employing activities that combine storytelling with digital technology has proven an effective method of engaging tech-savvy students while enhancing their language acquisition. This study will demonstrate the value of using digital storytelling with L2 learners by presenting a successful use of the project in a Korean-language course held at a Canadian university.

In L2 classrooms, learners often play a passive role, one with limited opportunities to practice expressing themselves in the target language. This limitation can stem from a large class size or time constraints. One way to overcome such limitations is to design activities that actively engage all students and that focus on individual learners' interests. The widespread use of digital communication devices is beneficial for developing this kind of activity. Exploiting technology in the L2 classroom gives students more opportunities to experiment with self-expression. Digital storytelling is one of the ways to increase students' opportunities to practise, while simultaneously allowing for personal relevance.

Developing and implementing digital learning activities while also navigating institutional structures can be quite challenging. Understanding the research behind using this type of learning activity is vital to instructor confidence and to acceptance by administrators of language-learning programs. Also important is the availability of articles on how to implement a digital learning activity, as well as evidence of successful results in learners' language acquisition. The following sections present a literature review of the previous research, instructions for a digital storytelling activity, and a discussion of the analysis results and student evaluations of the activity.

Literature Review

Digital storytelling is the creation of narratives that are digitized by inserting video, sound, and images into a story (Ohler, 46; Robin, 222). More specifically, learners are encouraged to engage in active writing using computer technology, as digital storytelling involves the traditional process of choosing a topic, researching stories, writing scripts, and developing intriguing stories (Robin, 222). The goal of digital storytelling is to deliver messages to the audience and to receive emotional reactions from the audience (Malita and Martin, 3061). Digital storytelling as an educational tool began to spread after Joe Lambert and Dana Atchley, the founders of the Center for Digital Storytelling (CDS), introduced the digitalized narrative form in the 1990s. According to the Center for Digital Storytelling website, "[CDS] is an international non-profit training, project development, and research organization dedicated to assisting people in using digital media to tell meaningful stories from their lives" (CDS, n.d.).

To support the creation of digital storytelling, the CDS developed the seven elements of digital storytelling: point of view, a dramatic question, emotional content, the gift of your voice, the power of the soundtrack, economy, and pacing. Similarly, H. Kim and Lee provided four elements that constitute the framework of a good story: points of story, feeling, authentic voice, and audience awareness. They explained that points of story, also called a "tellable" topic, "advises, informs, or warns the audience about ways of the world" and that authentic voice is the writer's opinions, arguments, attitudes, or position (H. Kim and Lee, 2). These two sources provide an initial reference point for developing digital storytelling activities.

Some empirical research has focused on using storytelling for the language development of elementary school students. In a study with Canadian elementary students ranging from ages ten to twelve, Campbell examined whether digital storytelling enhances engagement and motivation to create writing. The study revealed that most of the students showed improvement in the levels of story writing – as indicated by a strong Beginning-Middle-End (BME) structure – and identified story problems. They also increased their level of self-confidence vis-à-vis writing (389–90). Verdugo and Belmonte examined the effect of digital storytelling on listening comprehension with a group of six-year-old Spanish children learning English. They found that the experimental group performed better on the final test than the control group, and thereby recommended the use of technology in language learning (95–6). Park and Chung examined the effects of digital storytelling by dividing elementary school students into upper and lower proficiency groups. They found that digital storytelling worked well for both groups, and especially helped improve the speaking and writing skills of the lower group (244).

In relation to digital storytelling in upper-level education, some studies considered the assessment of using digital storytelling in secondary and higher education. Tahriri and others investigated the effects of digital storytelling on oral skills with intermediate English as foreign language (EFL) learners. They found that the group using digital storytelling outperformed the control group in oral production (148–9). Tsou and others developed a digital storytelling website that enables teachers and learners to construct new stories or edit existing ones, record sound effects, and record their own voices. In their study, they suggested that the degree of understanding content and complexity of sentence production could be evaluated through story recall. The results indicated that the learners working with the digital storytelling website used more complex sentences than the control group learners and described the story in more detail (26). P. Kim explored the effect of digital storytelling on the development of writing ability in EFL college pre-service teachers. She found that students who engaged in digital storytelling performed markedly higher on the post-test than the pretest, which measured writing skills in terms of accuracy, syntactic complexity as well as an analytical scoring evaluation method (89–94). In a study with fifty university students, H. Kim and Lee examined pairs of personal narrative scripts: one for in-class storytelling and one for digital storytelling use in participant-generated movies. Both types of scripts were analysed in terms of story framework – including point of story, authentic voice, feeling, and audience awareness. The researchers found that using digital storytelling allowed students to express more richly their ideas using images and music along with the writing script (7). In comparison to in-class storytelling, the results of the study showed that digital storytelling provided the students with a greater opportunity to become a better storyteller in terms of audience awareness, richer emotions, and unexplored topics (8).

In sum, regarding the effectiveness of using digital storytelling, extensive research has noted that digital storytelling improves understanding of content (Robin, 224), provides access to a variety of cultures, increases language fluency and accuracy (P. Kim, 90–5; Park and Chung, 243), increases critical thinking (Yang and Wu, 347–9), increases personalizing learning experience (Castañeda, 53–5; Grigsby et al., 62), and is a popular method of learning foreign languages that can be highly motivating (Yang and Wu, 349). These studies give instructors confidence in using digital storytelling as an alternative to passive or limited language practice.

In addition to the enormous benefits listed above, the process of digital storytelling creation also allows students to acquire multiple types of literacy: digital literacy, multicultural literacy, technological literacy, visual literacy, and information literacy (Robin, 224). According to Robin, digital literacy is "the ability to communicate with an ever-expanding community to discuss issues, gather information, and seek help," and is thus relevant to twenty-first-century communication skills (224). In contrast to learners in the past, today's learners grew up with digital media (Prensky,

1). As such, they possess quite proficient computer skills, and are capable of using and producing digital material. The creation and dissemination of digital media has changed the way this generation interacts with society. Instead of phone or face-to-face interaction, they rely more on text messaging and social media. These avenues of social interaction open the way for strangers who share the same interests to present ideas. This trend in communication has highlighted the importance of the ability to understand and communicate through digital literacy (Gee and Levine, 50).

Despite the abundant studies demonstrating the benefits of digital storytelling, there is a lack of research on how digital storytelling is employed in the classroom and how students perceive writing assignments through revising multiple drafts to create digital storytelling. Thus, to fill the gap in the literature, this study presents a digital storytelling application process as well as the students' perception of writing and feedback on their drafts.

Developing a Digital Storytelling Activity

This digital storytelling project was an assignment used in an advanced-level Korean course (Modern Standard Korean III) at a Canadian university in 2016. The goal of the project was to enhance students' writing and speaking ability by having them tell their personal experiences in a narrative form. The students were asked to create sentences on their own but write a draft in a narrative form that included indirect quotation and plain form in Korean. The class was composed of twenty-seven undergraduate students. Each student selected a topic of their own interest and prepared a first-draft script, which was then revised several times based on feedback from an instructor who is the second author. Each student produced a short three-minute video using images, music, film, or sounds on the basis of the script to enhance the story.

For this particular assignment the instructor limited the range of possibilities to those that fit the topic of "Introduce Toronto to Korean people who plan to travel to Toronto, Canada." Students were asked to select a place in or near Toronto that they wished to write about in Korean in a storytelling manner, with the focus on the content and writing skills rather than the elaborate use of media. Verbal expression was the primary goal, while other elements of the story were used to support the delivery of content. The instructor provided the assessment rubric (see the appendix to this chapter) in advance so that students could focus on the main goals of the project.

Digital Storytelling Project Plan. The project was planned for a seven-week time block. The process of creating digital storytelling in the classroom is shown in table 15.1. The plan is divided per week, and each week specifies the tasks that the instructor and students need to complete.

The digital storytelling project and its relevant information were introduced to the class in the first week. Students selected a place in Toronto and began to

Table 15.1. Lesson plan for digital storytelling

Week	Instructor's plan	Learner's plan
1st week	Announcement of DST production and introducing a sample Teaching indirect quotation (~고 하다) and plain form (ㄴ/는)다	Searching a topic
2nd–4th week	Introducing DST writing scripts and presenting writing tips Providing feedback on DST scripts	Writing DST script (1st draft) Modifying DST script based on instructor feedback Revising and resubmitting DST script (2nd draft)
5th–6th week	Holding a workshop on how to use iMovie Checking the recorded video with students	Producing DST adding photos, video clips, subtitles, and sound in iMovie
7th week	Evaluation and feedback Survey	Sharing and presentation Answering survey questionnaire

research information for their stories. The instructor asked each student about the topic and discussed the direction of the project. The instructor taught the grammatical expressions necessary to create the DST script.

On the second week, the instructor showed a DST script sample with relevant images to give students an idea of the expectations for the project. Students then began to explore their subjects and wrote the first draft of their scripts. They individually submitted their first drafts (with images) online. The instructor provided feedback on the content and grammar of the first draft. Figure 15.1 is an example of a first draft.

During the third and fourth weeks, students used the instructor's ongoing feedback to revise and resubmit their scripts several times. Figure 15.2 is an example of a script revision.

In-Class Media Workshop. During the fifth week, the instructor conducted a two-hour media workshop in which students learned to use computer software to edit, insert images and subtitles, and add voiceovers and sounds to augment their completed script. Since the majority of students used Apple computers, a free, easily accessible software program called iMovie Maker for Mac was introduced to the students. For video production, the instructor asked students to pay close attention to the feedback on their scripts. Before recording the video, the instructor asked the learners to match the content of the narration with the video image and sound. The students were also asked to consider their project as an exchange between a speaker and an audience, and to think about making

로열 온타리오 박물관이란 말 그대로 캐나다 온타리오 주 토론토에 위치한 박물관이다. 웅장하고 품위가 있어 보인다. 그것은 캐나다에서 제일 크고 가장 많은 소장품과 수많은 문화 유산들을 보관되어 있는 박물관이라고 듣는다. 그리하여 민족문화의 전당이라고 할 만하다. 지리적 위치가 우월하는 만큼 거기로 도착하는 방법이 많다. 예를 들어 말하면 지하철 1 호선이나 2 호선으로 타도 된다. 세인트 조지에서 내리고 나가고 나서 박물관이 보인다. 3 분 정도 걸으면 정문에 도착한다. 홈페이지에 의하면 영업시간은 오전 10 시부터 오후 5 시반까지이라고 한다.

Commented [Office5]: Please use indirect quotation properly in the sentence.

Commented [Office6]: 지리적 위치가 좋은 만큼 거기로 가는 방법이 많다.

Commented [Office7]: 말하면 should be deleted.

Commented [Office8]: 2 호선을 타면 된다.

Commented [Office9]: 내리고 나가서 보면

Commented [Office10]: 5 시반까지라고 한다. '이' is not needed in the sentence.

Figure 15.1. Digital storytelling project: First draft

로열 온타리오 박물관이란 말 그대로 캐나다 온타리오 주 토론토에 위치한 박물관이다. 웅장하고 품위가 있어 보인다. 그것은 캐나다에서 제일 크고 가장 많은 소장품과 수많은 문화 유산들을 보관되어 있는 박물관이라고 들었다. 그리하여 민족문화의 전당이라고 할 만하다. 그래서 많은 사람들 (이) 거기에 가보고 싶다고 생각한다. 지리적 위치가 좋은 만큼 거기로 가는 방법이 많다. 예를 들어 지하철 1호선이나 2호선을 타면 된다. 세인트 조지에서 내리고 나가서 보면 (↳ 내려서 나가면) 박물관이 보인다. 3분 정도 걸으면 정문에 도착한다. 홈페이지에 의하면 영업시간은 오전 10시부터 오후 5시 반까지라고 한다. 박물관에 들어가자마자 왼쪽에 매표소가 보인다. 보통 표 한 장에 17달러다. 표를 산 후에 바로 가도

Figure 15.2. Digital storytelling project: Second draft

their content easier for the audience to understand. After the workshop, the instructor invited the Korean studies librarian of the university to introduce how to use proper citation methods, as well as provide details on copyright issues for the image or audio material that the students wished to insert into the project.

On the sixth week, the students finalized their digital storytelling project. They uploaded their project to the university's media archive and provided links to access their archived projects to the instructor. They then spent time practising recording their scripts.[1]

On the final week, students presented their projects to the class. After the presentations, the instructor evaluated each presentation using the rubric that was given to students at the beginning of the project. The DST criteria comprised 10 per cent of the overall course grade, with 5 per cent allotted to both the script and video. The script was evaluated for appropriate topic selection, grammar, sentence composition, use of proper image, and expression of opinions and emotions. The video was evaluated in terms of pronunciation, narration, and audience awareness. To evaluate the effectiveness of the project from the learner's point of view, a survey questionnaire was distributed to all of the students.

Results of Student Feedback

The survey questionnaire was designed to investigate the extent to which the students perceived the effectiveness of the instructor's feedback, and to what extent they were satisfied with their own drafts. The questionnaire consisted of four items measured on four-point Likert scales and open-ended opinions about feedback and draft satisfaction. First, the questionnaire asked the learners to self-assess their proficiency level and composition skills using a four-point scale. The results showed that 11 per cent of the learners mentioned that their overall proficiency level was excellent, 56 per cent said good, and 41 per cent chose fair. Second, for composition skills, 55.5 per cent said good, 40.7 per cent chose fair, and 3.7 per cent said poor. None of the learners self-evaluated their composition skills as excellent.

The third question asked whether the instructor feedback on their first draft was effective. As shown in figure 15.3, 81 per cent of learners reported that it was very effective to write scripts and get feedback from the instructor before creating their project, while 19 per cent said it was useful. By writing scripts and receiving feedback from the instructor, learners could plan the content of writing in advance and reduce the burden of composition. The learners replied that feedback regarding words and grammar was the most useful. The practice of writing for digital storytelling is meaningful in that it allows learners to acquire new words and grammar, as well as vocabulary and grammar that they learned in class.

The next question asked about the students' satisfaction level towards their first and second drafts after they were revised. Figure 15.4 shows that 23 per cent said they were very satisfied, 58 per cent said satisfied, while 15 per cent of learners reported they were slightly satisfied. Script revisions not only expose

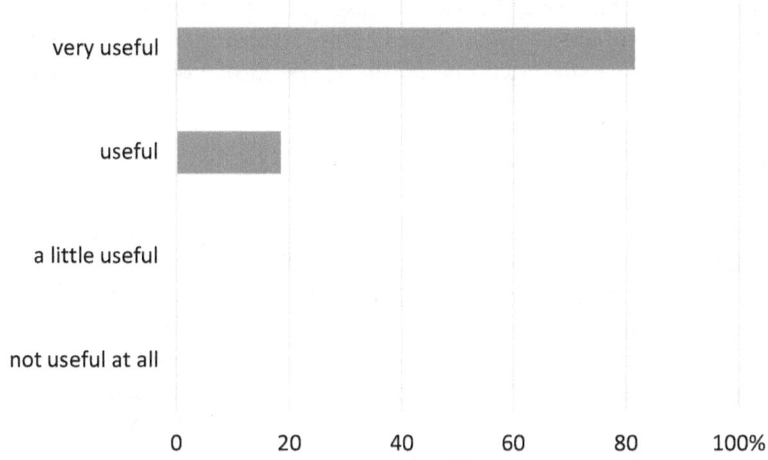

Figure 15.3. Effectiveness of feedback on the first draft

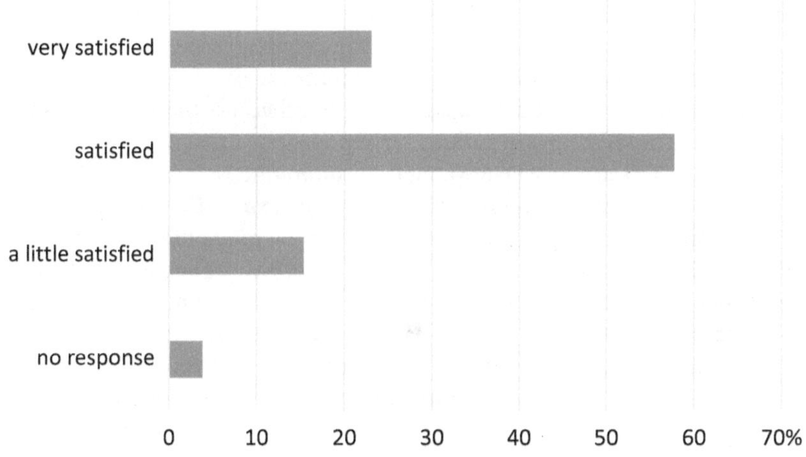

Figure 15.4. Satisfaction with revised scripts

the learner's satisfaction with their own script, but also suggest that multiple drafting is effective when considering writing as a series of recursive processes rather than a final product. More specifically, several learners responded with statements such as: "Sentences I didn't know how to properly word improved," "I feel like there aren't any awkward or strange sentences after the revision," and "When I read through the essay, I feel like I can express my thoughts better and it makes more sense."

After writing the script, the learners responded that they spent an average of 3.26 hours to practice pronunciation before recording the narration. In addition, the learners suggested that feedback, specifically on pronunciation, is quite beneficial.

Conclusion

This study presented a practical application of a language learning activity using digital storytelling. This project is meaningful in that it provided the learners an opportunity to express their opinions or thoughts in Korean by expanding their story with voice, image, and sound, and then sharing it with other learners. During the project students were able to practice certain grammar points that they had learned from the course, such as using Korean plain style speech and indirect quotations, and expand their writing skills with new vocabulary and sentence patterns which were not covered in class.

The results of the student evaluation survey led to the conclusion that writing scripts and producing videos for digital storytelling are helpful in learning Korean. In the survey, all respondents said that instructor feedback was useful for rewriting scripts, and 81 per cent of the learners were satisfied with their scripts after two draft revisions. This suggests that script writing improved writing skills through feedback and provided students with confidence and satisfaction. Speaking skills also improved through digital storytelling, because the learners read the script multiple times for the recording. Na and Na stated that digital storytelling is a tool that helps learners who are unable to communicate in a L2 language, like Korean, effectively, since it can maximize a story by expressing the ideas in one's own voice and using images in parts that are difficult to express with just words (253). Based on the results of students' perception of writing and feedback as well as potential applications of digital storytelling in L2 education, we can conclude that digital storytelling is an effective learning tool that instructors of L2 courses can use to enrich their instruction, enhance grammar and vocabulary learning, and motivate students to become more responsible for their own learning.

Appendix

Assessment Rubric

Essay	Poor	Fair	Good	Very Good	Excellent
(1st Draft)					
The student uploaded the essay on Blackboard by the designated due date.	1	2	3	4	5
The student chose and visited an appropriate tourist attraction.	1	2	3	4	5

Essay (*continued*)	Poor	Fair	Good	Very Good	Excellent
The essay was well organized using the required elements.	1	2	3	4	5
The essay contained new information using indirect quotations.	1	2	3	4	5
The student pasted at least five pictures related to the story.	1	2	3	4	5
(2nd Draft)					
The student submitted the hard copy by the designated due date.	1	2	3	4	5
The student used plain style accurately.	1	2	3	4	5
The student revised the 1st draft according to teacher feedback.	1	2	3	4	5
The essay contained some personal opinions or emotions.	1	2	3	4	5
The script used accurate grammar and correct spelling.	1	2	3	4	5
Average					/5

Video	Poor	Fair	Good	Very Good	Excellent
The student presented the video at the designated time.	1	2	3	4	5
The video reflected teacher feedback on the 2nd draft.	1	2	3	4	5
The student had sufficient oral practice for recording.	1	2	3	4	5
The narration matched the video.	1	2	3	4	5
The video presentation was easy for the audience to understand.	1	2	3	4	5
Average					/5

NOTE

1 For a sample work, see https://youtu.be/q1e7T2C-q6k.

WORKS CITED

Campbell, Terry A. "Digital Storytelling in an Elementary Classroom: Going Beyond Entertainment." *Procedia: Social and Behavioral Sciences* 69 (2012): 385–93, doi:10.1016/j.sbspro.2012.11.424.

Castañeda, Martha E. "'I Am Proud That I Did It and It's a Piece of Me': Digital Storytelling in the Foreign Language Classroom." *CALICO Journal* 30, no. 1 (2013): 44–62, doi:10.11139/ cj.30.1.44-62.

Gee, James Paul, and Michael H. Levine. "Welcome to Our Virtual Worlds." *Educational Leadership* (2009): 48–52.

Grigsby, Yurimi, et al. "(Re)Claiming Voices: Digital Storytelling and Second Language Learners." *Acta Technologica Dubnicae* 5, no. 1 (2015): 60–7. doi:10.1515/atd-2015-0034.

Kim, Heyoung, and Jang Ho Lee. "The Value of Digital Storytelling as an L2 Narrative Practice." *The Asia-Pacific Education Researcher* 27, no. 1 (2017): 1–9. doi:10.1007/s40299-017-0360-3.

Kim, Pirae. "Implementing Digital Storytelling and Students' Writing Ability Development in an EFL College Classroom." *Multimedia-Assisted Language Learning* 21, no. 1 (2018): 77–106. https://doi.org/10.3991/ijim.v13i07.10798.

Malita, Laura, and Catalin Martin. "Digital Storytelling as Web Passport to Success in the 21st Century." *Procedia: Social and Behavioral Sciences* 2, no. 2 (2010): 3060–4. doi:10.1016/j.sbspro.2010.03.465.

Na, Eun-young, and Eunju Na. "A Study of Korean Language Teaching Using Digital Storytelling Class Project for American College Learners." *Korean Education* 99 (2014): 235–60. doi:10.15734/koed.99.201406.235.

Ohler, Jason. "The World of Digital Storytelling." *Educational Leadership* 63, no. 4 (2005/6): 44–7.

Park, Punahm, and Haeok Chung. "The Effects of Proficiency-Levelled Elementary English Classes Using a Creative Digital Story Writing Method." *The Modern English Society* 17, no. 1 (2016): 227–50. doi:10.18095/meeso.2016.17.1.11.

Prensky, Marc. "Digital Natives, Digital Immigrants Part 1." *On the Horizon* 9, no. 5 (2001): 1–6. doi:10.1108/10748120110424816.

Rasmussen, Eric Dean. "Center for Digital Storytelling." *Mastering the Art of French Cooking and Systems Theory*, retrieved Jan 18, 2021, from https://elmcip.net/node/2820.

Robin, Bernard R. "Digital Storytelling: A Powerful Technology Tool for the 21st Century Classroom." *Theory Into Practice* 47, no. 3 (2008): 220–8. doi:10.1080/00405840802153916.

– Educational Uses of Digital Storytelling. digitalstorytelling.coe.uh.edu/archive/7elements.html.

Tahriri, Abdorreza, et al. "The Impact of Digital Storytelling on EFL Learners' Oracy Skills and Motivation." *International Journal of Applied Linguistics & English Literature* 4, no. 3 (2015): 144–53. https://doi.org/10.7575/aiac.ijalel.v.4n.3p.144.

Tsou, Wenli, et al. "Applying a Multimedia Storytelling Website in Foreign Language Learning." *Computers & Education* 47, no. 1 (2006): 17–28. doi:10.1016/j.compedu.2004.08.013.

Verdugo, Dolores Ramírez, and Isabel Alonso Belmonte. "Using Digital Stories to Improve Listening Comprehension with Spanish Young Learners of English." *Language Learning & Technology* 11, no. 1 (2007): 87–101.

Yang, Ya-Ting C., and Wan-Chi I. Wu. "Digital Storytelling for Enhancing Student Academic Achievement, Critical Thinking, and Learning Motivation: A Year-Long Experimental Study." *Computers & Education* 59, no. 2 (2012): 339–52. doi:10.1016/j.compedu.2011.12.012.

16 A Pedagogical Module for a Place-Based and Multiliteracies-Based Digital Storytelling Project for Language Learning

ANGELA LEE-SMITH

Introduction

One of the main challenges that language practitioners and researchers face is transforming literacy instruction to better accommodate the needs of language learners in the twenty-first century. As such, this chapter offers a timely insight regarding how to design multiliteracies-focused project modules for language learners of all levels by integrating multiliteracies and standards frameworks together, both of which have yet to be incorporated widely and proactively, towards practices in foreign-, second-, and heritage-language education. Language teaching practitioners, researchers, and graduate trainees may agree that there are few instructional materials, learning tasks or projects that are designed for learners with limited proficiencies, particularly when compared to learners at higher proficiency levels – namely intermediate to advanced levels. Thus, the model project presented here is for learners of the Korean language (one of the less commonly taught languages) at a beginner level, but the project can be easily applied to many other languages at all levels.

This chapter presents students' collaborative projects in a beginner-level language class, which showcased each student's skills in a multimodal storytelling project designed through incorporating place-based (Gruenewald and Smith, viii–xxiii), multiliteracies-based (Paesani et al., 37–48), and standards-based (NSCB) frameworks.

Storytelling is a meaningful and personalized application of language that fosters within language learners ways in which they can express themselves in the target language. Language learners also have the opportunity to work on expanding their vocabulary and grammar by formulating appropriate sentence structures in their cohesive storytelling. In addition, they can improve their speaking fluency, listening comprehension, and literacy through this project. These elements play an important role in advancing their language proficiency. This project is easily applicable across languages and levels, and the project's module, practical ways of assessments, learners' reflections, and pedagogical implications will be also discussed.

Pedagogical Framework

Multiliteracies-Based Approach

Multiliteracies – that is, multiple literacies – is a pedagogical approach founded by the New London Group that aims to render language instruction more inclusive of cultural, linguistic, communicative, and technological diversity. It is closely associated with multimodality – multiple modes of meaning making. For example, this can include technologies, communication channels, and mediums that differ from traditional pedagogy, which tends to focus on mono-modal teaching and learning.

The multiliteracies approach emphasizes the significance of situating language that is used within socially complex multimodal contexts that are commonly found in the twenty-first century (Cope and Kalantzis, 7; Allen and Paesanim, 123; Warner and Dupuym, 4).

The multiliteracies model suggested by Cope and Kalantzis presented the four phases of the learning process, all of which are summarized in figure 16.1. In this model, the various stages are as follows:

- Situated Practice – Learners observe and experience new situations or content and reflect on their own familiar experiences and perspectives
- Overt Instruction – Learners understand the new situations or content presented on a deep level by conceptualization
- Critical Framing – Learners critically view, interpret, and evaluate social and cultural contexts by analysing such contexts
- Transformed Practice – Learners transfer the meaning-making practice by appropriately and creatively applying what they have learned to real world situations and tasks

These four phases do not necessarily always follow in a linear order, and each phase can thus be applied without adhering to a fixed order in actual classroom practices.

Place-Based Approach

Connecting students to places can enhance learning (Gruenewald and Smith, 135). Place-based learning is an approach that makes use of geography – places – to create authentic, meaningful, engaging, and personalized learning in a variety of subjects; in this case, language is the designated subject.

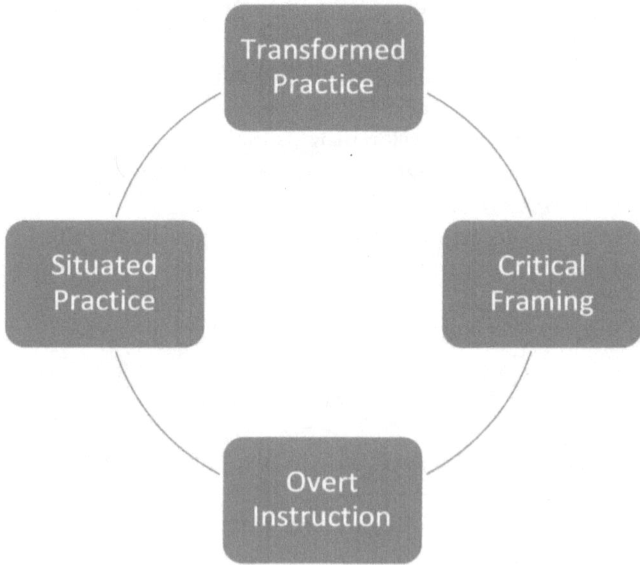

Figure 16.1. The multiliteracies model (adapted from Cope and Kalantzis)

Place-based learning activities enhance the authenticity of the learning experience and connect these to local contexts and communities (Sobel, 7; Holden and Sykes, 15). Also, it engages students in meaningful language uses and makes language learning more relevant to the daily lives of students (Holden and Sykes, 159–60; Godwin-Jones, 12). Practically any particular place, including the students' own "place" – home, campus, neighbourhood, town, or community – can serve as a valuable resource in place-based learning.

Standards-Based Approach

The *World-Readiness Standards for Learning Languages* (NSCB) guides language learners to develop the skills required for communicating adequately with cultural competence, in order to allow them to participate in multilingual communities within today's globalizing world. Through implementing the standards approach, language classrooms can provide learners with opportunities to develop well-roundedness in the five "C" standard goal areas: communication, cultures, connections, comparisons, and communities.

Indeed, the five standard goal areas can be summarized as follows:

- Communication – Learners communicate effectively enough to function in various situations

- Cultures – Learners interact appropriately with cultural competence and understanding
- Connections – Learners use the language to function in academic and career-related situations
- Comparisons – Learners develop insights into the nature of language and the concept of culture through comparisons of the language and cultures studied vis-à-vis their own
- Communities – Learners participate in multilingual communities both at home and around the world

Storymap Project: My Happy Place

Project Overview

- Applicable Proficiency Range: Novice to advanced proficiency
- Applicable Languages: All
- Education Setting: Foreign- and heritage-language learners in K-12 and higher education settings
- Project Description: This sample is a multimodal and place-based written and oral digital storytelling project. It is a collaborative student assignment that will be done in a first-semester Korean class (beginner level with seventy instructional contact hours) in a private college in the United States and will share each student's storytelling about "my happy place" at the campus and local area, in multimodal meaning-making ways: visual, aural, linguistic, textual, and spatial modes (e.g., video, images, music, mapping, technology).
- Project Rationale: Storytelling is a meaningful and personalized language application and encourages language learners to express themselves in the target language. Students will also have an opportunity to expand their vocabulary and grammar to formulate appropriate sentence structures that will facilitate a cohesive narrative and improve their speaking fluency, listening comprehension, and literacy through this project. These elements play an essential role in advancing their language proficiency.
- Project Goals and Objectives: Through this project, students demonstrate their communicative competence in the target language:
  (a) Interpersonal communication: Learners interact and negotiate meanings in spoken or written conversations to share information, reactions, feelings, and opinions on the project topic.
  (b) Interpretive communication: Learners understand, interpret, and analyse what is heard, read, or viewed concerning the project topic.
  (c) Presentational communication: Learners present information, concepts, and ideas to inform, explain, and narrate the project topic

through appropriate media and adapting to the various audiences – listeners, readers, or viewers (adapted from NSCB, 36).

- Major Tasks: Each student will create an oral storytelling video, mapping, and a written text on the StoryMap platform,[1] an online designated project site for the class.
- Project Duration: Two weeks outside of class time
- Primary Genre: Narrative

Project Module

- Pedagogical Approaches and Assessments: Multiliteracy framework, place-based, standards-based, proficiency-based, task-based, and project-based
- Context (function) and Content (topic): Narrative (written and spoken) digital storytelling; "my happy place" on campus and in the community
- Tasks: (a) Making video storytelling about "my happy place" and publishing it
  (b) Writing a story about "my happy place" and publishing it
- Multiliteracies Framework and Standards Goals:
  (a) Critical framing; interpersonal communication/cultures
  – Students discuss general feelings about their college life.
  (b) Situated practice; connections
  – Students research, introduce, and talk about their "happy place." (e.g., Why are you happy when you are in this place? What do you do here? Whom are you with in this place? How often do you come here? How much time do you spend here? Talk about your most memorable experience or moment in this place.)
  (c) Overt instruction; interpretive communication/connections/comparisons
  – Students watch and listen to previous students' storytelling videos and understand the oral and written texts.
  (d) Transformed practice; presentational communication
  – Students present their oral storytelling about the topic "my happy place." Instructors provide proficiency-based speaking rubrics.
  (e) Overt instruction/critical framing; presentational communication comparisons/communities
  – Students write about their happy places and edit, assess, and revise. Instructors provide proficiency-based writing rubrics.
  (f) Transformed practice; presentational communication
  – Students present their final products on the platform StoryMap.
- Assessments: Performance assessment and self-assessment
  – 15 per cent of the final grade: oral production 50 points/written narration production 50 points/multimodal production 50 points (mapping, multimedia, text, and digital storytelling).

- Reflection on Teaching and Learning, Experience-Based Learning
  - Critical Framing: Students respond to the given survey questionnaire on the project. Instructors may record the project reflection and outcome (e.g., classroom action research or portfolio).

Project Outcomes and Pedagogical Implications

The final products of the project show that learners were provided with the opportunity to demonstrate communication and multiliteracies competence through meaningful applications of the language. The final outcome of this project illustrated that students can do the following:

(a) Students can integrate pronunciation, vocabulary, expressions, and grammar into their language skills – listening, speaking, reading, and writing.
(b) Students can produce and understand written, oral, and visual texts.
(c) Students can use multiple modes of meaning-making systems (oral and written text, motion, and/or image) through multiple mediums (such as picture, symbol, sign, text, audio, video, gesture, music, technology, etc.) to convey and communicate, with clarity. Place-based learning activities enhance the authenticity of the learning experience and connect these to local contexts and communities (Sobel, 7; Holden and Sykes, 15). Also, it engages students in meaningful language uses and makes language learning more relevant to the daily lives of students (Holden and Sykes, 159–60; Godwin-Jones, 12). Practically any particular place, including the students' own "place" – home, campus, neighbourhood, town, or community – can serve as a valuable resource in place-based learning.
(d) Students can venture out of their comfort zones and perform beyond their designated proficiency level through working on the project.

Each student in the course produced their video spoken component, written text, and mapping on the project platform that provides a digital story-map tool, as seen in figure 16.2 above. The written texts and spoken components in the videos, in general, clearly show that the students are creative in their use of the language. Students' final products indicate that they can communicate information (e.g., simple facts and ideas), make presentations, and express their thoughts about familiar topics using sentences and series of connected sentences through spoken and written language.

The participating students shared their written reflections on the benefits of working on this project as a part of their language-learning process in the course. This project provided the students with the opportunity to integrate a variety of language skills.

Figure 16.2. Project final site sample

Excerpts 1. Student Reflections I

- *I thought that this project covered every aspect, from writing to speaking. Moreover, the topic was easy to write about using varied grammar and vocabulary.*
- *While working on this project, I was able to demonstrate my understanding of particles [case markers], subjects, locations, etc., while receiving feedback on my work. It has also assisted me in practicing my speaking skills.*
- *It was a culmination of everything that we had learned throughout the course.*
- *It really helped me exercise the grammar concepts I had learned into speech in a more practical way.*

Also, through working on the project, students applied what they learned in the classroom to meaningful and authentic uses of language that expanded their competence level.

Excerpts 2. Student Reflections II

- *This project allowed for a direct application of the language skills I had learned in class. It really did push me in my Korean skills simply because I had to speak rather than read and talk about things.*

- *The project is so unique in that it really helped reinforce the material we learned. Also, it helped me see my progress throughout the semester.*
- *I think that by doing this video it really helped me exercise the grammar concepts I had learned into speech in a more practical way. I think the project is a cool way to get a practicum out of the course outside of our usual class storytelling.*
- *This project helped me to improve my speaking immensely and pushed me to look back and survey the grammar I had learned in order to create a cohesive story.*
- *By working on this project, it really pushed us to use the full extent of our language ability to express our thoughts. Instead of just sentences, we had to speak in paragraphs and tell a story, which were very good exercises. I think it appropriately challenged us and our language skills.*

Furthermore, this project helped students gain confidence in their learning by highlighting what they *can* do rather than what they cannot do. Students need to have positive learning experiences and become encouraged to further develop their language proficiency.

Excerpts 3. Student Reflections III

- *I practiced writing longer, speaking more clearly, and gained confidence with Korean.*
- *I really enjoyed this project! It was a very fun way to apply grammar and vocabulary.*
- *My vocab was not versatile enough to cover some of the topics I wanted to, but I had the opportunity to search for new words that I wanted to use and learn them. It is amazing to see what I can do with the language as a beginner.*
- *It made me realize I could actually say quite a few things in the language only after one semester.*

Students were encouraged to expand their proficiency (language skills) by working on a storytelling project, which promoted the learners' interests and their creative and personalized language use. In proficiency-oriented teaching practices for authentic and meaningful tasks or activities such as this project, there is a need to guide students in order to ensure that they are aware of the proficiency goals and the features or criteria expected in the standard proficiency level (i.e., novice, intermediate, advanced level). To help students meet the project goals, the instructor guided them to communicate appropriately and accurately by building upon what they already know, what they can do, and what they need. Consequently, the project allowed students to practice diverse learning styles and strategies while fostering a range of language skills. At the same time, it kept students motivated and engaged by functioning as the centre of their learning.

Excerpts 4. Student Reflections IV

- *I learned how to write in longer form in Korean, which I really enjoyed. I also got much better at Korean grammar through writing the paragraphs, so I really enjoyed that. Filming the video was also really fun!*
- *I thought it was good to be able to attempt to speak about myself on a more intimate level.*
- *I feel much more fluent when talking about the things I talked about in the video.*

Lastly, but on an equally important note, project-based learning can help compensate for some of the limitations of textbook learning, particularly for students at the beginner level. Language textbooks should correspond to the learners' needs and reflect on the uses that learners will make regarding the language (Cunningsworth, 8); however, no commercial textbook will ever be a perfect fit for a language program (Richards, 251–70). Therefore, language textbooks should be regarded as just one of the many resources that teachers can draw upon to create useful lessons; as such, teachers may need to adapt and modify textbook exercises, as well as carefully design their learning tasks or projects, to ensure that the lessons are practical and meaningful to the learners.

Excerpts 5. Student Reflections V

- *I think the project is a cool way to get a practicum out of the course.*
- *I really liked the project because it helped me practice how to have a real conversation and tell my story without being prompted by a specific question.*

Conclusion

The chapter showcased implementing multiliteracies and standards-based learning projects and designing a practical project module and its significant benefit of promoting meaningful applications of what students learn in the classroom. The place-based project presented in this chapter can serve as a model that provides language learners with opportunities to make meaningful and personal connections to local places and communities and work as a foundation for deeper engagement and interactions as they further develop their proficiencies.

The project module, designed with the multiliteracies approach and the standards for learning a language, illustrated the application of hands-on information, including the project rationale, goals and objectives, activities and materials, assessments and outcomes, and the students' self-reflection. The project module presented can serve as a template that language educators may adopt and implement in their everyday teaching practices.

The integration of multiliteracies and the standard approaches through the digital storytelling project, "My Happy Place," has several advantages for language learners, even at the beginner level. Colleagues in the field of language education may wish to expand further and refine the existing curriculum, and they would benefit from designing project modules that adopt the principles presented in this chapter. Therefore, it would be worthwhile to create a collaborative repository of project modules for language learning that could be shared with language practitioners in both K–12 and higher education settings.

Appendix

Sample Text of Student Writing

제 행복한 곳은 제 방입니다. 제 방이 벤자민 프랭클린 안에 있습니다. 제 방은 엔틀이왜 "E" 삼 층에 있습니다. 그래서 저는 보통 엘리베이터에 가고 나서 방에 걸어서 갑니다.

저는 방에 있을 때마다 보통 친구들이 같이 있습니다. 왜냐하면 방에서 친구들하고 삽니다. 제 친구들 이름이 *A, B, C, D하고 E 입니다. 그래서 저는 친구 다섯 명하고 같이 한 방에서 삽니다. 방 친구가 많이 있습니다!

저는 방에 있을 때 자주 숙제하고 공부합니다. 숙제가 많이 있을 때마다 친구들을 안 봅니다. 그런데 숙제를 일찍 끝내면 방에서 친구들하고 보통 이야기할 수 있습니다. 저는 가끔 A 씨하고 B 씨하고 한국어 말하기를 연습합니다. 하지만 저는 방에서 친구들하고 넷플릭스 영화 봅니다. 보통 저녁에 A 씨하고 D씨하고 한국 음악을 듣습니다. 그리고 저는 방에서 친구하고 노래하고 춤 추기를 좋아합니다. 제 친구들이 정말 재미있어서 저는 안 바쁠 때마다 방에서 친구들하고 항상 같이 있습니다. 그리고 피곤할 때 저는 방에서 자고 쉽니다. 저는 제 방을 진짜 좋아합니다.

저는 매일 수업이 끝나고 나서 방에 항상 갑니다. 저녁 식사때 까지 저는 방에 있습니다. 그리고 저녁 식사하고 나서 방에 옵니다. 그래서 저는 매주 열여섯 시간 동안 방에 있습니다. 하지만 주말에 가끔만 밖에 갑니다. 그래서 저는 주말에 방에 항상 있습니다. 저는 자주 방에 안 있고 싶습니다.

여기에서 제 경험이 지난주에 있었습니다. 추석 방학을 끝냈을 때 저는 텍사스 집에서 예일까지 여행했습니다. 그리고 방에 가고 나서 친구들을 봤습니다! 우리가 일 주 동안 안 봤습니다. 그래서 우리가 아주 신났습니다. 우리가 방을 크리스마스 장식하고 이야기했습니다.

저는 방에 있을 때 항상 참 행복합니다. 왜냐하면 방에 있을 때 저는 쉬고 친구들하고 같이 있을 수 있기 때문입니다. 그래서 제 방이 제일 행복한 곳입니다.

[Translation]

My happy place is my [dormitory] room. My room is in Benjamin Franklin [building], Entryway E and on the third floor. Because it is on the third floor, I usually take the elevator and walk from there to my room.

Since I live with my friends, they are usually in my room with me. Their names are A, B, C, D, and E. I live with all five of my friends in a room. I have many roommates!*

I usually do my homework and study when I am in my room. Every time I have a lot of homework, I do not see my friends. But if I finish my homework early, I can have casual conversations with my friends in my room. I often practice speaking in Korean with A and B. But I watch Netflix movies with my friends in my room. Usually, in the evening, I listen to Korean music with A and D. And I like singing and dancing with friends in my room. My friends are really fun to be around, so whenever I'm not busy, I'm always with my friends in my room. And when I am tired, I sleep in my room and rest. I really like my room.

Every day, I go straight to my room after my classes end. I am in my room until dinner time and come back promptly after dinner. As a result, I am in my room for sixteen hours every week. However, on the weekends, I go out sometimes; but otherwise, I am usually always in my room on the weekends. Often, I don't like to be in my room.

Here, I had an experience last week. After Thanksgiving break, I travelled to Yale from my home in Texas. And after I came into my room, I saw my friends again! We hadn't seen each other for a week, so we were very excited to be reunited. As we continued our usual conversations, we decorated our room for Christmas.

I am always very happy when I am in my room, because when I am in my room, I can rest and talk with my friends. This is why my room is my happiest place.

(*Names have been replaced with A, B, C, D, and E.)

NOTE

1 https://storymap.knightlab.com is an open-source, mapping, and adaptable media storytelling site developed by Northwestern University Knight Lab.

WORKS CITED

Allen, Heather Willis, and Kate Paesani, "Exploring the Feasibility of a Pedagogy of Multiliteracies in Introductory Foreign Language Courses," *L2 Journal* 2 (2010): 119–42. DOI:10.5070/L2219064.

Cope, Bill, and Mary Kalantzis, editors. *Multiliteracies: Literacy Learning and the Design of Social Futures*. Milton Park: Routledge, 2000.

Cunningsworth, Alan. *Choosing Your Coursebook*. Oxford: Macmillan Heineman, 1995.

Godwin-Jones, Robert. "Augmented Reality and Language Learning: From Annotated Vocabulary to Place-Based Mobile Games." *Language Learning & Technology* 20, no. 3 (2016): 9–19. llt.msu.edu/issues/october2016/emerging.pdf.

Gruenewald, David, and Gregory A. Smith, editors. *Place-based Education in the Global Age: Local Diversity*. Mahwah: Lawrence Erlbaum Associates, 2008.

Holden, Christopher L., and Julie M. Sykes. "Complex L2 Pragmatic Feedback via Place-Based Mobile Games." In *Technology and Interlanguage Pragmatics Research and Teaching*, edited by Naoko Taguchi and Julie M. Sykes, 155–84. Amsterdam, Netherlands: John Benjamins, 2013.

Holden, Christopher L., and Julie M. Sykes. "Leveraging Mobile Games for Place-Based Language Learning." *International Journal of Game-Based Learning* 1, no. 2 (2011): 1–18. https://doi.org/10.4018/ijgbl.2011040101.

National Standards Collaborative Board. World-Readiness Standards for Learning Languages, 4th ed. 2015.

New London Group. "A Pedagogy of Multiliteracies: Designing Social Futures." *Harvard Educational Review* 66, no. 1 (1996): 60–92. https://doi.org/10.17763/haer.66.1.17370n67v22j160u.

Paesani, Kate, et al. *A Multiliteracies Framework for Collegiate Foreign Language Teaching*. New Jersey: Upper Saddle River, 2016.

Richards, Jack. *Curriculum Development in Language Education*. Cambridge: Cambridge University Press, 2001.

Sobel, David. *Place-Based Education: Connecting Classrooms and Communities*. Great Barrington: The Orion Society, 2004.

Warner, Chantelle, and Beatrice Dupuy. "Moving toward Multiliteracies in Foreign Language Teaching: Past and Present Perspectives and Beyond." *Foreign Language Annals* 56, no. 1 (2018): 116–28. https://doi.org/10.1111/flan.12316.

17 Using Facebook as a Resource for e-Tandem Language Learning in Higher Education

CHRISTINE SCHALLMOSER AND PIA RESNIK

Introduction

The past two decades have seen increasingly rapid advances in the field of technology-enhanced learning and telecollaboration. E-Tandem language learning, a more specific type of the latter (El-Hariri, 49), usually involves two language learners of different first languages (L1s) acting as the other tandem partner's target language (TL). They support each other in the learning process via digital tools such as Skype or Facebook, by alternating roles between language learner and expert of their own language (Stickler and Lewis, 238). Not only does learning in Tandem – either integrated into language courses or carried out independently – provide a platform for learners to improve their language skills, but they can also learn more about their target culture and exchange additional knowledge (Brammerts, 11–17), for example about student life in their respective national setting.

Reciprocity and autonomy are the two main criteria of Tandem language learning (Brammerts, 11). While reciprocity implies the commitment of both tandem partners to their own learning and to the support of their partner's learning (Little, "Introduction," 1), autonomy is the "ability to take charge of one's own learning" (Holec, 3) and encompasses both partners' ability to plan and monitor their learning and reflect on it, which in turn requires metacognitive awareness and metalinguistic knowledge (Little, "Counselling," 25).

In our e-Tandem scheme, we make use of Facebook for various reasons, one of them being its worldwide popularity, especially among adolescents and students. By the end of 2018, with its continuously increasing number of users, Facebook had 2.27 billion active users (i.e., users who logged in to the platform at least 30 days before the measurement taken by Facebook), and it is the first social media network with numbers surpassing the one billion thresholds (Statista). Although these data must be read with caution, since the measurements have been carried out by Facebook itself and their estimated rate of false active user accounts at 3–4 per cent (Facebook) is rather low, a more critical source confirms that Facebook is used by 84 per cent of internet users in our target group's age range – that is, eighteen- to twenty-nine-year-olds (Guimarães). The potential of social media in education has also been highlighted by researchers (e.g., Greenhow), and Facebook is widely accepted among our students, too. Indeed, they continuously point out that they prefer social media to email for communication. We therefore utilize Facebook as a communication tool to bring together students from tertiary institutions in Austria, the UK, and the USA. This paper offers insight into the implementation of this innovative practice of technology-enhanced language learning, sheds light on its advantages and challenges, and provides solutions by drawing on our experience and participants' voices in answers to open-ended survey questions.

Literature Review

Tandem Language Learning

Since Tandem language learning originated as part of an exchange program for German and French youth in 1968, a considerable amount of literature, for instance on intercultural learning in Tandem (Künzle and Müller) and more generally on autonomy (Lewis et al.), has been published. With the increased availability of the internet and its expansion across millions of private households in the 1990s, attention has started to shift to the electronic form of learning in Tandem. Little has pioneered the field, not only providing guidelines for Tandem language learning via the internet ("Counselling") but also evaluating empirical data on the use of email Tandems. This has indicated that the method is highly appealing to students, as "it involved them in modes of language use that seemed to them significantly different from anything offered by their previous language learning experience" (Little, "Introduction," 51). More recent studies on e-Tandem language learning have, for instance, investigated task design (e.g., El-Hariri), peer feedback in e-Tandem settings (e.g., Fondo Garcia and Appel), and learners' views on e-Tandem learning (e.g., El-Hariri). While the need for information and communications technology (ICT) to further language students' oral skills has been confirmed (e.g., Appel et al., 17), recent evidence suggests that teachers should indeed take advantage of social media as they provide a more authentic communication environment where students feel comfortable talking at any time and place (Sung and Poole, 98). We therefore followed this lead, aiming to make a contribution to this emergent area of research.

Theoretical Framework

Aiming for participants to provide mutual support in language learning, our project adopts the core principles of Tandem learning as outlined above:

reciprocity and autonomy. More precisely, our approach is inspired by scholars such as Dam and Little, according to whom autonomy constitutes the most effective way of learning (e.g., Dam; Little, "Discourse," 16). This suggests the usefulness of implementing e-Tandem learning as a complementary method (Vetter, 46) in higher education. Furthermore, they consider learning as a social phenomenon rooted in collaboration. This aligns well with our social-interactive perspective (Schwienhorst, 429) based on Vygotsky's sociocultural theory, according to which social interaction is related to conscious awareness of both ourselves and others (Vygotsky, 29–30). From this perspective, the learner-expert relationship in Tandem learning settings provides a framework that assists the mediation process and the internalization in language learning (Sung and Poole, 99). Schwienhorst further suggests there is an inherent connection between a social-interactive perspective of learner autonomy and an individual-cognitive one (429). The latter, drawing on Kelly's theory of personal construct (33), puts an emphasis on the fact that most learners endeavour to continuously advance and increase their range of constructs, a process in which the incorporation of new constructs tends to be evaluated against the latest repertoire of constructs and requires the skill of carefully reflecting upon learning. We therefore aim to assist the development of our participants' reflection skills with both specific tasks and the invitation to create a language portfolio.

Project Design

At the beginning of each term, students of German at King's College London, the University of Cambridge, University College London, the University of Kent, the University of Oxford, and/or the University of Texas at Austin as well as students of English at the University of Vienna and the University College of Teacher Education, Vienna/Krems, are recruited to participate in our e-Tandem scheme. Crucially, we are pairing students who are doing a degree in very similar disciplines to minimize the occurrence of potential problems related to living in different learning contexts (Schwienhorst, 432). Indeed, our e-Tandem scheme opens up the possibility to compare technical terminology and course-specific phrases (St. John, 62), as well as to discuss the difference between studying at degree level and student life more broadly in Austria, the UK, and the USA.

In the first instance, participants are contacted in class or via email. They are provided with an information sheet on our approach to e-Tandem learning, its benefits (such as learner autonomy), complemented by suggestions to make use of both the Common European Framework of Reference for Languages (Council of Europe) and the European Language Portfolio (Council for Cultural Cooperation). Students are encouraged to express their interest in participating via email, and those who do receive an invitation to join the

Facebook group we set up for the e-Tandem scheme, a new one for each round. Furthermore, participants are asked to share both their Facebook name and their current language level, based on the level of the language course they attend at the time, as well as any other languages they know. This enables us to match them more suitably.

In addition to being notified regarding forms of data collection linked to the project to improve our understanding of its strengths and weaknesses, students are sent a confirmation of these having received ethical approval by the Research Ethics Office of King's College London. They also receive the codes of conduct of their own and their partner's university. Once accepted as a Facebook group member, students can also find the abovementioned details on our approach to e-Tandem learning in the respective group description. They are first introduced to their Tandem partners by means of a direct message, in which we are also included so they can contact us should they encounter any problems. They are then guided towards learner autonomy through various tasks, disseminated via Facebook event invitations.

In these events, students are asked to organize meetings via Facebook voice/ or video call, Skype, WhatsApp, or FaceTime. The focus of these meetings lies in spoken interaction, since our students expressed their wish to improve oral communication skills rather than writing skills due to their advanced knowledge of the TL. In these weekly meetings, they discuss a range of topics, which are always described in both German and English. The first meeting is focused on getting to know each other, themselves as language learners, and discussing what they expect from the Tandem sessions (e.g., with regard to correction, mutual support, or controlling a fair distribution of using the languages concerned). The following session deals with popular culture, where they familiarize their partners with popular movies, TV series, books, and music that is popular in their country within their age group (always with a focus on making recommendations on what to read, listen to, or watch to improve their language skills). In the next meeting, students discuss studying and living in the countries concerned, thereby providing insight into tertiary education and everyday life in the country the TL is spoken in, which assists in preparing for their year abroad. In the following week, the topic is politics. Depending on the tandem partner's country of residence, they either discuss Brexit (UK), its media coverage in the different countries, and potential benefits of and downsides to leaving the EU, or they discuss contemporary issues related to US and Austrian politics. In week five, the focus is on tourism, where travel adventures, students' own preferred travel styles, and destinations are exchanged.

After having received the five weekly tasks via event invitations, they are expected to have developed the skills necessary to proceed on their own. Consequently, they only receive two more reminders to arrange meetings in the form of postings to the group. Facebook offers numerous advantages here: not only does it support synchronous communication, but it is also an inherent element of most of our students' everyday life. Furthermore, the option to create events facilitates an engaging presentation of tasks, students can be reached with ease, and the regular reminders prevent students from forgetting about their meetings (Sung and Poole, 109). It also provides a platform for participants to get to know each other as friends (Resnik and Schallmoser, 546). This, in turn, minimizes the risk of perceiving each other as mere pen pals, which could risk trivializing the e-Tandem partnership (Schwienhorst, 432).

Challenges and Solutions

Little identifies participant dropout as one of the challenges in e-Tandem language learning, both when language courses form an integral part of a degree and, even more so, in extracurricular settings ("Conclusion," 51). This is a challenge we also experienced in our e-Tandem scheme. Although language classes constitute a core part of our participants' degree courses, the e-Tandem scheme is voluntary, and some students do drop out. Nevertheless, we suggest offering such schemes irrespective of any module and without a link to assessment, since only then is the potential of fostering autonomy fully realized (Tatzl, 70–1). Some students emphasized that it was not the time difference between their countries of residence that had a negative impact on the frequency of e-Tandem meetings, but rather their busy schedule. To avoid students' dropping out and ensure regular attendance of meetings with their Tandem partners, we suggest the introduction of an official learning contract (Knowles). This specifies goals, obligations, and an individualized schedule of meetings as a formal framework that helps them explore and, ideally, confirm their readiness to actively engage in such a learning scheme in advance. Furthermore, we are planning to refine our matching process. While it will still be based on their language level, we are in the process of developing a survey for future participants. This aims to increase participants' level of engagement by better capturing their interests beyond their studies.

Overall, the participants appreciated that the e-Tandem scheme provided a platform for autonomous learning, and they reported a positive link between e-Tandem language learning and their learner autonomy. However, the majority of participants so far have not made use of the European Language Portfolio (Council for Cultural Cooperation), a tool that could foster reflection on language learning and language itself, which is an essential process in learner autonomy (Schwienhorst, 430). Further research needs to be done to investigate the necessity of portfolios in e-Tandem language learning. One possible method of encouraging the use of portfolios is their inclusion in the aforementioned learning contract. In their initial expression of interest in participating in the e-Tandem scheme, only a minority of students mentioned that security and privacy concerns related to the use of Facebook were at issue. In these cases, we offer an introduction to their Tandem partner and the delivery of weekly tasks via email. While this results in a higher workload for the organizers and a less appealing presentation of tasks, the respective students were very happy to be offered this option.

Another challenge we faced is based on the fact that, when studying a language in the countries concerned, language competence modules still heavily draw on L1 users as a reference group. To a certain extent, this is idealized (see Cook, 14–15) as foreign language (LX) users (Dewaele, "LX user," 238) *per definitionem* cannot become "native speakers" of anything other than their own L1(s). Still, L1 varieties are valued highly by learners and teachers alike as target models to which they orient themselves in the process of learning and teaching another language (Young and Walsh, 131–5). In Austria, for instance, it is common to specialize in either American or British English in pronunciation classes when studying English at the tertiary level. This initially prevented some students from participating in the e-Tandem scheme, since it used to be a collaboration between a UK and an Austrian university only. This problem was solved by also contacting potential partners in the USA. Additionally, students' high valuation of L1 varieties of the TL became apparent when noticing that they very much disliked being matched with LX users of the target language, some even dropping out as they often did not see any advantages in lingua franca Tandem sessions. Occasionally our students use the TL at C2 level. This reduces the likelihood of perceiving potential gains when learning from a LX user living in the country concerned on the level of linguistic mastery, in case this partner's proficiency is lower than their own. As previous research has demonstrated the various benefits of, for example, English and German lingua franca telecollaboration in school settings (Kohn and Hoffstaedter), such as developing intercultural communicative competence (Kohn, 246), raising students' awareness of potential benefits in the information sheet they receive at the beginning might be one way of overcoming these misconceptions.

Additionally, it is crucial to pay close attention to the task design itself. In order to reduce artificiality as much as possible, we tried to provide them with tasks appropriate for their age group. This, we hoped, would foster communication with their partner on topics they are genuinely interested in (Little, "Counselling," 28). When designing the tasks, we also aimed at highlighting students' role as cultural mediators (Roberts et al., 2, 229), giving their partners authentic insights into their cultural backgrounds. Here, attention needs to be paid to the contexts the partners come from. We overcame this challenge by designing US- and UK-specific tasks where needed (e.g., when discussing national politics) and, consequently, setting up different Facebook groups.

Finally, a further obstacle that needs to be taken into account when setting up an e-Tandem scheme in higher education is its launch date. A particular challenge in our case was the mismatch between the Austrian (semesters) and UK (trimesters) academic years. This initially led to dropouts as more relaxed and highly stressful periods frequently collided in the countries concerned. Besides having found the right time to implement the scheme, our experience also showed that teacher mediation is useful here to remind students of not necessarily perceiving the e-Tandem meetings as extra effort they put into their language-learning experience, but as useful practice they can also exploit when preparing for oral exams, for instance.

Benefits

At this point, students' perceived benefits of the tandem scheme will be briefly mentioned, based on answers to open-ended questions included in a web survey, which fifty-two Tandem partners completed three months into the scheme. Their self-perceived benefits will be included exemplarily to give participants a voice and to include an emic perspective in this paper (Dewaele "Inner Speech," 8). Overall, 84.6 per cent observed an improvement of their language skills through learning in Tandem, including fluency of speaking, pronunciation, selective comprehension, content-aimed listening and grammar. These students also mentioned having broadened their vocabulary base, frequently explaining that they learned vocabulary they "would not normally use in the classroom" (female, 28, TL German).

The same number of respondents, furthermore, reported the Tandem sessions caused them to enjoy the use of the language more.[1] Nearly half of them mentioned that authentic communication was crucial. Participant no. 19 (female, 19, TL German), for instance, wrote: "It helped me build my confidence up by providing me with real life situations where I can use the FL ... it was a very practical experience!" The sessions were often described as fun and relaxed. Participant no. 43 (female, 21, TL German) explained that she enjoyed "having normal chats in the foreign language, like I would with friends in my native language." Approximately one-third of participants mentioned cultural mediation as a key aspect they enjoyed, such as talking about current political issues like Brexit and "hear[ing] the opinion of someone who will probably be affected by it" (female, 23, TL English). Students also enjoyed getting "an insight into one of Britain's top universities and ... education in general" (female, 20, TL English). Participant no. 31 (female, 25, TL English) summarizes the basic tenor underlying the responses: "I profited enormously by perceiving an 'inside' view of the Anglophone culture." Not only did the Tandem sessions make some students appreciate the TL culture more (male, 30, TL German), but they also "enjoyed the confidence boost that came from knowing that [their] tandem partner could understand" them, which often also decreased their foreign language (classroom) anxiety.

Sharing common interests was also mentioned frequently. To put it into participant no. 32's (male, 30, TL German) words: "it felt very satisfying to be able to articulate my interests in German with someone who understood my point of view and shared an interest in the subject." This often made students spend a considerable amount of time talking about topics they became excited about, clearly illustrating heightened learner agency and their taking charge of their own learning (Holec, 3): "[t]ime went by so fast and we always talked for 1–2 hours" (female, 21, TL English). Three months into the program, nearly half of them had already visited each other or had concrete plans to do so.

Indeed, approximately 75 per cent of participants mentioned that the e-Tandem sessions made them more autonomous as language learners, which was reflected in them soon choosing the topics they talked about themselves "because [they] quickly found common interests" (female, 21, TL English). All of them mentioned time management in this context, referring to what language to use when, as well as finding time for the meetings. Teaching and correcting each other, in addition to taking notes during the Tandem sessions, were other frequently occurring aspects that clearly illustrate improvement on this level.

Conclusion and Guidelines

Research into e-Tandem language learning demonstrates numerous potential benefits of such a mutual learner-expert relationship that goes far beyond improving learners' language skills. These include increased learner agency (e.g., Kohn and Hoffstaedter, 357–60; Little, "Counselling," 28–9), heightened motivation (Ushioda, 122), and cultural mediation and pragmatic competence (Kohn, 246), but also increased foreign-language enjoyment (Resnik and Schallmoser, 557).

This paper reported on the implementation of such an e-Tandem scheme via Facebook to support students enrolled in language degrees at the tertiary level outside the classroom in Austria, the UK, and the USA. It demonstrated that Facebook can be used successfully as a platform, where students engage creatively and cooperatively in language learning, which is, according to Kohn, often neglected in traditional teaching contexts (244). However, it was also stressed that it requires careful planning and consideration from the teachers, in order to avoid a high dropout rate (Little, "Conclusion," 51). Besides designing tasks that students find appealing (Little, "Counselling," 28), they should also meet the learners' needs with regard to the skills they aim to improve. Thus, taking learners' own views into account is crucial (see e.g., El-Hariri, 54–9). In only this way can the potential of fostering learner autonomy and increasing learner agency be exploited fully. Moreover, to give students the chance to be "ambassadors" of their own culture – that is, to foster cultural mediation – the tasks need to be designed accordingly, something that worked nicely in the e-Tandem scheme presented in this paper. Further obstacles include the timing of the launch date, which requires consideration depending on the academic institutions involved, but also the L1s of the Tandem partners. The paper suggests that awareness raising of the benefits of developing intercultural communicative competence and, consequently, lingua franca Tandem schemes (Kohn, 246) might help to counteract students' unwillingness to participate in a Tandem partnership with a LX speaker of their TL who is immersed in the respective cultural background.

Additionally, the paper demonstrated that even students at an advanced language level require guidance towards learner autonomy and explicit initial instructions on the useful implementation of such an e-Tandem scheme. Our approach is to provide students with a detailed handout and explanations, encourage them to use language portfolios, and initially give them guided tasks. This could be complemented by learning contracts or agreements (Knowles). Overall, our project demonstrated that teachers should indeed take advantage of social media, as they can be used successfully when teaching and learning an LX. Besides providing an authentic communication environment for students where they seem to feel at ease and comfortable talking, they foster learner autonomy by giving students the opportunity to practice at any time and place. Further research into the use of e-Tandem language learning at the tertiary level is much needed to explore and understand its benefits and effects in greater depth.

NOTE

1 For a detailed analysis of links between e-Tandem language learning and foreign language enjoyment, see Resnik and Schallmoser, 541–64.

WORKS CITED

Appel, Christine, et al. "SpeakApps 2: Speaking Practice in a Foreign Language through ICT Tools." In *CALL Design: Principles and Practice; Proceedings of the 2014 EUROCALL Conference, Groningen, The Netherlands*, edited by Sake Jager et al., 12–17. Lancaster: Research-publishing.net, 2014, doi:10.14705/rpnet.2014.000187.

Brammerts, Helmut. "Tandem Language Learning via the Internet and the International E Mail Tandem Network." In *A Guide to Tandem Language Learning via the Internet. CLCS Occasional Paper 46*, edited by David Little and Helmut Brammerts, pp. 9–21. Dublin: Trinity College Dublin CLCS, 1996.

Cook, Vivian J. "Premises of Multi-Competence." In *The Cambridge Handbook of Linguistic Multi-Competence*, edited by Vivian Cook and Li Wei, 1–25. Cambridge: Cambridge University Press, 2016.

Council for Cultural Cooperation. *European Language Portfolio (ELP): Principles and Guidelines*. Strasbourg: Council of Europe, 2000. www.coe.int/portfolio.

Council of Europe. *Common European Framework of Reference for Languages: Learning, Teaching, Assessment. Companion Volume with New Descriptors*. Strasbourg: Council of Europe, 2018, www.coe.int/langcefr.

Dam, Leni. *Learner Autonomy 3: From Theory to Classroom Practice*. Dublin: Authentik, 1995.

Dewaele, Jean-Marc. "From Obscure Echo to Language of the Heart: Multilinguals' Language Choices for (Emotional) Inner Speech." *Journal of Pragmatics* 87 (2015): 1–17. https://doi.org/10.1016/j.pragma.2015.06.014.

– "Why the Dichotomy 'L1 versus LX user' is Better than 'Native versus Non-Native Speaker.'" *Applied Linguistics* 39, no. 2 (2018): 236–40. https://doi.org/10.1093/applin/amw055.

El-Hariri, Yasmin. "Learner Perspectives on Task Design for Oral-Visual eTandem Language Learning." *Innovation in Language Learning and Teaching* 10, no. 1 (2016): 49–72.

Facebook. "Form 10-Q 3Q." Investor Relations. 2018. investor.fb.com/financials/sec-filings-details/default.aspx?FilingId=13033054.

Fondo Garcia, Marta, and Christine Appel. "Synchronous Tandem Language Learning in a MOOC Context: A Study on Task Design and Learner Performance." In *CALL Communities and Culture – Short Papers from EUROCALL 2016*, edited by Salomi Papadima-Sophocleous, et al., 144–9. Research-publishing.net, 2016. doi:10.14705/rpnet.2016.eurocall2016.552.

Greenhow, Christine. "Youth, Learning, and Social Media." *Journal of Educational Computing Research* 45, no. 2 (2011): 139–46. https://doi.org/10.2190/EC.45.2.a.

Guimarães, Thiago. "7 New Statistics About Facebook Users That Reveal Why It's Such A Powerful Marketing Platform." *BI Intelligence*. Business Insider, 3 Dec. 2014. www.businessinsider.com/aprimer-on-facebook-user-statistics-2014-9?r=US&IR=T.

Holec, Henri. *Autonomy and Foreign Language Learning*. Bergama: Pergamon, 1981.

Kelly, George A. *The Psychology of Personal Constructs. A Theory of Personality*. Norton: Norton & Co., 1955.

Knowles, Malcolm S. *Using Learning Contracts: Practical Approaches to Individualizing and Structuring Learning*. San Francisco: Jossey-Bass Publications, 1986.

Kohn, Kurt. "POA Meets ELF in Intercultural Telecollaboration." *Chinese Journal of Applied Linguistics* 41, no. 2 (2018): 244–8. https://doi.org/10.1515/cjal-2018-0017.

Kohn, Kurt, and Petra Hoffstaedter. "Learner Agency and Non-Native Speaker Identity in Pedagogical Lingua Franca Conversations: Insights from Intercultural Telecollaboration in Foreign Language Education." *Computer Assisted Language Learning* 30, no. 5 (2017): 351–67. https://doi.org/10.1080/09588221.2017.1304966.

Künzle, Beda, and Martin Müller, editors. *Sprachen lernen im Tandem. Beiträge und Materialien zum interkulturellen Lernen. Erste Europaische Tandem-Tage, Freiburg (CH) Dezember 1989*. Freiburg/Schweiz: Universitatsverlag, 1990.

Lewis, Tim, Jane Woodin, and Elke St. John. "Tandem Learning: Independence through Partnership." In *Promoting Learner Autonomy in University Language Teaching*, edited by Elspeth Broady and Marie Madeleine Kenning, 105–20. London: AFLS/CILT, 1996.

Little, David. "Learner Autonomy and Learner Counseling." In *A Guide to Tandem Language Learning via the Internet. CLCS Occasional Paper 46*, edited by David Little and Helmut Brammerts, 23–34. Dublin: Trinity College Dublin CLCS, 1996.

– "Introduction." In *Evaluating Tandem Language Learning by e-Mail: Report on a Bilateral Project. CLCS Occasional Paper No. 55*, edited by David Little, et al., 1–5. Dublin: Trinity College Dublin CLCS, 1999.

– "Conclusion." In *Evaluating Tandem Language Learning by e-Mail: Report on a Bilateral Project. CLCS Occasional Paper No. 55*, edited by David Little, et al., 51–4. Dublin: Trinity College Dublin CLCS, 1999.

– "Learner Autonomy as Discourse: The Role of the Target Language." In *The Answer is Autonomy: Issues in Language Teaching and Learning, Selected papers from the LASIG conference at Treffpunkt Sprachen in Graz, Austria*, edited by Anja Burkert et al., 15–27. Britain: IATEFL, 2013.

Resnik, Pia, and Christine Schallmoser. "Enjoyment as a Key to Success? The Effect of Tandem Language Learning on Students' Foreign Language Enjoyment." *Studies in Second Language Learning and Teaching* 9, no. 3 (2019): 541–64. https://doi.org/10.14746/ssllt.2019.9.3.6 .

Roberts, Celia, et al. *Language Learners as Ethnographers*. Bristol: Multilingual Matters, 2001.

Schwienhorst, Klaus. "Learner Autonomy and Tandem Learning: Putting Principles into Practice in Synchronous and Asynchronous Telecommunications Environments." *Computer Assisted Language Learning* 16, no. 5 (2003): 427–43. https://doi.org/10.1076/call.16.5.427.29484.

Statista. "Number of Facebook Users Worldwide 2008-2018." *The Statistics Portal*. Statista, 2019. www.statista.com/statistics/264810/number-of-monthly-active-facebook-users-worldwide/.

Stickler, Ursula, and Tim Lewis. "Collaborative Language Learning Strategies in an Email Tandem Exchange." In *Language Learning Strategies in Independent Settings*, edited by Stella Hurd and Timothy Lewis, 237–61. Bristol: Multilingual Matters, 2008.

St. John, Elke. "Benefits of Pairing Partners Sharing the Same Discipline." In *A Guide to Language Learning in Tandem via the Internet. CLCS Occasional Paper 46*, edited by David Little and Helmut Brammerts, 61–2. Dublin: Trinity College Dublin CLCS, 1996.

Sung, Ko-Yin, and Frederick Poole. "Investigating the Use of a Smartphone Social Networking Application on Language Learning." *JALT CALL Journal* 13, no. 2 (2017): 97–115.

Tatzl, Dietmar. "A Systemic View of Learner Autonomy." In *New Directions in Language Learning Psychology*, edited by Christina Gkonou, et al., 61–75. Berlin: Springer, 2016.

Ushioda, Ema. "Tandem Language Learning via e-Mail: From Motivation to Autonomy." *ReCALL* 12, no. 2 (2000): 121–8. https://doi.org/10.1017/S0958344000000124.

Vetter, Eva. "Combining Formal and Non-Formal Foreign Language Learning: First Insights into a German-Spanish Experiment at University Level." *SALi, Special Issue: Teaching and Learning Foreign Languages*, 2014, pp. 39–50.

Vygotsky, Lev S. *Mind in Society: The Development of Higher Psychological Processes*. Cambridge: Harvard University Press, 1978.

Young, Tony J., and Steve Walsh. "Which English? Whose English? An Investigation of 'Non-Native' Teachers' Beliefs about Target Varieties." *Language, Culture and Curriculum* 23, no. 2 (2010): 123–37. https://doi.org/10.1080/07908311003797627.

SECTION VI

Online and Blended Language Learning

18 Students' Insights on a Fully Online Language Course

MIHYON JEON AND AHRONG LEE

Introduction

Advances in technology have led to significant changes in student learning. A 2018 national survey, representing 92 per cent of all public post-secondary students in Canada, revealed that more than two-thirds of all Canadian public universities and colleges offer online courses for credit, and roughly one in five Canadian students took at least one online course in 2018–19 (Bates). Almost two-thirds of the institutions expected online enrolment to increase (Bates). Nearly all institutions that participated in the survey reported that the main benefit of online learning was increased student access, while the main barriers were inadequate training and support for instructors and difficulty in identifying resources (Bates). This increasing trend in online courses is not limited to Canada. For example, in 2016, US distance education enrolments in higher education had increased for the fourteenth straight year, and 31.6 per cent of all students in higher education were taking at least one distance course (Burkett). In fact, online education has been embraced as "a central strategy for enabling reform, modernizing schools, and increasing access to a world-class education" across the globe (Powell and Barbour, 77). The field of language education was initially more reluctant to join the online movement than were other fields, based on the assumption that online language learning may limit learners' exposure to authentic speech and deprive them of the chance to interact with classmates and instructors (Özçelik and Kent, 26). However, with the introduction of successful online language programs, there have been efforts to develop more online language programs to capitalize on the benefits of online learning in general (Özçelik and Kent, 26–7).

This chapter introduces a fully online Korean-language course that was offered at York University, Toronto, Canada, in the summer of 2018, after which it explores the students' evaluation of and reception to the online format in general and of each component of the course. A fully online language course entails language learning "in which learners and education providers are physically separated from each other, and learning is essentially supported by online education technologies" (Wang and Chen, 17). The online course was originally developed by Mihyon Jeon and Ahrong Lee in 2014–15 through support received from Ontario Online Initiative Funding. It was the only language course that received such funding in that year's round of competition. The first online course was offered in the regular academic year 2016–17 as one of the four sections of the first-year Korean-language course. Since then, it has been regularly offered in both the regular academic year and in the summer. It has been extremely popular, drawing more students than the initial course enrolment limit of thirty, which has now expanded to fifty-five.

Literature Review

The literature about online education has shown that student attitudes towards, and their perception of, online learning has been mostly positive. Weibe and Kabat claim, for example, that the studies about students' perception and evaluation of computer-assisted learning materials predominantly reveal positive outcomes (222–3). Ayers examines student attitudes towards the use of computer-assisted language learning (CALL) and finds that students appreciate the value of CALL, considering it an important and useful aspect of their learning (247–8). Ayers highlights that CALL, as a tool to supplement the classroom, needs to be incorporated into the curriculum closely (248). In their study about Iranian high school students' and teachers' attitudes towards CALL, Jahromi and Salimi find that both groups have positive attitudes towards the integration of IT in language education (158) and value the motivational and instrumental merits of CALL (171). Their study highlights the need for adequate training in computer literacy, as well as ongoing pedagogical and technical support (171–2).

In their study of online Asian language programmes in New Zealand, Tolosa and others reveal that overall both students and teachers perceive online language learning as useful, beneficial and motivating (51). On the other hand, their study also identifies technological difficulties and insufficient access to computers as barriers. It also shows that teachers are concerned with the limited amount of time and with the perceived lower level of authority to enforce out-of-class study (60). Based on their findings, they suggest a blended learning environment to strengthen students' language-learning potential (60).

In her study of learners in fully online Chinese-language courses at a New Zealand university, Sun investigates the difficulties that the learners encounter and the strategies that they adapt to cope with these challenges (18). While her study confirms that "fully online learning is personalized, self-directed, and self-regulated, with paired or small-group activities" (34), it identifies six major difficulties that learners encounter: "(1) following the schedule and studying regularly, (2) getting ahold of classmates and finding suitable time to work together, (3) teaming up to work collaboratively, (4) ensuring constant engagement with the class, (5) keeping self-motivated and being a self-directed learner, and (6) socializing" (18). As Sun rightly points out, in the distance-education literature there has been a lack of distinction between blended and fully online teaching and learning, and insufficient attention has been paid to fully online teaching and learning (20). This is especially true in the area of fully online language education. This chapter intends to shed light on understanding learners' experiences with and perceptions of fully online language learning. The following sections will introduce the online course and then examine students' experiences with and perceptions of the course.

Course Overview

The online course was intended for twenty-six weeks, during which students would earn six credits. The course was developed in Moodle, one of the most commonly used learning platforms or course management systems (CMS). As shown in figure 18.1 below, which depicts the first page of the course website, the course materials were organized into nine sections, with one introduction and eight subsections. The introductory section includes a promotional video and an introductory video about the course (see table 18.1 for the URLs), as well as the course syllabus. The grading components of the course consisted of two written tests (45%), two oral tests (23%), weekly practice quizzes (0.5% * sixteen times), two regular quizzes (8%), weekly recordings (8%), and weekly virtual meeting participation (10%).

Figure 18.2 shows the materials for Weeks 1 to 3. A typical week's material (as exemplified in Week 3) consisted of icons embedded with links to online lecture clips, animation clips, a practice quiz, and a resource folder. For lecture clips, we provided three separate videos on new vocabulary items, grammar points, and conversation practices, respectively. Students could practice three to four animation videos per week, each of which presented one conversation that was also introduced in the conversation lecture clip. The lectures and animation clips were posted on YouTube and students had access to their links via our Moodle website, as recommended by IT specialists. In this way, clips are loaded quickly and without lag time on student devices (e.g., laptop, smartphone, etc.). All of the files – conversation audio recordings, lecture PowerPoint slides, and a transcript of the lecture videos for each week – were provided in the resource folder.

Moodle provides for the creation of quiz functions, a capability we employed in our quizzes and tests. For practice quizzes, each set consisted of thirty to forty individual questions on average in the format of matching, cloze, drag and drop, short answer, and embedded questions. Students were given

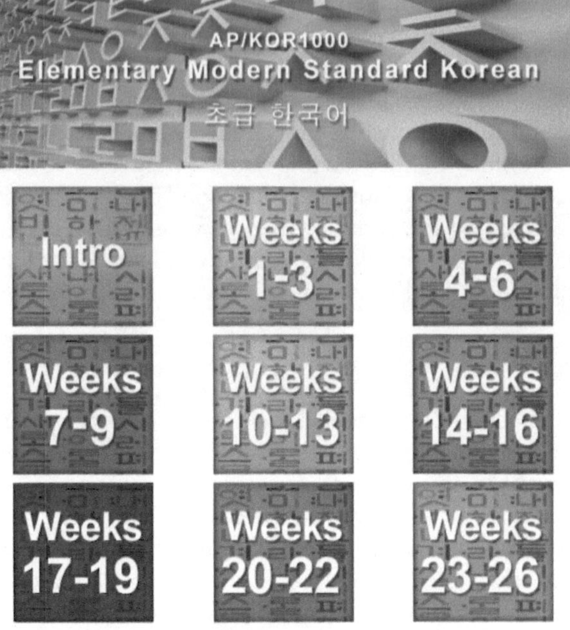

Figure 18.1. First page of the course website

approximately ninety minutes to complete a quiz and were allowed two more attempts to take the same quiz. Students were able to see which questions they did not answer correctly so that they could achieve a better mark on their next attempt. Then the highest scores achieved among the attempts were counted towards the final grade. After the quiz deadline, students could see the correct answers to all the questions.

There were two regular quizzes and two tests. For the weekly virtual meeting, the web conferencing software Adobe Connect enabled synchronous computer-mediated communication (CMD). The weekly virtual meeting was incorporated for the first time in summer 2018, in order to meet student demand for more synchronous interactions with the instructor as well as with peer students. The instructor and students logged in at a pre-determined time every week to go over the course materials and to have a Q and A session.

Both parties could see and hear each other, while the instructor ended up speaking more than the students. Adobe Connect was used also for the two oral tests, during which PowerPoint slides with picture cues were shared with the students.

Figure 18.2. Weeks 1–3 page

Student Evaluation and Response

The following section reports the survey and interview results with the students. Out of a total of forty-five students, thirty-three students completed the survey and forty students participated in the interview with the instructor at the end of the summer session in August 2018. Both the survey and the interview were conducted online. Table 18.1 summarizes the survey results.

Online Format in General

To the question about the overall satisfaction with the online format in general, close to 85 per cent of the students responded positively, 30 per cent extremely satisfied, 45 per cent very satisfied, and 9 per cent somewhat satisfied. Students' satisfaction with the online format in general came from the high level of flexibility, accessibility, and convenience that the online format offered. In terms of flexibility, students appreciated that they could study the course materials

Table 18.1. Student survey results

	Extremely dissatisfied	Very dissatisfied	Somewhat dissatisfied	Somewhat satisfied	Very satisfied	Extremely satisfied
Online format	0 (0%)	2 (6.06%)	3 (0.90%)	3 (0.90%)	15 (45.45%)	10 (30.30%)
Lectures	1 (3.03%)	1 (3.03%)	2 (6.06%)	3 (0.90%)	13 (39.39%)	13 (39.39%)
Animations	1 (3.03%)	0 (0%)	3 (0.90%)	6 (18.18%)	11 (33.33%)	12 (36.36%)
Virtual meetings	0 (0 %)	3 (0.90%)	0 (0%)	12 (36.36%)	9 (27.27 %)	9 (27.27%)
Recordings	1 (3.03%)	1 (3.03%)	2 (6.06%)	6 (18.18%)	11 (33.33%)	12 (36.36%)
Practice quizzes	1 (3.03%)	1 (3.03%)	2 (6.06%)	5 (15.15%)	10 (30.30%)	14 (42.42%)
Online tests	4 (12.12%)	1 (3.03%)	6 (18.18%)	7 (21.21%)	9 (27.27 %)	6 (18.18%)
Oral tests	1 (3.03%)	0 (0%)	2 (6.06%)	6 (18.18%)	13 (39.39%)	11 (33.33%)

at their own pace and schedule: "It allowed me to complete the course at my own pace;" "I am able to look at the resources whenever I have time before the next quiz/meeting;" and "I can do the schoolwork on my own schedule and I appreciate that the resources are always available to look over." Students also found that the online format made the course highly accessible. The high level of flexibility and accessibility made students perceive the course as convenient. A few students mentioned that they liked that they could access the online materials anywhere and review them repeatedly until they thoroughly understood the concepts. Some students highlighted that it was very convenient to take the course because they could do so at home instead of needing to travel to school. One student noted that the course was accessible even if she was travelling during the summer.

Online Lectures

The students' responses showed a high level of satisfaction with the online lectures: 39.39 per cent extremely satisfied, 39.39 per cent very satisfied, followed by 0.9 per cent somewhat satisfied. Only one student out of thirty-three rated very dissatisfied and extremely dissatisfied respectively. The interview data provided a more in-depth understanding regarding how students perceived the online lectures. Many students commented that the online lectures were very helpful and that these were well organized and easy to understand as the lectures "explained everything clearly."

A few students commented that they liked the lecture format in which an instructor simulated teaching a lesson to a student named Michael. A student indicated that, "[t]he conversation between the teacher and the student was relatable." Another student said, "I also liked the incorporation of the simulated student: "Michael's involvement, including his mistakes, jokes, etc., made learning a new language fun and less intimidating!" The format of the lecture recordings was overall well-accepted by the students, although one student reflected that sometimes Michael gave the answer too quickly – that is, before the student was able to think of it on her own. Two students emphasized that they liked the fact that the online lectures allowed them to repeat the lectures as needed: "I liked that I could watch the online lectures more than once to better understand all the lecture content;" and "The online lecture can repeat whenever you want, and it's better than in-class lecture." The following were suggested to improve the online lectures: 1) moving at a slower pace and 2) addressing common questions that students may have.

Online Animations

The online animations were well accepted by the students: 36.36 per cent extremely satisfied, 33.33 per cent very satisfied, and 18.18 per cent somewhat satisfied. The majority of students reported that the online animations were helpful in learning conversations and proper pronunciations, as well as for practicing speaking skills. One student reported that, "[t]he online animation was one of my favourite things about the course. They really helped me practice what I was learning and also helped me better my speaking and listening." Another student said that, "[o]nline animations were great for practising speaking Korean. It helped me to become more fluent orally as I did not have many other speaking partners to practise my Korean (other than my weekly submission partners). At first, I found that the animations went a little too fast at the beginning of the course, but this pace was more manageable once I improved my reading and speaking skills." On the other hand, one student expressed her dissatisfaction with the online animations: "There were no contexts whatsoever for every online animation, but just straight up dialogues. I eventually skipped watching [the] online animations." One section of each week's online lecture provided an explanation of the dialogues that were reintroduced in the online animation section. A better introduction of the course content would have helped this student to utilize the online animations in conjunction with the online lectures.

Weekly Virtual Meetings

The weekly virtual meetings were overall well accepted by the students. The majority of them expressed their satisfaction: 27.27 per cent extremely satisfied, 27.27 per cent very satisfied, and 36.36 per cent somewhat satisfied, while 9.09 per cent rated very dissatisfied. Many students reported that the weekly virtual meetings were helpful in that they provided a review of the content as well as provided a chance to "virtually" meet with the instructor and classmates and to ask the instructor questions. One student reported that these "virtual meetings were excellent reviews of weekly content. I also really enjoyed that we all had the ability to talk with the Professor in person and ask our questions directly. Meetings were very helpful as I could clarify any misunderstandings and obtain a more comprehensive understanding of the weekly content." Since the weekly virtual meetings required that all the participants log in at a preset time each week, however, some students faced a time conflict and therefore had to miss the actual meetings. Although they had a chance to play the recordings of the meetings, they did not have a chance for a synchronous communication with the instructor online. One student commented, "[i]t was difficult to attend and participate as the meeting times were on my workdays/times." Another student reported that there were some muted parts in some recorded meeting sessions. A student who had travelled abroad while taking the course said that he had difficulty in attending the sessions because of an unstable internet connection.

Weekly Recording Submissions

Many students found the weekly recording submissions helpful as they provided them with a chance to practise speaking in Korean with their partners, thereby motivating them to be on task each week. A student reflected that "[w]eekly recordings are helpful in getting the chance to speak Korean with your partner where otherwise there would not be much opportunity." Another student said that "[t]he recording submissions were fun, and I liked my partner, so it was helpful. Especially since saying the words out loud to someone else makes you realize your mistakes."

Out of all the activities for the online course, the weekly recordings relied on students' autonomy most: students as a pair had to determine when to meet virtually, to decide the content, and to make and submit the recordings. Lacking set class meeting times as well as a physical meeting place like a classroom, arranging a virtual meeting time could be challenging. The characteristics of the activity as a form of pair work also posed a special challenge those students whose partners were not cooperative. A student expressed her disappointment with the weekly recordings, as demonstrated in the following quote, "When my partner did not practise the conversation materials, this was wasted time and it ultimately did not help to improve my knowledge or speaking ability. My mark depended on the reliability of my other partners. It was very frustrating for me when a partner did not work hard." This issue of unequal participation and contribution has been reported as common problem of online collaboration in the literature (Sun, 32–3).

A few students reported that there were some technical challenges associated with meeting online, such as recording and submitting, which would not have been an issue in a face-to-face class. Such technical difficulties have been reported in previous research. For example, according to Jennings and Bronack, students could struggle with slower internet connections, unclear voices, and muffled microphones, which impede the effectiveness of online education (103–4).

Weekly Practice Quizzes

Weekly practice quizzes were also well accepted. Most students commented that taking the weekly practice quizzes helped them to test their knowledge and to prepare for the tests. A few students said they were motivated to watch the lectures and materials on time each week so that they would be ready to take the quiz. One student especially liked that she could retake the quiz up to two times. This helped her to better prepare for the tests, because after the first attempt she could find the right answers to missed questions. Another student also added, "I was glad that I got to review what I got wrong and was able to re-do them until I got a 70 percent or above."

While a few students expressed that they were satisfied with the quiz questions themselves in terms of the coverage and the level of difficulty, some students pointed out challenges that they had faced with the quiz content and form. One student found that a few quiz questions about vocabulary were not covered in the lectures. Another student suggested that more listening comprehension questions would be helpful. A student commented on the length of time allotted for their completion: "The practice quizzes were helpful, but I felt that at some weeks there were too many to complete in one week." The same student expressed difficulty with using the Korean keyboard. Three students commented that their answers with minor variations were graded as incorrect by the Moodle system. This issue stemmed from the fact that the Moodle quiz system can only recognize the pre-input answers as correct. The list of possible answers input by the developers could not cover all the possible alternative answers. After each quiz deadline, the students could view the correct answers and were encouraged to contact the instructor if any markings were in doubt. Even so, the students viewed this issue as a technical challenge.

Online Tests

Out of all the activity types, the online tests were rated with the lowest level of student satisfaction: 33.33 per cent rated from extremely to somewhat dissatisfied, while 66 per cent extremely to somewhat satisfied. Student responses to the online tests from the interview data were similar to those of the weekly practice quizzes in terms of the fact that the tests were helpful in learning the Korean language. For one student, the online tests worked well and helped her to assure her progress. However, many students found the online tests more difficult than the weekly quizzes: "I find that the tests were extremely difficult, especially the final test." One student pointed out that the online tests were frustrating, and the format was different from that of the quizzes: "It may be because of my lack of preparation even though I thought I was prepared. It might have to do with the fact that I was so used to the practice quiz format, that I assumed the tests would be similar in format." She also commented that she did not like that some questions were worth more than others. The student responses to the online tests were most divergent among the course activities depending on the individual students. For example, one student felt the test time was long enough, while another student reported it was not long enough. In addition, many students commented that the tests were difficult, while a student reported that the tests were primarily based on the lectures and quizzes and, thus, were not very difficult.

Online Oral Tests

Overall, student responses to the oral tests were positive. Most students commented that the oral tests helped them to improve their Korean in general and oral skills in particular: "I found the oral test to be really helpful in improving my oral skills. In practicing for this test, I greatly improved my speaking skills. Also, due to my preparation for the oral test, I felt like it also helped to improve my knowledge for the third test, which took place a week later." One student reflected that she liked the format and loved being able to talk to the instructor one-on-one, finding it engaging and relaxing. Two students reported some issues, however: the connection was not very smooth, and the volume of the instructor's voice was a little low. There were two students who pointed out the nerve-racking nature of the oral test itself, which is not specific to an online format: "The oral tests may not reflect the speaker's ability as they may get nervous and stutter or mess up" and "I prepared for the oral tests. But I was too nervous during the tests, so I didn't know if I completed them well."

Discussions

Although the course in general and the different activities in particular were well accepted by the students, the fully online format entailed its own challenges unique to that format. This section discusses the challenges that the students faced and ways to assist students to overcome them. The most commonly reported challenge was the low level of human interaction with the instructor and with classmates in comparison to a face-to-face format. The nature of the course made this challenge even harder to overcome, since learning a language involves human interaction, especially for developing oral skills.

Although students wanted to have more synchronous interactions, having such interactions caused difficulties in arranging virtual meeting times. This resulted in the absence of many students from the weekly virtual meetings, and in the difficulty of working with a partner for the weekly recording activity. The oral tests were mediated by synchronous computer communication (CMC) with the highest level of student participation, because of the nature of the tests. Students were also encouraged to set up a virtual office hour via Adobe Connect whenever they needed any assistance from the instructor, which would allow synchronous conversation. However, not many students requested such a meeting. Email correspondence was another way for students to interact with the instructor, although it was written and asynchronous.

Based on the student responses, the best way to encourage synchronous CMC that is practical in this particular online course setting is to increase the number of one-on-one virtual meeting times between the individual student and the instructor through Adobe Connect. This can be practiced through increasing the number of oral tests or through creating an activity that grants participation marks, although it would take up more time of both the instructor and the students. Another way is to better utilize the Adobe Connect meetings. Breakout rooms in Adobe Connect can be set up as platforms in which groups of students can interact with each other to practice the target language (see Chang in this volume for more information about Adobe Connect).

Tandem learning can be incorporated to encourage student interaction, which is a form of language exchange that allows learners from different countries to learn each other's language and culture in reciprocal cooperation (Blake, 27). This method first started in face-to-face contexts and has transformed into e-Tandem, where learners are linked via various forms of electronic communication (Cziko, 25), including CMC. For this context, native Korean-speaking learners of English can be paired up with native-English speaking learners of Korean via CMC (through utilizing e-Tandem websites such as verbling.com, lang-8.com, and language-exchanges.org).

The second most commonly reported issue was related to technical aspects, such as network problems (e.g., unstable and slow internet connection) and difficulty in recording and submitting weekly conversations. The former problem is beyond the control of the course participants, while the second issue can be improved through a more comprehensive discussion of the technical requirements for the course. It can be helpful to add a comprehensive technical help page, a FAQ (frequently asked question) section, and a Q and A forum dedicated to technical issues in the online course website. Of course, solid tech support and training within an educational institution must be available in case any class participant requires such support. More fundamentally, the infrastructure for online (and blended) education such as necessary software and hardware in both institutional and individual levels is the prerequisite for any successful online education.

More general issues surrounding online (and blended) education and potential solutions are worthy of further discussions here. Online education can be challenging for both teachers and students especially in the primary stages. On the teacher side, there is a need for technical training to become familiarized with numerous tech resources and online education tools and then to choose and utilize suitable ones for their class, which can result in a heavy workload. Furthermore, creating and managing a successful online learning community requires a lot of work from teachers. On the student side, it can be challenging to adapt to the online learning environment, as it requires more cognitive load. For example, the learning objectives may be neglected while students are occupied in using the tech devices. Especially when online education is not tailored to individual student needs, students can easily be distracted and lose motivation, which may be one of the most serious defects of online (and blended) learning.

AI (artificial intelligence)-powered education can provide tools to engage and motivate students by providing personalized language learning experience to each learner. Through big data processing and machine learning algorithms, AI tools not only provide instant feedback and assessment of progress, but also customize personalized learning materials (Pokrivcakova, 139). Some examples of AI tools include:

1. Machine translation: tools to translate a text from one natural language to another
2. AI writing assistants: tools to help writing process
3. Chatbots: computer programs to simulate intelligent human language interaction
4. Intelligent Tutoring Systems (ITS): computer-based learning systems designed to simulate one-to-one personal tutoring
5. Intelligent Virtual Reality (IVR): tools to create an authentic virtual reality and game-based learning environment. (Pokrivcakova, 140–4)

Conclusion

This chapter discussed a fully online language course as well as students' response to the course. Students have reported some advantages and disadvantages about the online format and each activity within the course. Students appreciated the flexibility and convenience of the online format, while expressing some dissatisfaction regarding the low level of (especially synchronous) interaction with the instructor and the classmates as well as some technical issues. Furthermore, the chapter suggested some potential ways to encourage more interaction through CMC and to help learners to deal with technical difficulties. The results of this study cannot be generalized to represent all language learners in fully online courses. Nevertheless, the study contributes to the understanding of student experience in and perception of fully online language learning. There is still a long way to go to improve the online language course to meet student needs and to tap into the full potential of the online format. Of course, this includes improving the course content itself, since an online format alone cannot provide a high-quality course.

WORKS CITED

Ayres, Robert. "Learner Attitudes towards the Use of CALL." *Computer Assisted Language Learning* 15 (2002): 241–9. doi:10.1076/call.15.3.241.8189.

Bates, Tony. "Summary of the 2018 Survey of Online Learning in Canadian Colleges and Universities." *Online Learning and Distance Education Resources*, The Canadian Digital Learning Research Association. 31 Mar. 2019. tonybates.ca/2018/12/20/summary-of-the-2018-survey-of-onlinelearning-in-canadian-colleges-and-universities/.

Blake, Robert J. "The Use of Technology for Second Language Distance Learning." *The Modern Language Journal* 93, no. 1 (2009): 822–35. https://doi.org/10.1111/j.1540-4781.2009.00975.x.

– "Current Trends in Online Language Learning." *Annual Review of Applied Linguistics* 31 (2011): 19–35. journals-scholarsportal-info.ezproxy.library.yorku.ca/details/02671905/v31inone/19_ctioll.xml.

Burkett, Rick W. "2018 Babson Report – Grade Increase: Tracking Distance Education in the United States." Virtual Chalkdust Considere Media Group. 16 Jan. 2018. virtualchalkdust.com/2018babson-report-grade-increase-tracking-distance-education-united-states/.

Cziko, Gary A. "Electronic Tandem Language Learning (eTandem): A Third Approach to Second Language Learning for the 21st Century." *CALICO Journal* 22, no. 1 (2004): 25–39. www-jstor-org.ezproxy.library.yorku.ca/stable/24149442.

Jahromi, Seyed Abolghassem Fatemi, and Farimah Salimi. "Exploring the Human Element of ComputerAssisted Language Learning: An Iranian Context." *Computer Assisted Language Learning* 26, no. 2 (2013): 158–76. dx.doi.org/10.1080/09588221.2011.643411.

Jennings, Morgan, and Stephen C. Bronack. "The Use of Desktop Video Conferencing as a Medium for Collaboration between Beginning Instructional Designers and Intern Teachers." *International Journal of Educational Telecommunications* 7, no. 2 (2001): 91–107.

Özçelik, Öner, and Anber Kennedy Kent. "Research-Informed Online Language Course Design and Development for Least Commonly Taught LTCLs: The Case of Introductory Dari, Pashto, and Uyghur." *Journal of the National Council of Less Commonly Taught Languages* 18, no. 1 (2016): 25–61. https://doi.org/10.10122/issn.1930-9031.2016.03.08.

Pokrivcakova, Silvia. "Preparing Teachers for the Application of AI-Powered Technologies in Foreign Language Education." *Journal of Language and Culture Education* 7, no. 3 (2019): 135–53. doi:10.2478/jolace-2019-0025.

Powell, Allison, and Michael Barbour. "Tracing International Differences in Online Learning Development: An Examination of Government Policies in New Zealand." *Journal of Open, Flexible and Distance Learning* 15, no. 1 (2011): 75–89.

Sun, Susan Y. H. "Learner Perspectives on Fully Online Language Learning." *Distance Education* 35, no. 1 (2016): 18–42. dx.doi.org/10.1080/01587919.2014.891428.

Tolosa, Constanza, et al. "Learning an Asian Language Online in the Context of Communities of Online Learning." *New Zealand Language Teacher* 43 (2017): 51–61. www.researchgate.net/publication/321574062_CoOL_or_not_CoOL_Learning_an_Asian_language_online_in_the_context_of_communities_of_online_learning.

Wang, Yuping, and Nian-Shing Chen. "Engendering Interaction, Collaboration, and Reflection in the Design of Online Learning Assessment in Language Learning: A Reflection from the Course Designers." In *Computer-assisted Foreign Language Teaching and Learning: Technological Advances*, edited by Bin Zou, et al., 16–38, Pennsylvania: IGI Global, 2013.

Wiebe, Grace, and Kaori Kabata. "Students' and Instructors' Attitudes Toward the Use of CALL in Foreign Language Teaching and Learning." *Computer Assisted Language Learning* 23, no. 3 (2010): 221–34. doi:10.1080/09588221.2010.486577.

19 Preparing Future Global Professionals: Technology-Enhanced Group PBL Pedagogy

MONICA BROIDO AND DANIEL PORTMAN

Introduction

Apprenticing for a profession is no longer limited to technical and academic skills but requires competencies in human relations as well (Mills and Treagust, 2) through successful communication and cooperation. Schools and universities not only need to impart knowledge but also provide their graduates with the "soft skill" building blocks of constructing and maintaining such fruitful human relations. Much work in the job market is dependent on these relations for team problem solving. However, traditional academic instruction methods, such as lectures, often do not provide the opportunities students need to practice team problem solving. Such real-life problem-based thinking often requires more than "an analytic exercise on paper" (Steinemann, 216); thus educators are faced with the challenge of how to effectively integrate the necessary skills for successful communication and cooperation into their classrooms. These entail "ways of knowing" and "ways of working," which are deemed crucial for success in academia, work, and life. Such "ways" are embodied within the framework of the 4Cs of 21st Century Education: creativity, communication, critical thinking, and collaboration (Binkley et al., 18).

Our Teaching Context

Since Israel is a small country, focused on global markets, these 4Cs are critical for successful work and collaboration with international colleagues. In fact, intercultural competence, which relies heavily on the 4Cs, has been deemed by major industry stakeholders as part and parcel of English-language proficiency in building and maintaining successful business relations (Broido and Portman, 61).

The Interdisciplinary Center Herzliya (IDC), Israel's only private university, embraces employability and capacity building as important pillars for their graduates. At IDC, we were charged with developing the Advanced 2 English for Economics EFL undergraduate course, which we did in conjunction with the dean of the School of Economics, who informed us of the English-language skills these students need to become top-notch economists.

PBL Pedagogy

We found Project and Problem-Based Learning (PBL) pedagogy helpful in ensuring that students acquire the necessary soft skills alongside their academic goals. Within PBL, projects enable students to work collaboratively and sharpen the problem-solving and teamworking skills needed for their future professional lives, where sustained enquiry "in a rigorous, extended process of asking questions, finding resources, and applying information" (Armstrong and Brunskill, 60) is critical. In this chapter, we will refer to this pedagogy as encompassing both Problem and Project-Based Learning (PBL). A PBL course results in a student-centred environment. As such, learning occurs in small groups where students take joint responsibility for the discovery and delivery (Smith, 95) of their products.

Creating effective PBL in the classroom is no easy task. Complex problem-solving projects often overwhelm students, and therefore require high-resolution planning of tasks that are carefully scaffolded so that students are challenged. However, the assignment should still be clear and attainable – along the lines of Vygotsky's Zone of Proximal Development (Tudge, 157). Moreover, working on such complex projects is especially challenging when English is not the student's first language. According to Kornwipa Poonpon, the advantages of PBL in an EFL context are that it focuses on content learning rather than on specific language patterns, so that language learning becomes more incidental and natural (2). In addition, PBL leads to authentic integration of language skills, critically processing of information from multiple sources, and bridging between the use of English in class and in real-life contexts.

To successfully engage in collaborative projects within PBL, the Google Suite is an ideal tool. It provides what Roschelle and Teasley have referred to as a joint problem space: "a space created and maintained through constant coordination and communication among collaborators and serves as a basis for collaborative action" (70). Among its many advantages, the Google Suite is free, easy to use (since most people are acquainted with Microsoft Word), does not require the installation of software, and is both platform and hardware agnostic. By using this online platform, all the information is up to date and available to all the members of the group. Hence, if a group member is absent from class, they can contribute to the work remotely.

The Advanced 2 English for Economics Course

To build the Advanced 2 English for Economics course, we drew on the 4C benchmarks outlined in the "P21 Framework Definitions" ("P21," 2). P21 includes the 4Cs as well as two other skills: 1) information, media, and technology skills and 2) life and career skills. Keeping in mind that this is an exit-level semiprofessional course, we believe that the information, media, and technology skills are crucial in developing critical thinking in an academic context. In addition, as students are apprenticed towards becoming professionals, life and career skills are equally important for developing collaborative practices.

Advanced 2 English for Economics is taught as a PBL course. It consists of a series of progressive small group projects in applied economics, each integrating the aspects worked on in previous assignments. These small projects consist of pair or group activities that not only instruct students about economic issues, but also teach a skill required in the field. Examples of such activities include writing reports and making presentations to stakeholders. This approach ensures that students acquire the knowledge and skills they need to tackle the final integrative project to transfer such knowledge and skills into their future professional lives. Below are descriptions of the projects and the 4C benchmarks involved to successfully complete each project. Note that once a benchmark is mentioned, it should be assumed that it is needed for the subsequent projects.

Mini-Project 1: Would I Invest in [Country] Based on Its Economic Indicators?

Pairs of students are asked to decide if they would invest in a designated country. Their decision is based on macroeconomic indicators, such as gross domestic product and inflation rate. After learning about various indicators, students access indicator data from different sites such as trendingeconomics.com. They are then instructed to analyse the data and create a graph that best represents such data. Following their analysis, each pair presents a substantiated investment recommendation to their classmates.

Mini-Project 2: Would I Invest in [Country] Based on Its Investment Incentives?

In pairs, students must select another country in which to invest. This time, their decision must be based on investment incentives offered by the country, such as tax breaks. Students are informed where they can find tax incentive information, such as websites of governmental finance ministries or major consulting firms. They are asked to then identify five incentives each country offers and summarize the incentives in a table. Based on this information, pairs are asked to write a short summary explaining the logic behind their investment decision.

In these first two mini-projects, teams begin practicing collaboration, which are the life and career skills necessary for successful cooperation. As they are given a task to complete as a group, they implement the following initiative and self-direction 4C benchmarks: "utilize time and manage workload efficiently" and "monitor, define, prioritize and complete tasks without direct oversight" ("P21," 6). In turn, the instructor monitors their work and provides scaffolding and feedback when needed, prompting them to practice the life skills of flexibility and adaptability by "incorporat[ing] feedback effectively" ("P21," 6). Other important skills practised are "assum[ing] shared responsibility for collaborative work and valu[ing] individual contributions" ("P21," 4–5), while working together creatively in order to "develop, implement and communicate new ideas to others effectively" ("P21," 3). Such collaboration applies both during group work and when the group presents their recommendation to the rest of the class. Such work includes the communication benchmark of "articulat[ing] thoughts and ideas effectively using oral, written and nonverbal communication skills in a variety of forms and contexts" ("P21," 4–5).

In order to optimally reach these benchmarks, students employ critical thinking, as they "use technology…to research, organize, evaluate and communicate information" ("P21," 5). This applies to the websites they locate and research, as well as their shared Google Doc. In the shared Google Doc, students record information, and in Google Slides, they prepare presentations. Working in this manner, students collaboratively collect, share, mediate, translate, write, and maintain updated information available to all team members.

Mini-Project 3: How Easy Is It to Start a Small- or Medium-Sized Business in Israel?

In pairs, students are asked to learn and present an indicator from the current year's World Bank *Doing Business in Israel* report[1]. This report covers eleven indicators of the ease of doing business in Israel, such as registering property. Each pair reads the indicator's definition, how it was calculated, and the specific data about Israel in the report. Students are instructed to decide why specific indicators are important for measuring the ease of doing business in any country. As part of their final stage, each pair presents one out of eleven indicators to the entire class. Through such presentations, the class learns about all eleven indicators in preparation for their final project, described in the next section.

This mini-project includes the following 4C productivity and accountability benchmark: "demonstrate … attributes associated with producing high quality products [such as]:" "multi-task," "participate actively," "collaborate and cooperate effectively in teams," and "be accountable for results" ("P21," 7). Accordingly, teams must work in a manner that produces an accurate explanation of their assigned *Doing Business* indicator, so that their classmates eventually select and utilize appropriate indicators for their own final project.

Final Project: Should I Open My New Business in [Country] or [Another Country]?

Groups of three to four students are given the following realistic scenario: "You are economic consultants who have been hired by an Israeli firm in an industry [which the group chooses] to check the feasibility of commencing operations in two countries covered in the World Bank reports. You must analyze both countries and then recommend one." This major project requires the knowledge and capacities acquired through the progressive mini-projects completed during the semester. It presents students with a much more complex problem, where a wider range of different data is gathered and analysed from multiple sources. Following such analysis, the data is then synthesized so that a clear recommendation can be made.

The sources for this project include economic indicators, *Doing Business* reports, investment incentives, trade agreements with Israel, successful businesses in the same sector, and non-economic information such as regulations. Students are instructed to write a referenced 1,000-word report and present their findings to their classmates who are asked to play the part of industry stakeholders. Effective planning is crucial for this project. Different leaders tend to emerge, bringing into play the collaborative life skills benchmark of leadership and responsibility in "leverag[ing] strengths of others to accomplish a common goal" ("P21," 7).

As a project without any clear answers, different students grapple with various data, thus implementing the critical ICT literacy practice of "manag[ing] the flow of information from a variety of sources" and "evaluat[ing] information critically and competently" ("P21," 5). Critical thinking skills are required to make sense of the data and then "synthesiz[e] and mak[e] connections between information and arguments." Students are also asked to "identify and ask significant questions that clarify various points of view and lead to better solutions" ("P21," 4). To make a final recommendation, students must eventually arrive at a consensus by critically interpreting their data. This requires students to draw on the collaborative life and career skills of initiative and self-direction, so as to "respond open-mindedly to different ideas" ("P21," 6). Finally, given the many different sources of information obtained, students are responsible for properly documenting and acknowledging all of the different sources. They must document their data through the APA citation method, thus "applying a fundamental understanding of the ethical/legal issues surrounding the access and use of media" ("P21," 5).

While we have focused on the practice of the 4Cs from the students' point-of-view, Utecht proposes a fifth C: control. This allows instructors to facilitate the learning process through a highly scaffolded structure and a developed support system.

Google Docs for the Teacher: Implementing the 5th C

Though the benefits of PBL in supporting the acquisition and practice of the 4Cs are many, the management and monitoring of such projects can be quite challenging. Instructors need to present the problem or project, monitor each group's progress, guide students through difficult concepts, and troubleshoot when they encounter a dead-end in their research. In previous years, when integrating PBL projects into courses at our institution, a number of issues arose.

One surprising problem was that at times, groups containing strong students would receive lower than expected grades. Analysing our behaviour in class, we noticed that we often gave more time and attention to the weaker groups than to the groups that seemed to have things "under control." This resulted in the stronger groups sometimes misunderstanding certain issues or losing their way in the key parts of the project. Another problem we noted was the differential rate of advancement, as some groups took longer to complete certain parts of the project. They either had rushed, catching up at the end, or did not include everything the project required. In addition, students often found it difficult to approach long and complex projects while coordinating their group work efficiently and in a timely manner.

It became clear that we needed to find a way for instructors to scaffold the groups in an efficient and effective manner. We also had to find a method that would help students organize their work effectively and assist each other. Hence, a robust platform for teacher management was required. As collaborators on numerous projects of our own, we knew that Google Docs is an excellent tool for working synchronously with colleagues. Therefore, our solution came in the form of a whole-class Google Doc managed by the teacher. This one Google Doc includes a table with the team participants in one column, and session "deliverables" in the other column, thus helping students work through smaller sections. In each class session, new deliverables were added. At the end of the process, a record of all the research each group had done became clearly available to everyone in one place.

This table made it easy for students to consolidate all their research in one place. Before implementing this change, groups had divided the work among the different members, and they had each worked on a different document. This made it difficult for students to keep track of every member's work. Instead, this single class document enabled groups to learn from each other, as students were encouraged to look at other groups' work for guidance. With this new method, instructors are able to showcase examples of other groups' successful work. Equally important, we noticed that this system leads to class-wide collaboration, as it often encourages students to help other groups.

In addition, a single document enables instructors to see students' work and ongoing changes in real time. This grants instructors an ideal platform for formative feedback, providing a "bird's-eye view" of the entire process. Aside from walking around the classroom and engaging with the students face-to-face, with Google Docs, instructors are provided immediate access to all the work being created, so they can best direct their efforts in aiding groups, either in their research or in their writing.

Conclusions and Recommendations

Given our experience developing and teaching the Advanced 2 English for Economics course for future economists, we recommend that such professionally oriented EFL courses include group PBL enquiry projects as a way of developing the 4Cs. In agreement with Smith and others, this type of pedagogy of engagement serves to raise the level of academic challenge (91). This approach encourages achievement by setting high expectations and emphasizing the importance of student effort. Through PBL enquiry projects, students not only become intensely involved in their educational process, but they also apply the knowledge acquired throughout the course through producing text types similar to those they will encounter as economists. Equally important, PBL enquiry enhances the quality of student-teacher interaction. With this type of learning environment, students are able to learn from their instructors on a one-on-one basis (Smith et al., 92), especially important in an EFL context. Projects that simulate real-life tasks in a given discipline increase authentic language production. These provide vast opportunities for students' incidental learning and relevant connections to the material, while strengthening their English-language skills for their future professional lives.

The use of Google Docs in our courses has also contributed to streamlining and simplifying the groups' work processes. This platform helped reveal that the seemingly overwhelming complex demands of the project were not necessarily cognitive in nature but technical. With the introduction of Google Docs, the project became scalable and enjoyable. We also noted that after the adoption of a Google platform, the quality of the projects rose considerably when compared to previous years. We attribute this to the shared table and closer monitoring. With the shared table, there were clear daily deliverables, hence, there was less misunderstanding of the tasks. The shared document also allowed instructors to devote more time to all groups and have fruitful conversations with the students. It also helped students shift their focus to effective research and writing and away from mechanics. Students were able to show a greater ability to critically and creatively solve problems, while effectively express well-thought-out solutions. On the whole, Google Docs facilitated group-work practices by providing students with an efficient way to streamline their work, which is often adopted in future content-area coursework (Broido and Rubin, 712). It also provided a vehicle for more teacher control and involvement (the 5th C).

Preparing future economists to communicate in today's global environment entails proficiency in English, in conjunction with the 4Cs: creativity, communication, critical thinking, and collaboration (Binkley et al., 18). As argued throughout this chapter, a PBL pedagogy, supported by appropriate technology, provides a meaningful framework that can be used to develop students' disciplinary knowledge and professional skills.

NOTE

1 This report may be retrieved through the following website: www.worldbank.org/content/dam/doingBusiness/country/i/israel/ISR.pdf.

WORKS CITED

Binkley, Marilyn, et al. "Defining Twenty-First Century Skills." In *Assessment and Teaching of 21st Century Skills*, edited by Esther Care, Patrick Griffin, and Mark Wilson, 17–66. Springer: Dordrecht, 2012.

Broido, Monica, and Daniel Portman. "Building Bridges, Creating Competencies: ESP Capacity Building for the Israeli Information Technology Industry." *The Asian ESP Journal* 35 (2017). https://doi.org/10.1177/0092070305281619.

Broido, Monica, and Harriet Rubin. "Problem-Based Learning: Managing Complex Projects Simply." INTED 2017 Proceedings, 2017, 771–7. doi:10.21125/inted.2017.

Castro, Carolina V. "A First and Basic Approach to the PBL in the English Class." Grupo de Trabajo. Lulu.com. 2016.

Mills, Julie E., and David F. Treagust. "Engineering Education – Is Problem-Based or Project-Based Learning the Answer?" *Australasian Journal of Engineering Education* 3, no. 2 (2003): 2–16. www.battelleforkids.org/networks/p21.

P21 Partnership for 21st Century Learning. "P21 Learning Framework Definitions." 2015. static.battelleforkids.org/documents/p21/P21_Framework_DefinitionsBFK.pdf.

Poonpon, Kornwipa. "Enhancing English Skills through Project-based Learning." *The English Teacher* 10 (2017): 1–10.

Roschelle, Jeremy, and Stephanie D. Teasley. "The Construction of Shared Knowledge in Collaborative Problem Solving." In *Computer Supported Collaborative Learning*, edited by Claire O'Malley, 69–97. Berlin: Springer, 1995.

Smith, Karl A., et al. "Pedagogies of Engagement: Classroom-Based Practices." *Journal of Engineering Education* 94, no. 1 (2005): 87–101.

Steinemann, Anne. "Implementing Sustainable Development through Problem-Based Learning: Pedagogy and Practice." *Journal of Professional Issues in Engineering Education and Practice* 129, no. 4 (2003): 216–24. doi.org/10.1061/(ASCE)1052-3928(2003)129:4(216).

Tudge, Jonathan. *Vygotsky, the Zone of Proximal Development, and Peer Collaboration: Implications for Classroom Practice*. Cambridge: Cambridge University Press, 2019.

Utecht, Jeff. "The 4 Cs of Learning." *The Thinking Stick*. 10 January, 2016. www.thethinkingstick.com/the-4-cs-of-learning/.

20 A Guide to Synchronous Online Language Teaching

SEUNG-EUN CHANG

Introduction

Regardless of our preferences and choices, society is closely entwined with the online world, and the field of education is no exception. Given that language is a primary and essential tool to render the online world meaningful, language education and the online environment are inextricably linked. This chapter aims to maximize the benefits of synchronous online language education, emphasizing the special characteristics and challenges of online teaching rather than debating which format (online or traditional education setting) is more desirable. Also, rather than addressing issues of theoretical knowledge or their implications, the chapter provides practical issues and skills pertaining to the virtual classroom while touching on some controversial topics related to synchronous online teaching.

Given that students' expectations and perceptions towards online classes differ from those of the traditional classroom (Platt et al.), new teaching approaches and skills are expected for online language teachers (Hampel and Stickler). Hampel and Stickler (317) promote a seven-level pyramid of expected skills for online language teachers: 1) basic information and communications technology (ICT) competence, 2) specific technical competence, 3) awareness of constraints and possibilities, 4) online socialization, 5) facilitation of communicative competence, 6) creativity and choice, and 7) development of their own style (317). Providing room to create higher-level skills for each teacher with his or her own experience and expertise, this chapter is focused on the specific skills needed for teachers who have just stepped into the field of online or blended classes. Language teachers who are accustomed to a traditional classroom environment might feel out of place in a virtual classroom. This feeling of frustration can shift to confidence as teachers come to accept the special affordance of virtual settings and make a total transition in their mindset from a traditional classroom to an online setting.

To help guide this process, this chapter first introduces the basic features of online classroom settings that are available in most online class software applications. The following section offers basic, introductory guidance on online language teaching, including hands-on strategies in a synchronous virtual classroom. Specifically, it discusses how best to equip and orchestrate multimodal tools effectively, inclusive of breakout rooms, PowerPoint (PPT), video file sharing, and chat boxes. A detailed description and illustration will be provided through the application of Adobe Connect, one of several easily accessible software programs used within academic institutions. The chapter also addresses the benefits, challenges, and other relevant issues related to virtual classrooms, while providing examples and suggestions for how best to cope with them.

Basic Features of the Virtual Classroom

The basic layout of the Adobe Connect screen is illustrated in figure 20.1, and more features in the file uploading process are shown in figure 20.2. It offers a couple of options, and the layout can be changed according to the focus of the class. The online classroom involves basic features such as a microphone, camera, chat room, participants' list, participants' videos, opinion indicators (icons), the main screen, and breakout rooms. While most of these features can be used by simply clicking the button, and the manual for each tool is available online, this section will address some practical usage issues not mentioned in the manuals but potentially necessary for effective and smooth instruction. The practical issues related to these features are summarized as follows.

1. Fonts: Check which fonts are available in your language application. If the fonts that you used in your document are not available in the application, the PPT format will be distorted in presentation mode because each font has a slightly different size, and thus different fonts will cause size differences within each slide. Please ensure that you use a supported font when you prepare a document.
2. PDF file: In light of the font issue described above, I have used the PDF file format to keep my original fonts and sizes. However, PDF files are not smoothly implemented, and whenever I used the "arrow" or "draw" functions on the PDF screen, the letters and pictures in the PDF were not stable and started lagging. Please make sure to use PPT files, not PDF.
3. Video embedded in PPT: Videos embedded in a PPT file do not work in this application. Video files need to be prepared in a separate manner, and the most efficient way is to use the Pods feature, which is described in Section 2 below.

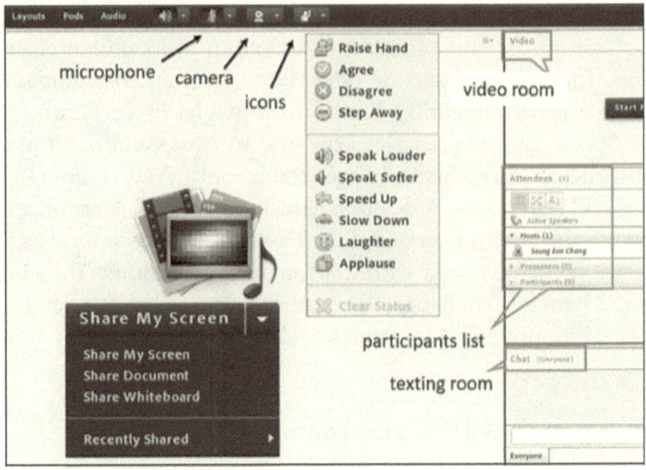

Figure 20.1. File uploading process

4. File size limit: If the size of the document file (e.g., PPT) is too large, it cannot be embedded in the application.
5. PPT running: The Adobe Connect (and most other online class platforms) screen does not show the next PPT slide in advance. In order to keep track of which slide comes next and ensure a smooth transition to the next one, I usually open the summary of all PPT slides on another computer or on a paper copy to track all PPT flows in one glance.
6. Additional file upload using Pods: Related to file uploading, the Pods feature is very useful and efficient. If you like using videos during class, you do not have to remove the current PPT file on the main screen and upload the video file, and then upload the original PPT file again to return to the main file. You can keep your original PPT file that is already open in a main screen and click the "Pods" button on top of the basic features in the application. You have several options, then, to choose from additional screens. I usually use two features among others for the video screening and announcement.
   a) Video: Click "Share" and "Add New Share" from the "Pods" menu. Then you can upload any relevant video file before the class begins and hide it, so only the main teaching material is shown at the beginning of class in the main room. When you need to show the video, you can go to "Pods" and select the file that you previously created. Then you can keep your original PPT file as it is and add as many additional video files as you need. After you show the video, you can hide it again, and then it will disappear from the main screen.

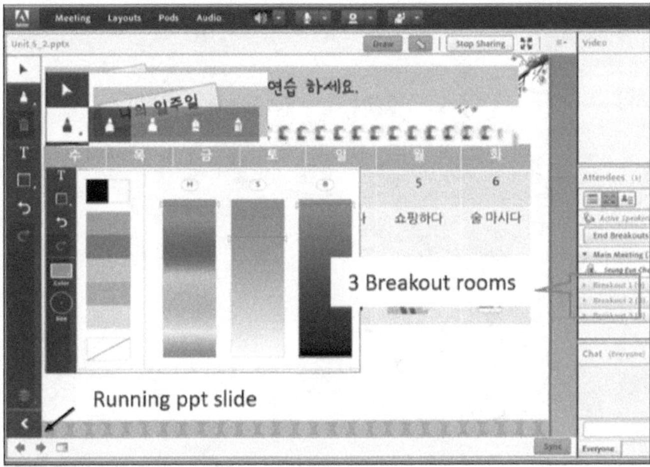

Figure 20.2. More features on uploading files in a virtual classroom

b) Announcement: Likewise, you can add "Notes" from the "Pods" options whenever you have an important announcement for the students. A sample announcement using the "Notes" feature is given in figure 20.3. As in figure 20.3, you can create the notes over the main PPT material, and you can hide it when class begins.

7. Restriction on file type: There is a restriction for video and audio file types, and you need to check what kinds of file types are available in your application. Currently only mp4 and mp3 formats are available in this application.

A number of effective strategies in language teaching and learning have been developed related to group projects or group activities that successfully grab students' attention and interest and inspire a more dynamic and exciting classroom environment (Jacobs et al.; Johnson et al.). At the same time, the effect of individually tailored language teaching has also been proposed, and no teacher can doubt its positive impact on learners despite the practical difficulties to implement it (Keefe and Jenkins; Smith and Throne). If teachers like to combine and practice these two ideal models of educational concepts in class, a synchronous virtual language classroom will help create an effective environment.

This practice is available in the virtual classroom using the "Breakout Room" feature, which is available in most online course applications (with slightly different names according to the application), including Adobe Connect and Blackboard. The "breakout room" is one of the most significant functions in the synchronous online language class and is illustrated in figure 20.2. By using this

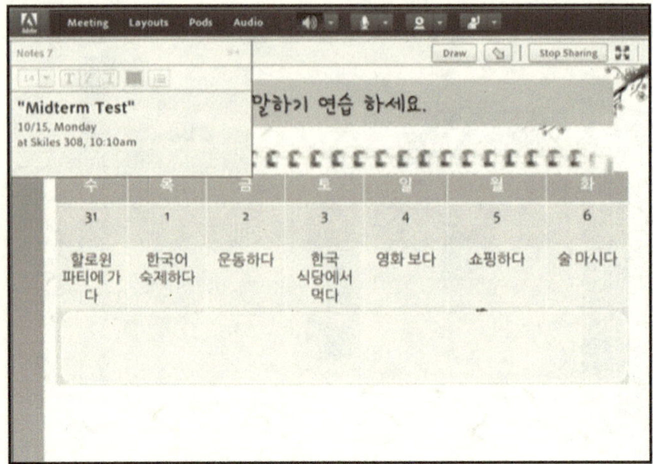

Figure 20.3. Use of "note" feature

feature, teachers can enable students in small groups of two or three to practice speaking together or perform relevant pair work in each breakout room. Teachers can shuffle the members in each room, manage the number of breakout rooms, and set the number of participants. This exercise is useful for interactions not only among students, but also between students and the teacher. By entering each room, teachers can observe students' interactions, get involved in their activities, or communicate with each student via a more personal, individualized, and unmediated mode with a specific topic or issue for each student.

Personalized interaction: Teachers create pairs or groups of students according to their proficiency level, interests, goals, or needs and prepare individually tailored material in each room if necessary. Teachers can manage the number of assignments (e.g., fewer assignments for the rooms of students who usually need more time to complete them), level of difficulty, and different skills (speaking, writing, reading, or listening) or topics of interest, depending on the students. Students are typically more motivated by receiving a personalized atmosphere and set of assignments. In addition, to amplify the individualized character of the online classroom, one-on-one activities with a teacher, such as one-on-one oral quizzes or one-on-one speaking practice, can provide a great opportunity for students to improve their oral and aural competency. One-on-one oral activities with teacher are challenging in a traditional class setting but are fairly manageable and flexible in the online format through the use of webcams, and thus frequent oral activities or quizzes might offer great convenience both for teachers and students.

Student-driven interaction: Students cannot afford to be distracted or laid back in a breakout room, as there are only a few people (usually two or three) or students alone with a teacher. Limited time is spent watching other students' performance, but every student is nevertheless expected to be actively involved in every activity. Especially in a breakout room, students are expected to operate the tools for themselves by managing the PPT slides and audio function as needed. Students are not just receivers or lone participants within the virtual classroom but are active leaders.

Issues in practice: One thing to note is that the breakout room feature is a totally separate space from the main screen room. This means that you need to upload the relevant teaching material in each room separately, because the file in the main room is not transferred to the breakout room. For example, if you have three breakout rooms, then you need to upload the file three times, that is, one for each room. I usually make separate PPT files for the breakout room, which includes only pair work materials such as speaking practice, pair activities, or games apart from the main teaching materials. I establish the rooms prior to when the class begins and upload the files in each room; this way students can see the file as soon as they enter the breakout room, with no waiting time for the file upload.

Dynamics in Silence

It is important to render the virtual classroom appropriate for communication, and the audio quality plays a key role in effective communication. Even with little noise or feedback, participants are easily distracted and disturbed. While active and cheerful conversations and interactions are usually encouraged in a traditional classroom, audio control is necessary in a virtual classroom, but this does not mean that the class is inert or passive. Instead, it creates a more focused classroom atmosphere, and students can still participate in class actively and effectively during application tools lacking audio. Here are some tips for well-controlled and organized audio quality in an online classroom.

Audio control: To avoid audio distortion and feedback, ensure that the following conditions are met.

- Students turn off their microphone unless they are told to turn it on. If all students turn on their microphone, it can cause excessive levels of noise and feedback. Students can express their need to speak using the opinion icons, such as "raise hand," "agree," or "disagree," illustrated in figure 20.1. These features are discussed in greater detail in below.
- All participants use a USB headset. This is required equipment. If even one student does not use the appropriate headset, it causes echoing and noise throughout the entire virtual room.

- There is only one Adobe Connect window open on your computer. If you open (i.e., log into) more than two Adobe Connect windows on the same computer, it will cause an echoing or howling sound.

Icons: Whenever students have any questions or comments, students are encouraged to use the "Icons" tool. Most applications have opinion icons such as "raise hand," "yes," "no," "agree," "disagree," "laugh," "applause," and "slow down." This icon feature is used to express students' opinions or situations, but it is also used as the designated symbol for questions or activities. Without the aid of a webcam video, audio, or touch-screen technology, students can still answer your questions, and teachers can simply check students' answers by using this icon feature. Any kind of two-option activities or games can be conducted using the "agree" and "disagree" features in the opinion icons,; for example, true or false, (1) or (2), O or X, and so on. You can designate the "agree" symbol for true answers, (1) or O, and "disagree" for false answers, (2) or X, and have students answer the game or activities with these two opinion icon symbols. For example, you can present some listening questions after showing a drama clip. If the question is correct based on the drama, students are expected to click the "agree" symbol while listening to your question. Both teacher and students can check all other students' answers at the same time. This kind of activity helps students to be alert and attentive during class lessons and activities.

Chat box: Text messaging is another useful tool, especially when participants have a quick note or audio problems that arise. Typing practice in a target language is also accommodated with this tool.

Concentration and Salience with No Face

Most people agree that interactions are livelier when communicating face-to-face, and educational researchers have also found great positive value with using webcams in online classroom settings, such as the feeling of co-presence, the socio-affective aspect (Manstead et al.), or psychological closeness between interlocutors (Cunningham). However, researchers also observe that not all participants feel comfortable with this approach, and some learners feel considerable personal discomfort when using a webcam (Burger; Telles). Several extant works in the literature also discuss the additional cognitive demands on teachers and students when the webcam is turned on, because they should be aware of their webcam image and ensure that they can see each other well during the class (Develotte et al.). These emotional and cognitive weights easily distract the participants and prevent them from paying full attention to the lesson itself. Also, while the socio-affective function of using a webcam has been well recognized, the pedagogical benefits of using a webcam in a virtual classroom have not been investigated in depth, and therefore remain unanswered. A recent study, which involved twenty experienced online language teachers and twenty adult learners who were interviewed about their attitudes towards webcams, reported that most teachers and students only used webcams at the beginning of their lessons for socio-affective reasons and stopped using webcams after the first two to three weeks (Kozar).

My own personal experience concurs with the literature regarding the negative effects of using webcams, and there are other ways to confirm the co-presence and command of students' attention without entirely relying on the webcam. Practical benefits with no webcams are suggested from the perspective of both teachers and students in the following section.

Creating professional practice for the teacher's side: Teachers are conducting multimodal tasks in a virtual classroom. These include drawing, erasing, making arrows, managing PPT slides and breakout rooms, checking students' opinion icons and chat boxes, as well as providing the oral instructions of the lesson at the same time. All of these performances and busy movements of teachers are displayed in a more exaggerated fashion through face-focused video webcam rather than in a traditional classroom. The class instruction could be delivered in a more professional, smooth, or even graceful way with no webcam showing the inner mechanics of the class. Instead, teachers can devote more effort and attention to their teaching materials and voice teaching as they are more salient without a face webcam.

Creating a concentrated environment for the students' side: For the same reason exemplified above, students can be easily distracted by the teacher's busy work and movement through the video. Students can focus more on the teaching material on the main screen room and on the teachers' voice when only these two modes are presented to them, compared to the case in which three different modes (i.e., webcam, teaching materials, and voice) are presented at the same time in a virtual classroom. Also, teaching material in a main room appears to be more salient alone than when another visual mode is turned on. Even without webcams, teachers can attract and retain students' full attention by frequently calling upon individuals for the questions or activities.

Reducing pressure for both sides: Both students and teachers can pay more attention to the lesson itself and fully enjoy the flexibility of online classes with no visual images through webcam and with no additional pressure (Develotte et al.).

Conclusion

This chapter provided both basic and practical suggestions and guidelines for online classes to create effective and professional synchronous online language courses in a skillful manner. The samples and examples are offered to demonstrate how synchronous online language courses can be dynamic and effective in a more focused and individualized way through the unique attributes of a virtual classroom. This chapter also briefly addressed some issues such as the use of a webcam and the practice of personalized and student-driven learning. These topics present ongoing controversy, and each topic deserves further attention and consideration depending on the teacher's own experience and approach. Teachers can also build up their own style and creativity to integrate their teaching expertise and philosophy successfully into their online teaching (Hampel and Stickler), based on the introductory competences exemplified in this chapter.

WORKS CITED

Burger, William. *Exploring the Complex Computer-mediated Communication Needs of Learners in a Multilingual, Multicultural Online Learning Environment*. Raleigh, NC: North Carolina State University, 2013.

Cunningham, Jennifer. *Students' Perception of Experience in an Online Classroom using Videoconferencing*. Minneapolis, MN: Capella University, 2009.

Develotte, Christine, Nicholas Guichon, and Caroline Vincent. "The Use of the Webcam for Teaching a Foreign Language in a Desktop Videoconferencing Environment." *ReCALL* 22, no. 3 (2010): 293–312.

Hampel, Regine, and Ursula Stickler. "New Skills for New Classrooms: Training Tutors to Teach Languages Online." *Computer Assisted Language Learning* 18, no. 4 (2005): 311–26. https://doi.org/10.1080/09588220500335455.

Jacobs, George, et al. *The Teacher's Sourcebook for Cooperative Learning*. Thousand Oaks, CA: Corwin Press, 2002.

Johnson, David, et al. *Circles of Learning: Cooperation in the Classroom*, 5th ed. Edina, MN: Interaction Book, 2002.

Keefe, James, and John Jenkins. *Personalised Instruction: The Key to Student Achievement*, 2nd ed. Lanham: Rowman and Littlefield Education, 2008.

Kozar, Olga. "Perceptions of Webcam Use by Experienced Online Teachers and Learners: A Seeming Disconnect between Research and Practice." *Computer Assisted Language Learning* 29, no. 4 (2016): 779–89. https://doi.org/10.1080/09588221.2015.1061021.

Manstead, Antony, et al. "Facing the Future: Emotion Communication and the Presence of Others in the Age of Video-mediated Communication." In *Face-to-Face Communication over the Internet: Issues, Research, Challenges*, edited by Arvid Kappas and Nicole C. Krämer, 144–75. Cambridge: Cambridge University Press, 2011.

Platt, Carrie Anne, et al. "Virtually the Same?: Student Perceptions of the Equivalence of Online Classes to Face-to-Face Classes." *Journal of Online Learning & Teaching* 10, no. 3 (2014): 489–503.

Smith, Grace, and Stephanie Throne. *Differentiating Instruction with Technology in Middle School Classrooms*. Eugene, OR: International Society for Technology in Education, 2009.

Telles, Joao. "Do We Really Need a Webcam? The Uses that Foreign Language Students Make Out of Webcam Images during Teletandem Sessions." *Letras & Letras* 25, no. 2 (2010): 65–79.

Conclusion: The Future of Teaching and Learning Language in a Complex Global Setting

The twenty chapters included in this volume are diverse in linguistic and cultural terms, yet manifest similar threads in focus. These approaches aim to create dynamic spaces for in-class discussions of decolonization, critical thinking, and socio-political consciousness to foster language learning in a global environment and to promote an internationally aware citizenry. While implementing technology and enhanced learning, and adapting to the ever-changing field of pedagogy, they attest to agile ways of blending old and new approaches to carry forward in the twenty-first century.

Responding to the call for developing practical approaches and sharing theoretical and pedagogical perspectives for the teaching and learning of the three Ls in multilingual fields, the contributors have explored aspects of the study, implementation, and renewal of these methods. The arrangement of the book juxtaposes perspectives to enrich our views on the creation and revision of traditional, blended, and online language courses in multiple languages, including a diverse corpus of texts and theory from various disciplines. This journey has taken us from discussions of postsecondary policies, curriculum development, and critical pedagogy into specific examples of courses that teach host, heritage, and foreign languages, linguistics, and literature. It invigorates discussion on how to update and integrate inter-artistic approaches and experiential education. This volume also celebrates, while also cautioning about, the challenges in current surges of online and blended learning. It addresses how incorporating various degrees of technology-based resources in teaching can enhance the learning process at different undergraduate year levels. It presents student-affirming assessment tools and classroom resources and activities that respond to twenty-first-century concerns and competencies. This volume highlights how learning is rooted in historical and socio-cultural realities and imaginaries, yet operates in concrete contexts that are constantly changing and evolving.

The volume includes some long-standing pedagogical devices such as oral tradition, autobiographies, and Socratic conversation circles to inform written composition, language acquisition, and multicultural literacy. The book also boldly unites various perspectives, including new forms and results-based discussions for implementing experiential education and language teaching, online and blended language learning formats and inter-artistic approaches, as well as sample techniques and studies. Together they reveal the status of learning and teaching in second-language acquisition, the main objective here and in the courses and curricula represented. The samples and data draw from specific courses that share common recommendations concerning the integration of innovative approaches and methods. It is hope that this knowledge sharing will extend the dialogue between instructors from a range of languages including Korean, Portuguese, Spanish, English, German, and Hindi-Urdu as second languages, and others by extension. Enhancing access to such information in one volume is one part of this process. Scholars and faculty members teaching courses in other cultural areas and across the three L fields may find the suggested track record of innovations presented in this volume of timely inspiration for implementation in their courses.

Throughout this journey, *Curriculum Design and Praxis in Language Teaching: A Globally Informed Approach* has provided readers with theoretical and hands-on suggestions that will serve to enhance curricula design to reinforce students' socio-cultural engagement and linguistic development, both inside and outside of their language learning classrooms. Bridging successful teaching and learning ideas across the three Ls of pedagogy – languages, literatures and linguistics – here espoused, the amplification of these aspects has reached across cultures, languages, and geographical spaces. The weaving of the chapters into seven sections finds points of contact among the current research. The approaches represented in this volume share practices borne out of interdisciplinary classwork and innovative course design developed in the last ten years. New digital approaches, online advancements in technology platforms, social media tools, and various community engagement formats complement a variety of methods and samples. Each chapter, case study and approach has provided a breadth of evidence testifying to the vibrancy of the research being conducted in nations across the world –Canada, as well as Austria, England, Israel, Mexico, New South Wales, Spain, and the United States. As we have seen in the research presented by scholars working in these postsecondary education settings, the techniques are transferable to other cultural and linguistic areas.

Balancing between "canon and cornucopia," as John Miles Foley has described the task of taking stock of integrated collections such as this one, the book reveals the similar challenges that the pedagogues and learners face across diverse languages. However, while Foley referred to something akin to "a digest of practical applications" in a prior collection related to oral traditions, the depth of resonances between the chapters of this collection speaks to a more consistent pattern. Innovative and task-based perspectives have exposed key issues such as dealing with shifting education paradigms to include the skills students will need to succeed and thrive in today's world. This requires developing skills such as critical thinking, collaboration, communication, and creativity through the utilization of TEL-based activities, experiential learning projects, and inter-artistic materials. The chapters collectively offer a comprehensive approach to studying social and ethical matters involving challenges and problems that are inherent to the scientific study of language. The enclosed templates reflect research methods ranging across different languages and disciplines that emphasize practical, clear purposes to ensure student success. This volume sets itself apart by addressing hitherto underrepresented languages, and in bridging various cultural milieus and curricular formats. Moreover, the pedagogical methods and real-world situational approaches in this volume integrate myriad ways to motivate students to engage with various analytical tools, develop ethical decision-making skills, and become increasingly more aware about socio-political consciousness, critical thinking, autonomy, and collaborative techniques for knowledge production and dissemination and engaged global citizenry.

The chapters each also actively address various cultural and linguistic perspectives in relation to multilingual multi-media and technology in critical ways. This volume gathers current pedagogical techniques aimed at advancing students' abilities to use these skills professionally and grow in greater self-directed ways in the future, while it also provides pedagogues with a dialogic forum to amplify their own teaching practice. One of the forerunning players in this field is AI and what implications it will have moving forward. As Yuval Noah Harari notes, "the rise of AI and biotechnology will certainly transform the world; but it does not mandate a single deterministic outcome" (461). The specific outcomes related to the teaching of languages and cultures is still to be explored, and AI in this context is still a moving target. Part of that challenge is the economic reality, so that only now are some less-funded language programs able to even fathom their integration into regular courses and classrooms. In the current and post-COVID-19 environment, we will be alert as to how to utilize online formats to reach parts of the world that cannot be accessed directly. Perhaps for that reason technologies such as augmented reality, VR and AR platforms – for instance, the Expeditions app – that allow students in world languages courses to "travel" virtually to other locations across the globe, will enhance this access; at the same time, it will raise questions, as it does so now in other formats, to issues of accessibility, equity, and other travel restrictions due to economic, political, social, or health issues. The use of robotics, such as the *Double Robot*[1] in classrooms to simulate in-class presence will serve to further close distances, as will enhancements related to Adobe Connect, Zoom[2], and other ways to creatively be more inclusive to various learning styles and teaching methods. These teaching industry trends and innovations in pedagogy will continue to evolve as remote teaching, online, and blended learning formats are further woven across languages, literatures, and linguistics curricula.

In conclusion, we hope that this volume will appeal to a broad readership of scholars and pedagogues in the fields of education within the three Ls, applied linguistics, and socio-linguistics. As a reading of the full volume demonstrates, the current practices, program re-visioning, and implementation of specific courses included here prove their extension into other arenas of learning and teaching beyond language education. It is our wish that that this volume, with its interdisciplinary and international orientation, will contribute to the generation of further conversations, directions, and questions that can be used to bring about change in making the pedagogy of the three Ls not only more effective in ensuring student success but also more accessible and socially equitable.

NOTES

1 See https://www.actfl.org/sites/default/files/tle/TLE_FebMar20_TechWatch.pdf (Feb./Mar. 2020).

2 See. for example, www.chronicle.com/article/8-Ways-to-Be-More-Inclusive-in/248460 (8 Apr. 2020).

Chapter Synopses

Section I: Critical Approaches to Curriculum and Pedagogy in Language and Pre-service Teacher Education

1 International by Default? Global Citizenship Education in the Language Classroom by Shobna Nijhawan

Considering the importance of language education of so-called "less commonly taught languages" in the post-secondary classroom in a day and age that highlights the ever-increasing importance of bilinguality, even multilinguality, and that registers high numbers of second language as well as heritage language learners, this chapter lays out how Hindi-Urdu has developed over the past decade at York University in Toronto. It addresses questions concerning university policies revolving around the internationalization of the curriculum, administrative and academic resources, as well as pedagogical challenges and experiments with a more communicative and project-based pedagogy. This chapter draws from experiences of teaching Hindi-Urdu and developing classroom materials for second language and heritage language learners at three proficiency levels. Special attention will be given to a description of the course design and to evaluation methods that are catered towards the *diverse* pedagogical requirements of heritage and "foreign" language learners in the mixed as well as the separate (heritage language and foreign language) classroom. This description addresses aspects of experiential education, blended learning, as well as the use of technology-enhanced learning materials for teaching grammar, vocabulary, and the two scripts (Nagari and Nastaliq) of Hindi and Urdu. It contemplates whether teaching a "foreign" or less commonly taught language, that is, Hindi-Urdu, is by default a contribution to the internationalization of the curriculum and gives examples of teaching and learning practices as they have been developed for and tried out in the classroom.

2 Socratic Circles, Critical Literacy, and Culturally Responsive Teacher Education by Hyunjung Shin and Geraldine Balzer

This chapter integrates dialectical learning circles, so-called Socratic Circles, as an experiential activity in pre-service teacher education courses. As faculty members from the University of Saskatchewan, Shin and Balzer share the manner in which such circles create a space for students' development in the areas of language, culture, and moral responsibility. The critical discussions described by Shin and Balzer involve the incorporation of topics, such as indigenous perspectives, that are of much relevance to their sociopolitical and pedagogical realities. They critically examine how the adoption of Socratic Circles not only provides students with opportunity to engage in lively discussion but also enables them to develop linguistically and culturally responsive pedagogies.

3 Developing Future English-Language Educators' Critical Language Awareness in Cross-College Discussions by Anuradha Gopalakrishanan and Leah Shepard-Carey

This chapter describes a learning activity performed through two different postsecondary institutions: Shepard-Carey's project aimed at fostering critical language awareness in future language teachers.

Specifically, her activity created discursive spaces for participants to share and reflect on issues of language, culture, and identity, and on how they may act as moral agents of change. In this chapter, Shepard-Carey discusses the educational contexts of her interuniversity project and how her study informed students' teaching ideologies and practices.

Section II: Designing Classroom Resources, Activities, and Assessment Tools for Student Engagement

4 Teaching with Case Studies by Lynn Burley

For undergraduate linguistics classes, as an alternative to relying on traditional lectures, readings, and discussions, Lynn Burley examines the significance of teaching linguistics with case studies. As argued by Burley, this pedagogical tool offers a more comprehensive approach to studying social and ethical matters involving the many questions and problems the scientific study of language presents. With case studies, students are exposed to knowledge through evidence-based problem solving. Following the discussion of this research method, the author offers templates for instructors to follow.

5 Conceptualizing the Significance of Studying Translingual, Autobiographic Narratives in ESL Classrooms at the Post-Secondary Level by Fernanda Carra-Salsberg

When studying the ontological meaning of a lived tongue, it seems like common sense to ask what occurs when the language that defines the self, while nurturing individuals' growth and sense of who they are, loses its dominant currency. Specifically, what occurs to postsecondary monolingual migrants and exchange students when immersed within a foreign linguistic reality that defies their pre-existing conceptualizations and subjectivity? By focusing on translingual essays and poems, as well as contextualized sections of book-length migrant memoirs, this chapter discusses the pedagogical importance of reflection and text-to-reader connection in learning English as a host language. It discusses approaches to memoir studies and the relevance of studying narratives that highlight intersubjective experiences, linguistic dislocations, identity shifts, and the overall socio-affective challenges students encounter as host language learners. By presenting a narrative-centred theoretical approach to host language acquisition, this chapter highlights the significance of creating a space for students to discuss and understand the emotional world of linguistic immersions and language learning. It argues that establishing a personal connection by discussing, understanding, and engaging with published translingual literature enhances students' willingness to reflect and learn, and thus to engage in active reading, critical thinking, and writing.

6 Classroom-Based Assessment Practices of College Korean-Language Teachers: A Qualitative Study by Hye-Sook Wang

In this chapter, Hye-Sook Wang discusses the challenging aspects of creating innovative assessments for language learners at the postsecondary level. Understanding the need for further research on this topic, this author conducted a study that integrated data from eight Korean language instructors. In this chapter, Wang shares her findings, gives examples of achievement and proficiency tests, and discusses the implications of her results for current and future foreign language instructors.

7 Classroom Activities for Student Engagement: "5 Minutes" and Survey Project by Myounghee Cho

This chapter shares two classroom activities that were conducted in Korean as a Foreign Language classes in a US college: 1) a practice of using five minutes before class that was effective in creating an engaging classroom environment and 2) a survey project that worked well to implement national standards that govern communicative and functional forms of language learning. The practice of using five minutes before class was designed to provide students with additional exposures to the target language and culture. The practice persuaded the teacher that it built a productive rapport between the teacher and the students that facilitated learner motivation and created an engaging learning and teaching environment for both the teacher and students. A survey project was designed with the purpose of familiarizing students with indirect quotation. The project, with guidance that identified language components that students required in the project (designing a survey form and conducting group discussions) and for the project (giving a presentation and reporting the results of the survey), helped students to enhance their proficiency in interpersonal, interpretive, and presentational modes of communication. This chapter presents the logistics and significances of the activities.

Section III: Inter-artistic Approaches to Language Teaching

8 Inter-artistic Approaches to Teaching Hispanic Culture: Literature and Music by Victoria Wolff

This chapter focuses on methodologies and successful practices for teaching the intersection of literature and music to better understand Hispanic culture. This contribution will be developed so that it offers practical advice and suggestions for both the undergraduate and graduate classrooms. Furthermore, its applications are for teaching Hispanic culture in the target language (Spanish) or for more general use (in English), beginning with established practices of connecting literature and music, as well as newer approaches that consider popular music and the relationship of music and society through experiential and community-engaged learning. Another important frame of reference is transatlantic studies, which seeks to uncover cultural linkages between Spain and Spanish America. Examples, therefore, come from diverse countries of the Hispanic world. Finally, Wolff's discussion is informed by theoretical perspectives from the sociology of music. The principal idea of this academic subfield is that musical art is the result of collaborative social and artistic interactions. As applied to the classroom environment, activities and outcomes are also defined by collaborative and artistic actions. Media, such as recordings and film, are included as additional resources that help bring new dimensions to the material.

9 E(xpanded) Dialogues between Literature and Music: Optimizing Synaesthetic Resources for Teaching Language and Literature by Maria Figueredo

This chapter offers an interdisciplinary and inter-artistic approach for teaching advanced Latin American and Caribbean literature in a Spanish-language literature and linguistics program, and the relevant connections to music. The sample course studies significant movements and interactions of literature and music as authentic expressions of cultural identity in Hispano America and the Caribbean by examining the textual and performative contexts in which musical forms are adopted in literature and literature is set to music. Examples drawn from course activities, assignments, and group work reflect key questions from course files, student feedback, and test scripts to provide empirical data from which to examine best practices for engaging with cross-disciplinary materials, in a cross-regional and trans-historical framework to foster language learning in concert with critical skills and literary analysis. Although geared mainly towards upper-level undergraduate students, Hispanic Studies, and literature courses, this groundbreaking pedagogical research is also transferable to graduate studies, as well as language courses of other literary and cultural traditions, to incorporate music and multimedia sound files to expand ways for interactive and community-engaged learning of language and culture.

10 When Art and English Language Instructors Collaborate by Tamara Warhol and Katherine Rhodes Fields

This case study discusses the benefits that arose from the collaboration between an artist and English-language instructor in an Intensive English Program (IEP) at a public university in the south-eastern United States. The two instructors constructed and implemented a curriculum that required students to create fine art projects and write a blog about the cultural differences among the students. As the course was based in an IEP, the English-language instructor was not teaching language to help students successfully participate in a university art course. Instead, the art instructor taught visual arts techniques to support English-language learning. Although not without its challenges, the curriculum and the collaborative pedagogy provided students with creative tools to help them improve their multimodal English skills. This case illustrates how collaboration between English-language and discipline specialists need not only be designed to support content learning through additive language instruction, but also may be designed to enhance English-language learning by teaching disciplinary skills.

Section IV: Experiential Education in Language Teaching and Learning

11 Communicating and Understanding the "Other" through Experiential Education: Portuguese Language and Culture in Toronto by Maria João Dodman, Inês Cardoso, and Vander Tavares

This chapter addresses the purpose and significance of experiential education within the curriculum of a foreign language university program. Dodman, Cardoso, and Tavares draw on theory and experiences from teaching Portuguese in a fourth-year undergraduate course. Aside from describing this pedagogical method with specific examples, they explain how fostering students' engagement with members of the Portuguese-speaking community of the Greater Toronto Area furthers their development at the linguistic, professional, and subjective levels.

12 Using Experiential Learning Theory as a Framework for Undergraduate Academic Communication Development by Maria Herke, Susan Hoadley, and Deanna Wong

Founded on pedagogical theory and experiences drawn from a discipline-specific academic communications course, this chapter debates the practices and approaches to the experiential learning approach. Delivery methods, teaching and learning activities, and assessment tasks are discussed in relation to the manner by which this student-centred approach to learning addresses students' multidisciplinary needs.

13 Words at Play: Language Learning at Work by Agustina Tocalli-Beller

This chapter stresses the significance of interaction and the exposure of humour as key components in the second-language learning process. Tocalli-Beller delivers the results of a recent study that involves a series of authentic material from newspapers, such as jokes, cartoons, and riddles. The method and choice of delivery, students' learning outcomes, and recommendations for future pedagogical work are addressed by the author.

Section V: Technology-Enhanced Teaching

14 Building Capacity for Twenty-First-Century Digital Language Teaching Practices by Geoff Lawrence

With a focus on digital technology as a collaborative tool in the language classroom, Lawrence discusses the importance of using social networks and information and communication technologies to explore genre, registers, and interaction. In his chapter, Lawrence outlines strategies from recent research that supports the pedagogical integration of digital approaches. Methodologies are outlined as a means to assess the value of technology integration. The role of mentorship programs and communities of practice are also discussed, as well as readings instructors may use as reference for their current and future technology-based practices.

15 Digital Storytelling in the L2 Classroom: Enhanced Writing Skills by Yujeong Choi and Na-Young Ryu

In this chapter, Choi and Ryu present an overview of a case study on digital storytelling as a pedagogical tool for all language-learning classrooms. This study involves twenty-seven students enrolled in an intermediate Korean language classroom. After outlining the procedures and survey results, Choi and Ryu describe the manner by which the project motivated students while greatly enhancing their language skills.

16 A Pedagogical Module for a Place-Based and Multiliteracies-Based Digital Storytelling Project for Language Learning by Angela Lee-Smith

This chapter stresses the significance of literacy in language-learning classrooms. Centred on a beginners' level language class, Lee-Smith presents a digital storytelling exercise that has been developed through place-based, multiliteracies-based and standards-based frameworks. This author explains the manner by which her project enhances students' interpersonal communication, interpretative communication, and presentational communication. She also stresses that such digital storytelling projects may be applicable to different languages at all levels of language learning.

17 Using Facebook as a Resource for e-Tandem Language Learning in Higher Education by Christine Schallmoser and Pia Resnik

This chapter discusses the significance of collaborative learning in foreign language classrooms. Schallmoser and Resnik explain the way in which they use Facebook to establish interactions between speakers of different L1s. Through such connections each student is the other's tandem partner in the target language (LX). The aim is for language learners to support each other's learning experience. Throughout the chapter, e-Tandem language learning is explained and supported with specific examples taken from their previous classes.

Section VI: Online and Blended Language Learning

18 Students' Insights on a Fully Online Language Course by Mihyon Jeon and Ahrong Lee

This chapter discusses an online Korean language course offered at York University in Toronto and students' reception and response to the course. In recent years, there has been an accelerating expansion of online language courses in both educational institutions and commercial organizations (e.g., Rosetta Stone), as well as various attempts to evaluate the effectiveness of online education. Most research regarding online language education focusing on post-secondary settings has found that it is as effective as its face-to-face counterpart, if not slightly more effective. This chapter aims to contribute to the growing body of research on the effectiveness of online language education by focusing on a case study of an online Korean language course. After introducing the development of the online course and the course itself, this chapter presents students' evaluation of and response to the course as a whole and to different elements of the course such as online lectures, animations, weekly virtual meetings via Adobe Connect, and conversation recording submissions. The data are drawn from surveys and interviews with students. This chapter concludes with the implications of online language education.

19 Preparing Future Global Professionals: Technology-Enhanced Group PBL Pedagogy by Monica Broido and Daniel Portman

Broido and Portman discuss how to develop twenty-first-century competencies through a group project-based learning (PBL) pedagogy in advanced English for an economics course. They demonstrate that PBL pedagogy facilitates learners' collaboration and creativity and helps learners to develop effective communication strategies, problem solving, and group decision-making skills. Briodo and Portman also show how the Google Suite can provide teachers both with a bird's-eye and detailed views of learner progress so as to effectively manage and support multiple concurrent projects in a PBL-based classroom.

20 A Guide to Synchronous Online Language Teaching by Seung-Eun Chang

This chapter addresses the special affordance and challenges of synchronous online language teaching and provides introductory and straightforward guidance for online language teaching with hands-on strategies and practice within a virtual classroom. Chang explains how to equip and orchestrate multimodal tools to facilitate the instructional conversations in a virtual environment, such as breakout rooms, whiteboards, PowerPoints, video and website sharing, and chat boxes. She introduces how to develop online course syllabi, quizzes, homework assignments, activities, and teaching materials and how to incorporate them effectively into a virtual learning.

Contributors

Geraldine Balzer is an associate professor of curriculum studies in the College of Education at the University of Saskatchewan. Her teaching focuses on ways of disrupting the hegemony of standard English and embracing a diversity of *Englishes*, incorporating Aboriginal and postcolonial literature into classrooms, and preparing teachers to be advocates for social justice. Her research focuses on decolonization and social justice. She works with teachers to explore the use of diverse literary texts and theories in order to engage students in critical thinking. She also studies International Service Learning and its impact on Canadian participants and host communities in Central America. <geraldine.balzer@usask.ca>

Monica Broido is the head of writing programs at Tel Aviv University. The programs include academic and scientific communication for PhD students in various faculties, and the Center for Language Excellence (CLE) where students or faculty are tutored individually on their language needs. She also teaches Spanish at TAU and is co-chair of the Israeli Forum for Academic Writing, an association dedicated to connecting people engaged in the teaching and research of academic writing in Israel. <famliabroido@gmail.com>

Lynn Burley is a professor of linguistics and interim chair in the Department of Languages, Linguistics, Literatures, & Cultures at the University of Central Arkansas. She teaches courses in educational linguistics, grammatical structures, phonology, semantics, and sociolinguistics. She was chosen as a STIRS Scholar by the American Association of Colleges and Universities in 2014 for her creation of the case study and facilitator's guide entitled "Should English be the Official Language of the United States?" She has also published on Siouan languages, teaching composition, and on the role of service in tenure. <lburley@uca.edu>

Inês Cardoso is an assistant professor at the University of Aveiro, Portugal. From 2013 to 2019, she was a sessional assistant professor, through a protocol with Camões, Instituto da Cooperação e da Língua, at York University. She holds a PhD in didactics; her research and publication records include Portuguese language teaching, writing research, teaching of writing, writing for professional development, teacher training, pedagogical tools, written and oral communicative genres, and students' relationship with language, writing, and knowledge. She is an associate of the Centro de Investigação "Didática e Tecnologia na Formação de Formadores" (CIDTFF, Research Centre on Didactics and Technology in the Education of Trainers). She coordinates the group "ProTextos – Ensino e Aprendizagem da Escrita de Textos." <inescardoso @ua.pt>

Fernanda Carra-Salsberg has been a postsecondary foreign-language educator since 2001. Born in Buenos Aires, Argentina, her interest in language, culture, migration, trauma, and identity formations stems from her repeated relocations as a child and an adolescent migrant, and from experiences as a foreign-language pedagogue. She teaches English as a second language and Spanish to heritage- and second-language learners at York University in Toronto, Ontario, Canada. Carra-Salsberg has earned a bachelor of arts degree with honours in Spanish language, literature, and linguistics at York University; a bachelor of education degree in language acquisition and history at OISE UT; and a master of arts degree in Spanish language and Ibero-American literature at the University of Toronto. In 2015 Carra-Salsberg completed an interdisciplinary doctoral degree at the Faculty of Education, York University. Her areas of expertise are host, foreign and heritage-language acquisition; child and adolescent migration; trauma studies; semiotics; language philosophy; and psychoanalysis. <fcarra@yorku.ca>

Seung-Eun Chang earned a PhD in linguistics from the University of Texas at Austin, specializing in phonology and phonetics. After ten years of teaching at University of California, Berkeley, she joined Georgia Tech in 2018. Her research interests include theoretical and experimental phonology and phonetics and Korean linguistics. Several influential phonetics journals have published her work, including *Language and Speech* and *The Journal of the Acoustical Society of America*. Her Korean-language teaching has also led to her involvement in various research efforts directly related to language teaching, and she is currently examining issues related to online language teaching. <seung-eun.chang@modlangs.gatech.edu>

Myounghee Cho is an assistant professor of instruction in Korean in the Department of Modern Languages and Cultures at the University of Rochester. She is interested in language pedagogy and developing effective instructional methods and materials. <myounghee.cho@rochester.edu>

Yujeong Choi is an assistant professor in East Asian Studies at the University of Toronto. She earned her PhD degree in linguistics from the University of Texas at Arlington in 2012. Her research interest includes second-language acquisition, Korean pedagogy, Korean linguistics, and educational technology. <yujeong.choi@utoronto.ca>

Maria L. Figueredo (PhD, MA and BA, University of Toronto) is an associate professor of Spanish at York University in Toronto. She teaches courses in Spanish language and Hispanic culture and literature. Her research specialization in the area of interrelationships between literature and music in Hispanic America include music as a subtext in women's writing and contemporary innovations in Spanish American literature. Recipient of the President's University-wide Teaching Award (2016), her passion for teaching strategies that foster intellectual growth and challenge students to achieve a higher level of critical thought and analytical writing has led to designing and leading experiential learning projects; *Enter Voczes*, a trilingual journal to publish student work in Spanish or Portuguese with English translation; and the Pan American games "Poet-Tree" project. Her community engagement experience has connected with her roles as coordinator of the Spanish program and undergraduate program director, languages and literatures, at York University. Her newest book is *Creation Sounds: Music, Gender and Performativity in Contemporary Latin American Literature* (2018, Common Ground). <mfiguere@yorku.ca>

Anuradha Gopalakrishnan is an adjunct faculty member at the University of Minnesota in the Department of Curriculum and Instruction. Her research interests include multilingual pedagogies, language-teacher education, and heritage language learning. Her multilingual and multicultural experiences shape her research work and influence her teaching. <gopal076@umn.edu>

Maria Herke has worked as an educator and researcher for almost two decades in the Department of Linguistics at Macquarie University. Her main research focus is communication strategies across a variety of professional contexts, including academic communication. Maria has presented her research at international conferences, runs workshops for external organizations and has published numerous papers and books including *Academic Culture: A Student's Guide to Studying at University* (4th edition, 2020), with Jean Brick and Deanna Wong, and *Academic Success* (2018), with Deanna Wong, Jean Brick, and Nick Wilson. She holds a PhD in linguistics and a bachelor of arts with first-class honours in linguistics, both from Macquarie University. <maria.herke@mq.edu.au>

Susan Hoadley taught in the higher-education sector in Australia for nearly twenty years before retiring as a senior lecturer from the Department of Linguistics at Macquarie University. Throughout her academic career, Susan focused on the development of language and communication skills in a diverse range of disciplinary contexts. From 2008, she was involved in leading teaching and learning, particularly curriculum and instructional design to develop communication and other graduate outcomes. Prior to joining the higher-education sector, Susan worked in the financial services industry for over ten years and has considerable business experience. She holds a PhD in education from Macquarie University, a diploma of education from the University of New South Wales and a bachelor of arts with first-class honours in linguistics from Macquarie University. Susan's industry background and education qualifications underpin her interdisciplinary approach to research and she has significant publications in language, education, and business journals. <susanhoadley@mac.com>

Mihyon Jeon is an associate professor of the Department of Languages, Literatures, and Linguistics at York University in Toronto. Her research interests include Korean-language education as a heritage language in North America, and English as a second language education in Asia. She focuses on language ideologies and maintenance issues among Korean immigrants in North America as well as native-speaking English teachers who teach English in Asia and their transnational experiences and identities. Her journal articles were published in *Journal of Sociolinguistics, Modern Language Journal, Journal of Multilingual and Multicultural Development, Heritage Language Journal, Language Culture and Curriculum, Language Awareness, Korean Language in America*, and *System*. She copublished a translation of a book titled *Media Literacy* (9th ed.) from English to Korean. <mihyjeon@yorku.ca>

Maria João Dodman is an associate professor at York University in Toronto, where she teaches in the Portuguese and Luso-Brazilian Studies program. Her research and her publication record in English, Spanish, and Portuguese reveal a wide range of interests: from early-modern Spanish and Portuguese literature to colonial encounters, contemporary Portuguese island culture, Brazilian north-east writers, and creative writing. <mdodman@yorku.ca>

Geoff Lawrence is an associate professor in English-language teaching and applied linguistics at York University in Toronto. Geoff is a teacher educator, researcher, and curriculum designer interested in exploring the potential of online, blended, and classroom-based English-language teaching and language teacher education programs. His research examines online and blended language teaching methodology, teacher beliefs towards pedagogical innovation, plurilingualism, and intercultural approaches in language and teacher education. <glawrenc@yorku.ca>

Ahrong Lee is an associate professor of the Department of Languages, Literatures, and Linguistics at York University in Toronto, where she teaches courses in elementary modern standard Korean and intermediate modern standard Korean. She is a member of the York Centre for Asian Research. She received her PhD in English (2009), concentrating in linguistics, from the University of Wisconsin–Milwaukee. Her research areas include Korean linguistics, second-language acquisition, foreign-language pedagogy, curriculum development, and the integration of technology in foreign-language education. <arlee@yorku.ca>

Angela Lee-Smith is a senior lector II and director of the Korean program in the Department of East Asian Languages and Literatures at Yale University. She specializes in Korean linguistics, language pedagogy, and materials development for heritage language (HL) and second language (L2) learners of Korean. Her research interests include HL/L2 pedagogy and materials development: project-based language teaching and learning for literacy, culture, and proficiency. She is certified as an ACTFL Oral Proficiency Interview (OPI) tester and a Writing Proficiency Test (WPT) rater in Korean. <angela.lee-smith@yale.edu>

Shobna Nijhawan is an associate professor of Hindi at York University in Toronto. Amongst her monographs in the fields of gender, nationalism, and Hindi literature are *Women and Girls in the Hindi Public Sphere: Periodical Literature in Colonial North India* (2012), *Hindi Publishing in Colonial Lucknow: Gender, Genre and Visuality in the Creation of a Literary "Canon"* (2018), and the edited volume *Nationalism in the Vernacular: Hindi, Urdu and the Literature of Indian Freedom* (2010). Her research on Hindi-Urdu language acquisition is published in *A Handbook on Heritage Language Education: From Innovation to Program Building* (2017), the *Journal of the National Council of Less Commonly Taught Languages* (2011) and the *World Hindi Journal* (2016). <shobna@yorku.ca>

Daniel Portman holds an EdD from the Open University in the UK, in which he researched interpersonal meaning enactment in job application letters by Israeli business administration students. Based in Israel, he develops curricula for, lectures in, and researches EAP/ESP at the Azrieli College of Engineering Jerusalem and the Interdisciplinary Center Herzliya. His research interests include the English-language needs of both tertiary students as they transition from student to professional as well as practicing professionals. <dfportman@gmail.com>

Pia Resnik is a professor of ELT research and methodology at the University College of Teacher Education, Vienna/Krems, Austria. In the past, she worked at the Departments of English at the Universities of Vienna, Graz, and Salzburg, Austria, and spent research visits at Newcastle University, UK, the University of London, UK, and Kasetsart University, Thailand. Her research interests include all aspects surrounding LX users of English – with a particular focus on emotions in multilingual contexts and the psychology of language learning. She is the author of the book *Multilinguals' Verbalisation and Perception of Emotions.* <pia.resnik@kphvie.ac.at>

Katherine Rhodes Fields is an artist whose work cross-pollinates traditional printmaking with contemporary processes, such as photography, digital media, and installation. She is professor and division chair of visual arts in the Center of Excellence for Media, Visual, and Performing Arts at Houston Community College. <katherine.fields@hccs.edu>

Na-Young Ryu is an assistant teaching professor of Korean in the Department of Asian Studies at the Pennsylvania State University. She holds a PhD in linguistics from the University of Toronto with a specialization in phonology and computer-assisted language learning. Her research interests include artificial intelligence (AI) in education, computer-based auditory training for foreign language learners, and sound variation and change. <nmr5569@psu.edu>

Christine Schallmoser is a senior lecturer in German language education and language director in the German Department at King's College London, UK, where she develops, manages, and teaches language modules across all levels, with a focus on culture, linguistics, and politics. She is also a Senior Fellow of the Higher Education Academy. Before joining King's, she taught German at the Goethe-Institut Buenos Aires, Argentina, and at Vienna University of Technology, Austria. Her research interest lies in foreign-language acquisition and learning, with a particular focus on learner autonomy, motivation, and emotions in foreign-language learning. <christine.schallmoser@kcl.ac.uk>

Leah Shepard-Carey is an assistant professor of education in graduate studies, specializing in TESOL and literacy education at Drake University. As a former public school educator, Leah's research interests include multilingualism, translanguaging, culturally sustaining approaches to language and literacy teacher education, and multilingual children's literacy learning. Her work has been featured in *TESOL Quarterly, Linguistics and Education, The Journal of Early Childhood Literacy, Language Awareness,* and *TESOL Journal.* <shepa090@umn.edu>

Hyun Jung Shin is an assistant professor in Curriculum Studies in the College of Education at the University of Saskatchewan. Her research focuses on globalization, transnationalism, and second-language education; political economy and study abroad; critical pedagogy and teacher education; and sociolinguistics. She published in multiple journals including *Journal of Sociolinguistics* and guest edited special issues of *Journal of Multilingual and Multicultural*

Development (with Joseph Park) and *Education Matters*. Her current work focuses on internationalization of universities and student mobility, decolonizing language teacher education, and adult ESL policy and pedagogies to support refugees and newcomer immigrants. <hyunjung.shin@usask.ca>

Vander Tavares is a PhD candidate in the linguistics and applied linguistics program at York University in Toronto. Vander is an instructor of both English as a second language (ESL) and Portuguese as a foreign language (PFL), having taught both languages at a number of post-secondary institutions in Canada. Some of his interests relate to multilingualism and international students, (second and foreign) language identity, and pedagogy. <vanderjuniort1@gmail.com>

Agustina Tocalli-Beller received her doctoral degree from the Department of Curriculum, Teaching and Learning at the Ontario Institute for Studies in Education of the University of Toronto, where she also worked as a research assistant with Merrill Swain. Her research interests include interaction in second-language teaching and learning, vocabulary learning, language play, and sociocultural and creative approaches to second-language classroom research. She has published several academic articles, classroom readers and pedagogical material with Rubicon Publishing, Macmillan, Oxford University Press, and University of Dayton Publishing. She has also published songs to learn language and many children's books in which through literature she addresses the topics of cultural identity, sociolinguistics differences, language performance, and linguistic creativity. <atocalli-beller@hotmail.com>

Hye-Sook Wang is an associate professor of East Asian Studies (Korean) at Brown University. Her research interests are in sociolinguistics and applied linguistics (KFL). She served the American Association of Teachers of Korean (AATK) as the elected president. She also served as editor-in-chief for *Korean Language in America*, the official journal of AATK for eight years. Her publications include *Rise of Korean Language Programs in U.S. Institutes of Higher Education: A Narrative History* (editor, 2015, Korea University Press), a number of course books including *Integrated Korean: High Advanced I, II* (co-authored, 2005, University of Hawaii Press), and many journal articles and book chapters. <hye-sook_wang@brown.edu>

Tamara Warhol is an associate professor of linguistics and TESOL in the Department of Modern Languages at the University of Mississippi, and from 2007–15 she served as director of the university's Intensive English Program. Using multimodal discourse analysis, she studies how people acquire and demonstrate expertise in classrooms, online, and in professional contexts. <twarhol@go.olemiss.edu>

Victoria Wolff (PhD McGill; MA University of New Mexico; BA University of North Carolina at Chapel Hill) is an associate professor of Hispanic Studies in the Department of Modern Languages and Literatures at the University of Western Ontario in London, Ontario, Canada. Her research is in the area of inter-artistic approaches to Hispanic studies (literature and music). Because of her diverse cultural and linguistic background, varied educational experiences, and adaptability to teach and learn new subject matter, she has taught a wide variety of undergraduate and graduate courses, in both Peninsular and Latin American literature and culture. She is also affiliated faculty of the Migration and Ethnic Relations Program. Victoria is twice the recipient of the Community Service Learning Award at Western. <vwolff@uwo.ca>

Deanna Wong was a lecturer in the Department of Linguistics at Macquarie University, where she taught academic communication, with a focus on academic communication in the sciences, and linguistics across a range of sub-disciplines. Her research focuses on the dimensions of human communication in spoken, online, and academic contexts, using corpus linguistic methodologies. She is a co-author of *Academic Culture- A Student's Guide to Studying at University* (4th edition, 2020), with Jean Brick and Maria Herke, and *Academic Success* (2018), with Maria Herke, Jean Brick, and Nick Wilson. She holds a PhD in linguistics and a bachelor of arts with first-class honours in linguistics, both from Macquarie University. <deanna.wong@gmail.com>

www.ingramcontent.com/pod-product-compliance
Lightning Source LLC
LaVergne TN
LVHW090806070826
844660LV00022B/1092

* 9 7 8 1 4 8 7 5 2 8 9 1 1 *